Settlement Houses
and the
Great Depression

Settlement Houses and the Great Depression

by *Judith Ann Trolander*

WESTERN ILLINOIS UNIVERSITY

Wayne State University Press, Detroit, 1975

Library of Congress Cataloging in Publication Data

Trolander, Judith Ann, 1942–

   Settlement houses and the Great Depression.

   Bibliography: p.

   Includes index.

   1. Social settlements—United States. 2. Social
action. 3. United States—Economic conditions—
1918–1945. I. Title.

   HV4194.T75 1974   362.5'0973   74-20994

   ISBN 0-8143-1529-1

PERMISSIONS

Chapters 2 through 6 first appeared in slightly different form as "The Response of Settlements to the
Great Depression" in *Social Work*, 18 (5): 92–101, 1973.

   Special thanks is extended to Lea Taylor for permission to quote from her papers as well as those of
her father, Graham Taylor; to Helen Hall for permission to quote from her papers as well as those of
Paul Kellogg; to Mrs. Arthur J. Kennedy for permission to quote from the papers of her husband.

   Appreciation is extended to the following for permission to quote from materials in their collections:

Archives of Industrial Society, University of Pittsburgh, Pittsburgh, Pa.
Case Western Reserve University Archives, Cleveland, Ohio.
Chicago Historical Society, Chicago, Ill.
City College Library, City University of New York, New York, N.Y.
Columbia University Libraries, New York, N.Y.
Jane Addams Memorial Collection, University of Illinois at Chicago Circle, Chicago, Ill.
Joseph Regenstein Library, University of Chicago, Chicago, Ill.
Lillian Wald Papers, Manuscripts & Archives Division, The New York Public Library, Astor, Lenox
   and Tilden Foundations, New York, N.Y.
Manuscript Collection, Library, University of Illinois at Chicago, Chicago, Ill.
Minnesota Historical Society, St. Paul, Minn.
Newberry Library, Chicago, Ill.
Schlesinger Library, Radcliffe College, Cambridge, Mass.
Social Welfare History Archives Center, University of Minnesota, Minneapolis, Minn.
State Historical Society of Wisconsin, Madison, Wis.
Urban Archives Center, Temple University, Philadelphia, Pa.
Western Reserve Historical Society, Cleveland, Ohio.

To Mother and Father

Contents

Preface

*T*HIS study is about what happened to the reform tradition of American social settlements. A leading agency of reform during the Progressive Era, settlement role in social change had altered drastically by the time of the second major reform period of the twentieth century, the New Deal. Ultimately, the reasons for the decline provide an important measurement of the role of private enterprise in solving social problems.

Prior to beginning research, I had written an article describing some reform activities in Cleveland's Hiram House during the Progressive Era. I had found that the director of Hiram House became outspoken against the New Deal in later years. His reversal in attitude made me wonder how prevalent the trend to conservatism was among other settlements. I began my research with the hypothesis that settlement houses during the New Deal were conservative in social outlook.

As the study progressed, however, it became increasingly impossible to label the whole movement as conservative. Too much liberal and even radical activity had taken place in certain cities, particularly in New York and Chicago. I discovered a widespread difference in tone or attitude toward social action among settlements in various cities. Indeed, one could not fail to be impressed by the tremendous difference in attitudes shown by settlements in New York or Chicago as opposed to those in Pittsburgh or Cleveland.

The discovery of the variation between settlements led to another question—what accounted for the differences in settlement attitudes? Why were settlements in some cities involved in social action programs while settlements elsewhere ignored social issues? An important factor seemed to be the impact of individual leaders in the settlement movement of the 1930s, strong social action advocates such as Lea Taylor, Glenford Lawrence, Helen Hall, Charlotte Carr, and

Lillie Peck. Yet, surprisingly, I found that the decisive factor was the presence or absence of a Community Chest within any given city. The explanation for why settlements varied in social outlook and why the settlement reform impulse weakened lay in the use of joint funding of private social agencies.

Although settlement boards retained control over personnel, the ultimate decisions as to the programs of individual houses were made by the Chests which controlled their finances. The response of the settlements to various social issues—the Hoover approach to relief, the New Deal, the radical approach to the Depression, and labor, housing, and race relations—shows that the correlation between the presence of the Chest and conservative social attitudes or non-involvement with social issues was particularly high in regard to unemployment, relief, and labor relations; when the issue was housing or race relations, however, the correlation was less clear. Significantly, when the issue was most directly related to economic problems, the attitude of the settlements was most likely to be determined by those who controlled their budgets.

The results of this study are based largely on seventy-seven manuscript collections, most of which relate specifically to forty-three settlements, approximately twenty percent of which were included in the National Federation of Settlements, United Neighborhood Houses of New York, or the Chicago Federation of Settlements during any given year of the Depression. A listing of each of the members of these three organizations is included in the Appendix.

Perhaps the most enjoyable aspects of the whole project were the places I visited and the people I met. In the preparation of the book, I have had the assistance and encouragement of a number of scholars and archivists. I especially thank David Van Tassel, professor of history, and Marjorie Main, professor of social work, both of Case Western Reserve University, and Allen F. Davis, professor of history at Temple University, for their invaluable suggestions in the preparation of the manuscript. I am indebted to archivists Frank A. Zabroskey, University of Pittsburgh; Philip S. Benjamin, Temple University; Elizabeth Shenton, Schlesinger Library, Radcliffe College; Ruth Helmuth, Case Western Reserve University; Kermit Pike, Western Reserve Historical Society; Archie Motley, Chicago Historical Society; Robert Fueglein, City College of the City University of New York; Mary Lynn McCree, University of Illinois, Chicago

Circle; and Andrea Hinding, Social Welfare History Archives, University of Minnesota. In addition, Helen Morton showed me the materials in possession of South End House, and Natalie Swimmer those at the Chicago Federation of Settlements. I also thank Frank W. McCulloch for his correspondence, and Lea Taylor for granting an interview. Finally, I express my appreciation to Henry Street Settlement, which, by allowing me to live for nearly a month at 265 Henry Street, gave me the opportunity to learn firsthand about residence in a settlement.

Abbreviations

AASW—American Association of Social Work

CCC—Civilian Conservation Corps

CWA—Civil Works Administration

CWCOU—Chicago Workers Committee on Unemployment

ERA—Emergency Relief Administration

FERA—Federal Emergency Relief Administration

LID—League for Industrial Democracy

MSW—Master of Social Work (degree)

NFS—National Federation of Settlements

NRA—National Recovery Administration

NYA—National Youth Administration

PWA—Public Works Administration

SASS—School of Applied Social Sciences at Western Reserve University

SERA—State Branch of Federal Emergency Relief Administration

SWHA, U. of Minn.—Social Welfare History Archives, University of Minnesota

TVA—Tennessee Valley Authority

WPA—Works Progress Administration

Introduction

$\mathcal{S}$ ETTLEMENT houses were founded in the major cities of the United States to bring about social change. The early settlement pioneers sought a new approach to the problems of the slums. By actually living among the poor, the well-to-do settlement residents hoped to gain new insights into poverty and to establish a new relationship with those they were trying to help—that of a neighbor. Experimenting with ways to alleviate some of the effects of slum life, the settlements became part of Progressive reform.

In the early days of the American settlement movement, roughly 1889 to 1914, immigrants were crowding into major cities, and labor unions were trying violently to wrest recognition from obstinate employers. At the same time, Herbert Spencer's "survival of the fittest" interpretation of Darwin's theory provided conservatives with an intellectual rationale for ignoring the plight of the poor. Yet settlement pioneers rejected Spencer, tried to respond to the needs of immigrants, and attempted to bridge the gap between rich and poor, laborer and employer.

By adopting certain innovations such as kindergartens, settlements induced the public schools to follow their example and incorporate new elements of progressive education into curriculums. Settlements led in establishing Americanization programs and public playgrounds and in getting housing regulations passed. Early settlement workers were active in attempts to regulate working conditions for women and children and encouraged labor to unionize. Finally, settlement workers became identified with political reform on the municipal and ward level. Indeed, settlement houses emerged from the Progressive Era with a strong heritage of social reform.

The Progressive Era, the dozen or so years leading to the outbreak of World War I, had been the first reform period of the twentieth century. It was a time of general prosperity, but also a time when white, Protestant, "old line" families, often of rural background, felt themselves losing power to the urban, immigrant, Catholic elements and to the new, huge corporations. This situation led to the Progressive concern with "democracy," which meant revising government machinery from the level of the ward boss to the United States Senate. It also meant breaking up monopolies. But the Progressives were concerned with much more. They believed that the environment, especially the urban environment, was the key to solving social problems. If children had playgrounds, perhaps they would be diverted from disruptive activities. If immigrants had language and citizenship classes, maybe they would abandon the ward boss. Progressive reform was wide-ranging, sometimes favoring the poorer and working classes, but more often championing the middle class. Consequently, not all Progressives supported all the reforms associated with the Progressive movement.

The methods of the reformers reflected a certain naive faith in their fellow men. High, moralistic overtones were characteristic. The Progressives believed that if they publicized bad conditions, if people read their descriptive and factual accounts of problems, society would respond, a solution would arise, and people would back it. Indeed, much Progressive energy went into making the larger society aware of social problems. Settlement houses, however, went further than mere publicity. They offered the middle and upper classes a chance to actually live in the slums of the cities, to observe the environment at first hand, and to become pragmatic experimenters in search of solutions.

The whole tone of the New Deal, from Franklin D. Roosevelt's inauguration to the outbreak of World War II, was quite different from the preceding reform period. While basic problems of poverty still plagued settlement neighborhoods, the New Dealers for half a dozen years thrust nearly all their energy into problems directly related to the economy. In place of Progressive prosperity and optimism, the New Deal had to cope with the worst depression in United States history and with a consequently faltering sense of confidence in the future. For a brief time, the business world was caught off-balance, the businessman was no longer a hero, and the federal government quickly moved into unprecedented areas. Machine politics ceased to be a major concern. Although Franklin Roosevelt had a fling at breaking up monopolies, the president's primary emphasis was on government regulation of big business. And while the Progressives had toyed with solutions to the urban environment, it was the New Dealers who put the federal government into welfare, housing, and labor programs.[1]

During the conservative 1920s other changes had affected settlement house programs. For example, legislation cut the flow of immigrants to a trickle. Meanwhile, schools and other public agencies took over many successful settlement programs, such as Americanization classes, kindergartens, and playgrounds. Settlements lost their youthful resiliency while trying to perpetuate themselves as institutions. As city after city adopted the Community Chest and private philanthropy became more centralized, settlements also lost their old independence. Furthermore, with the social work profession maturing, social services started to multiply and become more specialized. The amateurish, neighborly, "jack-of-all-trades" character of the settlement house was beginning to seem old-fashioned in a world which had become more professional, bureaucratic, and centralized.

Settlements approached the new reform era with their old methods, but with cramped operations. Publicity on behalf of the poor was still needed, but the larger society already possessed a sense of crisis. With many formerly well-off people impoverished, discovering poverty through residence in a settlement house was no novelty. Without money to hire new professional workers, throughout the 1930s settlements clung to residents, volunteers, and workers not trained in graduate social work schools. Consequently, the Depression staved off for a time the controversial impact of professionalization.[2] Lack of money also meant that settlements were limited in their efforts to experiment. Thus, the pragmatism of the Progressives carried over into the New Deal, but the sense of urgency and the magnitude of the Depression ruled out settlement-nurtured solutions.

Theoretically settlements still functioned as organizers for their neighborhoods. Yet objectives were a major problem. For what purpose were the poor being organized? In the Progressive Era, the settlements had dabbled in labor organizing and in pressuring for better housing and public services. By the time of the New Deal, however, most settlements sensed that such programs would get them into trouble with their local Community Chest, an umbrella organization which completely controlled the finances of its member agencies and which had first been introduced in 1913. Settlements had to do

something to survive. Therefore, they continued organizing their
neighbors for recreation and pressuring their staff to occupy the
residents' rooms, in what amounted to a rather hollow and irrelevant
response to the Depression. Significantly enough, the settlements that
functioned meaningfully as community organizers were those which
remained relatively independent of the business-dominated Community Chests.

Recent books have dealt with the failure of private enterprise
to solve social problems. In a study of Pittsburgh's urban problems,
Roy Lubove's *Twentieth Century Pittsburgh* notes the failure of the
city's business-dominated leadership to do much about poverty and
low income housing, emphasizing that as a whole Pittsburgh benefited
from large-scale and imaginative planning, but its poor people were
neglected. In *The Private City*, Sam Bass Warner, Jr. contends that
private interests are inimical to the general welfare. Francis Fox Piven
and Richard A. Cloward in *Regulating the Poor: the Functions of
Public Welfare* are even more critical of the business community.
These authors charge that the welfare system was organized to insure
a flexible pool of cheap labor for business. Furthermore, they say that
the liberalization of the welfare system under the New Deal was due
more to the need to check political unrest than the desire to eliminate
economic hardship.

Research into settlement archives from the New Deal period
shows the variations in social action among settlement houses, and
ultimately measures to what extent privately funded social agencies
can carry out programs of social change. Certain settlement leaders of
the thirties, aided by a decentralized system of financing, were able to
keep some settlement houses active in reform. For the most part,
however, by the time of the New Deal the effectiveness of the
settlement movement as a force in social reform had been curtailed;
its demise paralleled by the rise of the Community Chest.

1. Settlements and the Reform Tradition

*O*N January 28, 1913, headworker Robbins Gilman of University
Settlement in New York City faced his board of trustees and
acknowledged that his settlement had become "much concerned" with the Garment Workers Strike. When the strike began, the
settlement had immediately offered the use of its halls for strike
meetings. Consequently, striking girls in the whitegoods industry met
in the settlement house. When he discovered that the girls did not
have enough food, the settlement had provided them with lunches.

Gilman had gotten this support for the strikers past the
settlement's big contributors by disclaiming any intention of taking
sides on the economic issues involved in the strike. Instead, he had
stressed that by offering its facilities, the settlement was saving the
striking "girls from all sorts of evil influences." [1] Just what these "evil
influences" were is not clear, but his explanation apparently satisfied
the board. Robbins Gilman thus successfully made University Settlement a vehicle for furthering unionization in the garment trades.

Yet twenty-four years later as head of North East Neighborhood House in Minneapolis, Gilman could recall no connection
between his Minneapolis settlement and labor unions. Should a union
request to use settlement rooms, he said he first would have to get the
approval of his board and then check so "that such a policy would not
cause any discrimination against the Neighborhood House by the
Community Fund." He implied that such assurances were highly
unlikely because "the big contributors to the Community Fund" were
also the men responsible for the "open shop" policy which was
generally characteristic of Minneapolis.[2]

This was the same man. But in a different reform period and in
a different city, he had found himself forced to reverse his policies. By
Gilman's account, the key factor in this reversal was "the big

contributors to the Community Fund." These two incidents in his career illustrate what had happened to the settlement movement as a whole between the Progressive Era of the early twentieth century and the New Deal in the 1930s.

The United States settlement movement dates back to 1886, when Stanton Coit brought the idea from England and founded Neighborhood Guild in New York City. (This house had changed its name to University Settlement by the time Gilman became head-worker there.) It became known as the settlement movement because the purpose of its program was for people who were relatively well-off to "settle" among the poor. By living among them, the settlement residents would learn to know the poor as neighbors and then could better determine their needs. The next step for the settlement workers was to provide services to meet those needs. Hull-House, for example, began in 1889 with a kindergarten for children of working mothers, then soon added clubs and classes for other age groups.[3]

The early settlement workers realized that their neighbors were in need of far more than the settlement resources could provide. The wretched housing in the slums was one reason why settlement workers usually chose to live together in a settlement house rather than spread out through the neighborhood. Factory conditions were bad, wages low, undernourishment common, and politics corrupt. To combat these and other problems of the slums, early settlement workers placed emphasis on interpreting their neighbors to the larger community. They assumed that by calling people's attention to the horrible conditions in the slums, the community would then move to correct them. Therefore, the early settlement workers sought to help their neighbors on two levels—first, by providing immediate services, and second, by working to reform the physical and social environment of the slum.

An example of this dual approach is Robbins Gilman's response to the depression in the early months of 1914. Although the settlement was not supposed to be a relief-giving agency, in emergencies it did improvise relief programs on a limited scale. In the middle of winter, University Settlement housed 250 unemployed, homeless men in two large assembly halls. Settlement staff cleaned these floors daily, then gave each man a newspaper to lie upon. The heat was kept high while the men "slept" because the settlement had no blankets or other coverings to give them. At one point, Gilman managed to procure work relief for these men in the form of shoveling snow. Before the settlement sent the men out on this job, they were "given a simple breakfast of coffee and rolls." Some of the men did not have adequate boots, so Gilman also solicited boots for them.[4]

While doing his best to meet the men's immediate needs, Gilman pondered various reforms. He suggested that the federal government establish national employment exchanges and unemployment insurance, the latter in cooperation with the American Federation of Labor. To bring the unskilled worker into this scheme, Gilman proposed that the settlements themselves organize these workers into a union of sorts.[5] Gilman's ideas bore no fruit at that time, but the fact that he proposed them at all indicates that he was capable of responding both to an individual in need and to the broader social issues involved.

Depression and labor strife were really more characteristic of the 1890s than they were of the Progressive Era, and it was during the 1890s that the number of settlements in the United States rose from three to around one hundred.[6] It was also during this decade that the American attitude towards poverty began to change. Was poverty the fault of the individual or of society? The depression which began in 1893 challenged the American "assumption that earnest seekers could always find honest employment." [7]

Like the contemporary Social Gospel movement, settlement leaders began to see the causes of poverty in society and the slum environment. One by-product of the Social Gospel was the establishment of a number of "institutional churches" in the 1880s and 1890s. In some respects, these organizations bore a marked resemblance to settlements. Located in the poorer neighborhoods, institutional churches provided their neighbors with badly needed gymnasiums, libraries, and recreation rooms. However, the settlement attack on poverty was broader than the provision of immediate services. Settlements attacked poverty through the advocacy of labor legislation, public welfare, better housing, playgrounds, improved education, and democratic reforms.

The reforms that the settlement movement took up became an integral part of the Progressive Era, a period characterized by reform on many fronts. It was a time for attacks on big business and machine politicians, for experiments in education and housing for the poor, for establishing new government agencies and programs, for attempting to safeguard labor, and for feminism and prohibition. One might claim to be progressive on certain issues while denouncing others. Perhaps because the reforms of the Progressive Era were so wide-ranging, they were also shallow, but they were, nevertheless, significant. The aspects of the Progressive movement that most concerned the settlements were those that directly touched on the lives of their neighbors in the slums.

During the 1890s and the Progressive Era, labor unions struggled to establish themselves. As highly controversial organizations, unions had trouble winning support in the larger community. Yet a number of settlements risked their own reputations in defense of unionization. Besides meeting at University Settlement in New York, unions met regularly at settlements in New York, Boston, and Chicago.[8] Settlement workers also publicly endorsed the concept of labor organization.

Some of them even intervened in strikes. In most instances of employer-labor conflict, Jane Addams initially began with the idea of bringing the two sides together impartially for mediation or arbitration, but she usually ended by being on the side of labor.[9] During the tense Pullman strike in 1894 and in 1900 during the Chicago Building Trades strike, she spoke out in favor of collective bargaining despite the anti-strike feeling which was rampant. When Eugene Debs was arrested during the Pullman strike, two Hull-House residents organized a large protest meeting. Boston's Denison House hosted strike meetings and the settlement staff joined workers on picket lines. Further cooperation between settlements and labor occurred when a labor organizer became a member of the board at South End House and Sidney Hillman of the International Ladies Garment Workers Union moved into New York's Henry Street Settlement.[10]

The settlements had to pay a price for their support of labor. Both Hull-House and the University of Chicago Settlement lost donations because of their pro-union stance, and Elizabeth Peabody House in Boston had to return some contributions when it announced that its new building would be built with union labor. Nevertheless, labor got some badly needed support from leading settlements in the United States.[11]

When settlements joined the progressive campaigns to abolish child labor and improve the lot of the woman worker, they encountered similar opposition. Manufacturers' associations advised their members to make their contributions to private agencies "contingent on the promise that no part of the contribution should be used to promote the passage of, or to carry on propaganda for, any 'social-service labor program.' " [12] Undaunted, Hull-House resident Florence Kelley led the way when she began collecting information on child labor for the state of Illinois. She was widely imitated. In Jersey City, Whittier House organized a successful campaign to improve that state's child labor law. The settlement also investigated the bottle-blowing industry and subsequently founded the local Children's Protective League. In San Francisco, a settlement investigation helped secure the passage of a better child labor law in California. Boston settlement leaders were instrumental in gaining improvements in Massachusetts' child labor law. To strengthen their fight against child labor, settlement leaders supported the establishment of the federal Children's Bureau in 1912. Julia Lathrop, former Hull-House resident, became the first director.[13] The settlement campaign to abolish child labor was geographically widespread.

Two organizations came out of the Progressive Era devoted to the cause of the woman wageearner. The first was the National Consumers League, organized in 1899. Under Florence Kelley's direction, it sought to improve working conditions for women and children. The Women's Trade Union League was also formed with settlement help, and the first branches were located in settlements in New York, Boston, and Chicago. While leadership tended to come from the settlements in these cities, support for labor reforms came from settlements scattered around the United States during the Progressive Era.

The progressive attempt to bring about labor reforms was part of a new attitude towards poverty. Before 1900, poverty was widely regarded as a school for success; after 1900, poverty became associated in the public mind with poor food, inadequate housing, and health problems. To aid the children of poverty-stricken mothers, states initiated "Mothers' Aid" pensions. New York was one state where settlement workers led the fight. In 1912 Alice Gannett, then on the staff of Henry Street Settlement, and Richard Neustadt, along with his headworker, Robbins Gilman, formed an organization to work for the adoption of Mothers' Pensions. They faced the opposition of the Charity Organization Society and the Jewish Relief, who felt that the proposal for state welfare was a criticism of private charity.[14] The state established a commission to investigate the matter with Neustadt as chairman in 1913. This commission's report resulted in a Mothers' Aid Law which remained in force until the advent of the federal Aid to Dependent Children program in the 1930s.[15]

By the time of the New Deal, however, all three of these reformers had left New York. In 1937, Neustadt was director of the regional office of the Social Security Board on the Pacific Coast; Gilman was in charge of a Minneapolis settlement; and Gannett, then headworker of Goodrich House, was supporting reforms in Cleveland, but no longer using the settlement to further these reforms as she had in the Progressive Era.

The progressives decided that the key to solving social problems lay in the environment. One aspect singled out for special attention was housing. Settlement workers usually proceeded towards reform by first making a survey of the neighborhood, then publicizing the results, and finally seeking legislative action.

Cleveland's Hiram House, for example, made a study of housing in 1901. The report called attention to the small frame houses often crowded two or more on one lot with no running water, with garbage boxes, sheds, and manure heaps covering most vacant areas, and wooden balconies for fire escapes. Several families might be crowded into a single house.[16] Cleveland also had its tenements, but the dilapidated small frame house was more typical, not just in Cleveland, but in most other cities as well. Other settlements which carried out studies leading to more effective regulation of housing were South End House in Boston, Whittier House in Jersey City, Kingsley House in Pittsburgh, Union Settlement in Providence, Kingsley House in New Orleans, and settlements in Chicago and New York.[17]

Few reformers during the Progressive Era were ready to propose that the government itself actually go into the business of building housing for the poor. In fact, the only project of this kind at the time was that of the Massachusetts Homestead Commission. Significantly, Eva Whiting White, head of Elizabeth Peabody House, was on the commission. The project consisted of a dozen single-family, detached houses located in Lowell, Massachusetts. The Massachusetts Homestead Commission disbanded in 1919.[18] But public housing on a large scale for low income people was eventually to become a goal of the National Housing Association, organized in 1910 with the help of settlement workers from around the country.[19]

Another aspect of the slum environment which the progressives and the settlements decided to do something about was the lack of playgrounds. Cities were just beginning to recognize the need for public play areas for children, but left it to settlements in many cases to take the initial step. Chicago got its first playground in 1893 when Hull-House had some tenements beyond repair which were torn down and the vacant land equipped with play apparatus. The settlement operated the playground for ten years before the city took it over.[20]

Other settlements in New York, Chicago, and Philadelphia also ran playgrounds. In Boston, settlement workers put pressure on city authorities to provide better recreational facilities for children.[21] In Cleveland, Hiram House opened the first night-lighted playground; and headworker George Bellamy did much to develop the new occupation of playground director. Bellamy's playground program received national recognition in 1906, the same year that settlement leaders helped to form the National Playground Association. In 1910, he was offered the position of secretary of this organization, but preferred to remain as headworker of Hiram House. Bellamy again furthered the cause of playgrounds in 1912 as chairman of a committee which sought the passage of a $1,000,000 playground bond issue. The issue failed to pass; but two years later, he became Cleveland's first Director of Public Recreation. His objective in accepting the unpaid, temporary position was to keep the appointment of playground directors out of politics.[22] Thus, playgrounds are another example of a Progressive Era reform that attracted widespread support among settlements.

Like playgrounds, reforms in the areas of education, Americanization, and local politics were largely limited to the Progressive Era. Just as settlements preceded their local governments in establishing playgrounds, so many educational innovations made their appearance in settlements before being adopted by the Boards of Education. Hiram House, for instance, introduced kindergarten, manual training, and domestic education classes to Cleveland. The settlement also geared much of its efforts to helping immigrants to learn English and to succeed in American society. These activities were later adopted by the school board,[23] but Hiram House still carried them out on a limited scale long after the need to demonstrate their usefulness had passed. Educational projects were almost universal among settlements and were some of the major accomplishments of the movement.

When it came to municipal reform, settlements had a mixed record. Jane Addams fought a losing battle with her local ward boss, but Chicago Commons was successful in dominating its ward politics for two decades. South End House in Boston helped to dislodge a machine politician as mayor in 1907.

A number of municipal reformers had contact with the settlement movement, however. Economist Richard T. Ely helped to found the University of Wisconsin Settlement in Milwaukee. Newton D. Baker was connected with Goodrich House prior to being elected mayor of Cleveland.

Most importantly, settlement workers furnished reformers with the data they needed to attack urban problems. A former settlement resident, Paul Kellogg, directed the Pittsburgh Survey and received invaluable assistance from settlement workers in his research.[24] Settlements also furthered the cause of municipal reform through their own surveys and attempts to publicize bad conditions in the slums. While their efforts were not always successful, most houses were in sympathy with municipal reform.

The cause of the black was a major gap in Progressive Era reform, and here again the settlement record was mixed. Many settlement workers shared the prejudices of the period and either ignored the black or sought to relegate him to an inferior place. To keep blacks from mixing with their white clientele, some settlements established black branches. These included College Settlement in Philadelphia, which formed Starr Center, and South End House in Boston, which set up Robert Gould Shaw House for blacks. Other settlements, like Hiram House in Cleveland and Cambridge Neighborhood House in Massachusetts, welcomed blacks along with whites. A few settlements founded for blacks had no previous connection with white settlements. Altogether, by 1910 about ten settlements served primarily a black clientele. In addition, some settlements sponsored studies of the urban black. Greenwich House helped to finance Mary White Ovington's study of the New York black, *Half a Man*, and Philadelphia's College Settlement initiated W.E.B. DuBois's investigation, *The Philadelphia Negro: A Social Study*.

Probably the most significant contribution to the black cause on the part of the settlements at this time was their aid in forming the

National Association for the Advancement of Colored People. Henry Moskowitz, head of Madison House in New York, and two others who had been connected with settlements in the past, William English Walling and Mary White Ovington, drew up the initial plans for the NAACP. More than a third of those sponsoring the first NAACP conference were settlement workers, and the first reception of that gathering took place at Henry Street Settlement. Out of this conference came the formal organization of the NAACP with an executive committee of thirty-five members, eight of whom were settlement workers.[25] The NAACP was the most important accomplishment to come out of the Progressive Era for the black.

Clearly, the settlements were at the heart of much Progressive Era reform. Settlement support of labor unions and labor legislation was widespread. The same was true of laws to regulate slum housing, and efforts to establish playgrounds, Americanization programs, kindergartens, manual training, and domestic education classes. In the area of equal rights for blacks, the settlement record is certainly better than that of the progressives as a whole.

Settlement workers played key roles in the reform process. For example, they contributed their organizing ability and leadership. The number of reform organizations begun in the Progressive Era with settlement help is striking. A partial list includes the Consumers League, the Women's Trade Union League, the National Housing Association, and the NAACP. Another role settlement workers played in advancing reform was that of publicist. Jane Addams excelled in this part, both as a speaker and a writer. Other settlement leaders followed her example. The studies and surveys made by so many settlements also helped to publicize the needs of the poor and point the way to solving social problems. The settlements themselves served as demonstration centers or places of experiment in finding solutions to these problems. Finally, the settlements contributed the prestige of their movement to the reform cause.

This prestige was based on a variety of factors. First of all, the settlement was innovative. It was at the center of the exciting new profession of social work. As Jane Addams put it, "It was just 'wicked' enough to be popular." [26] During the Progressive Era, the settlement generated enough excitement to attract a large share of the leading reformers as well as a host of volunteers to staff its programs. Further prestige came from the social background of the settlement workers.

From the start of Hull-House, Jane Addams sought residents and support from Chicago's upper class, who accepted her as an equal.[27] Settlement workers invariably came from the middle and upper classes, and most possessed a college degree. The pioneers had a certain tendency to flaunt their educational ties in naming their institutions. More than one settlement bore the name "University Settlement" or "College Settlement." Others were named after specific colleges, such as Northwestern University Settlement and Hiram House. While well-educated, few workers had taken actual courses in social work, simply because they were not available. For example, the School of Applied Social Sciences at Western Reserve University did not open until 1916, and it was the first social work school to be part of a university from its beginning.[28] The prestige of social workers was not yet based on professional education.

The settlement workers of the Progressive Era were also distinguished by two other factors—age and volunteer status. The early leaders were all young people. Consequently, many were still around and actively in charge of their settlements during the New Deal. However, they no longer found it quite so easy to get volunteers. Many people referred to loosely in the Progressive Era as "settlement workers" were actually volunteers who derived their income from jobs outside the settlements but who made their homes in settlement houses and gave some of their spare time to settlement work. Good volunteers became harder to get as the settlements lost their initial innovative appeal.

The basic settlement program of clubs, classes, and recreation required a substantial investment in building facilities and staff, especially after volunteers became scarce. It was this basic program, and not the reform activities, which made settlement budgets substantial. To meet its expenses in the Progressive Era, each settlement individually solicited its own funds. Then, in 1913 in Cleveland, fifty-three charities, some of which were settlements, joined together for a major fund drive.

This Cleveland venture marked the start of the Community Chest system. The agency for distributing the Chest funds was the Welfare Federation. The intent was to rationalize fund-raising by having one large drive replace many smaller drives and for the funds from the large drive to be distributed to the member agencies in such a manner as to eliminate needless duplication and inefficiency among the charities. Under the Chest system, an agency's whole program was turned over to an all-powerful Welfare Federation for funding, since raising money outside the Chest was forbidden.[29]

The Community Chest caught on rapidly; and by the time of the Depression, the Chest financed settlements in all cities except New York and Chicago. Thus, the major difference between settlements in the Progressive Era and the New Deal was that in the earlier period each settlement was financially independent, whereas in the later period settlement budgets were controlled by a community-wide supervisory agency.

The number of settlements in the 1930s had not increased much since the Progressive Era. The National Federation of Settlements estimated that there were around 230 of them.[30] Of these, only 160 belonged to the National Federation in 1930.[31] Dues may have discouraged some from joining. Houses were supposed to pay $3.00 per $1,000.00 of income or a flat $10.00 fee annually.[32] Although these sums seem minimal now settlements were so hard pressed for money during the Depression that house after house found payment difficult or impossible. Yet, as the Depression worsened, the membership list of the National Federation remained remarkably stable. Once a settlement was admitted, it became the practice of the national organization to look the other way if the house fell behind in its dues. In spite of economic hardship, only a few settlements went out of existence during the Depression.

However, the main reason why a number of settlements did not join the National Federation was their religious connection. The Federation had strict, nonsectarian requirements for membership. Because of the absence of a Chest in New York and Chicago, a large number of settlements were dependent on various religious bodies for funds. Most of these settlements were admitted to the local settlement federations: United Neighborhood Houses of New York, and the Chicago Federation of Settlements. Their test for admission was the amount of proselytizing in the settlement's program. If a settlement with religious connections did not proselytize too much, it might be a member of a local settlement federation, but it could not be a member of the National Federation.

The settlements belonging to the National Federation were by no means evenly distributed around the United States. Nearly half were concentrated along the Eastern seaboard, with New York (35),

Boston (28), and Philadelphia (22) in the lead. After them came Minneapolis and St. Paul with a total of twelve, and Chicago and Cleveland with eleven each. Consequently, over half of the settlement houses were located in six metropolitan areas in the East and Mid-West. Only ten settlements were located along the Pacific Coast and just sixteen in the South.[33] The West was not only weak in numbers, but in "strength of leadership." Most of the people prominent in the movement came from the half dozen metropolitan areas which contained a majority of the settlements in the United States.

Regardless of where the settlement was located, the basic program consisted of a nursery, clubs, and classes, large group activities, special interest groups, and local units of national organizations, such as the Scouts. For example, if one were to have walked into Chicago Commons on a typical day, one might have found in a corner of the auditorium an English and citizenship class, and in another corner, a meeting of the Infant Welfare Society. The parlor would be turned over to school girls for table games, while the boys gravitated towards the game room and the gymnasium. The Commons was also fortunate to have facilities with which to conduct cooking schools and dressmaking classes.[34] During the early years of the Depression when staff size remained fairly constant while the number of people coming to the settlement increased, settlements reluctantly shifted somewhat from clubs to large group activities.[35] Later when the settlement staffs were augmented with a variety of workers under the federal work relief programs, a shift back to clubs occurred.

The music school settlements were a special breed. Although they had a number of settlement characteristics, their programs were built almost entirely around music. The National Federation included about a dozen music school settlements in 1930, but most were dropped by the National during the Depression.[36]

While settlements are associated with the branch of social work known as group work, virtually all settlements carried on a limited amount of casework as well. For instance, a settlement worker might assist an unwed mother in making arrangements for the birth of her child; or on the complaints of neighbors, she might talk to the family of a teenager who was bordering on juvenile delinquency.[37] Neighbors having trouble with the relief office often turned to the settlement worker. For example, at Chicago Commons when a family failed to receive its relief order for coal, the settlement's family service worker called the public relief station.[38] Meanwhile, until the missing order was found, the Commons provided the family with coal. Although relief-giving was not usually considered a function of the settlement, most houses could not avoid giving some of it during the Depression. The individual needs of their neighbors simply could not be ignored.

While recreational and educational activities, common to virtually all settlements, occupied the bulk of the settlement's space, a number of settlement leaders regarded social action and experimentation to be the major function of the agency. To some extent, however, recreation and social action were in opposition to each other. As Lillie Peck, the executive secretary of the National Federation of Settlements, conceded, "The fact that settlements have built up large institutional equipment which takes the major part of their budget, limits what they can put into experimental work, which is their major reason for being." [39] In a sense, the settlements mortgaged themselves to large contributors when they adopted a substantial institutional program. By the 1930s, settlements in certain cities had largely abandoned social action.

During the Progressive Era, settlements had served the cause of social action, first, by acting as advocates for their neighbors, and secondly, by serving as demonstration centers in the quest to find solutions to social problems. The New Deal altered the role of the settlements. Some settlement workers, particularly in New York and Chicago, still fulfilled the advocate role. However, the New Deal emphasis on large-scale federal experimentation left little place for the settlements.

A leading example of the 1930s settlement worker functioning as an advocate for the poor was Lea Taylor, head of Chicago Commons, president of the Chicago Federation of Settlements until 1937, and president of the National Federation from 1931 to 1934. As an advocate for her neighbors, she served on a number of committees relating to relief and social service, attended conferences, and testified before committees of the Illinois legislature and the United States Congress.

Taylor saw her role as that of an interpreter of her neighborhood to the larger community. She recalled times when she was the only person on a board or committee who had firsthand contact with or lived in a poor neighborhood. She could tell committees formulating relief regulations how her neighbors felt. For example, the chairman of the Illinois Emergency Relief Commission could ask her, "Do the people like this regulation?" and she could accurately say, "No." She served on a WPA committee in Chicago, and remembered how the work reliefers were accused of "leaning on their shovels." She could interpret why, knowing that some of the men arrived on the job having had nothing to eat.[40] She wholeheartedly shared the viewpoint of her successor to the presidency of the National Federation of Settlements, Helen Hall, who declared that "the social settlement, here and abroad, has from the beginning been an instrument of social reform, using first-hand knowledge to bring about changes in living conditions." [41]

During the New Deal, some social workers continued to see the role of the settlement as the initiator of experiments, whose successes would then be taken over and expanded by the government. Edith Abbott, a professor in the School of Social Service Administration at the University of Chicago, held this view. Consequently, she was disappointed when her study showed the Boston settlements to have "very little such experimentation in progress." Yet, she had several possible explanations. First, the pioneering spirit had left the settlements. Second, one could not expect innovation and experimentation to be continuous. Third, the reduced budgets of the settlements prohibited new and experimental undertakings. Finally, the country was primarily interested in experimental relief and recovery programs on the national level, not in small scale, local experimentation.[42] Of these four reasons, lack of money was probably the most decisive; for even if the other factors had not existed, reduced budgets made new undertakings almost impossible.

Some historians have advanced another reason why social workers in general turned away from social reform after the Progressive Era. They call attention to the rise of professionalism as seen in the establishment of social work schools and professional associations, the emphasis on casework as a teachable technique, and the prevalence of "professional" attitudes. Freud's impact on the United States at this time was partially responsible, as he focused attention on psychological problems at the expense of social problems. Also, because the leading early social work schools tended to be associated with private universities, they were directly under the control of large contributors, most of whom had conservative views. However, very few settlement workers actually had attended these schools before 1940 and almost none possessed the MSW degree. Consequently, most were excluded from the professional social work organizations and could not claim professional status in the full sense of the word. Thus, professionalism did not directly affect settlements during the 1930s.

What really had happened to the settlement movement between the time of the Progressive Era and the New Deal? In the formative years, settlements had been active participants in a variety of reforms. However, they also established institutional programs which demanded a sizeable portion of budget and staff time. Then came the 1920s. When the settlement movement lost its initial excitement, it also lost many of its best volunteers and residents. The number of settlements stabilized. Meanwhile houses outside of New York and Chicago lost their financial independence due to the rise of the Community Chest. By the time of the New Deal, consequently, reform was quite different from what it had been in the Progressive Era. The New Deal concentrated on economic measures, emphasized large scale reform originating with the federal government, and made major changes in American society. Yet well-to-do people who controlled the pursestrings of private charity were adamantly opposed to the New Deal. Furthermore, with the rise of the Community Chest, they had extended their control over private charity. Therefore, it is not surprising that settlements were more central to reform in the Progressive Era than in the New Deal.

2. Professionalism and Social Action

*D*URING the Depression, limited resources forced the Community Chests to curtail settlement budgets. Consequently, the houses were able to hire only a token number of social work school graduates and those only towards the end of the Depression. Community Chests did little to encourage membership in professional associations or other professional activities. It was not that the Chest saw professionalization as either hindering or abetting reform. It was simply that more immediate problems, ranging from hungry children to leaking roofs, took precedence. Besides, regardless of who was on the settlement staffs, it was the Chests, and not the staffs, that controlled agency policy.

Historians, however, have had a tendency to blame increasing professionalization in the field of social work for the declining commitment to reform.[1] Professionalism in social work takes on tangible form through social work schools and professional associations. It also has an intangible dimension, involving such abstractions as "professional" attitudes, ethics, values, manner, and even, lifestyle. The historians who emphasize professionalization as the key element inhibiting reform stress the social work schools' utilization of psychological concepts. In the process of focusing on individual adjustment, the schools neglected the need to reform society. Furthermore, they became the gateway to membership in the leading professional organization, the American Association of Social Work. Finally, the professional mystique dictated a clinical, neutralist approach to social work.

Recently, some scholars have challenged the belief that professionalism inhibits social action. For example, a 1970 study showed that more professionally oriented social workers tended to be more committed to social action. In other words, the influence of the profession acts as a counterweight to pressures for conservatism which the worker usually encounters on the job.[2] Yet the social work profession has had elements both favoring and opposing social change. During the 1930s, the settlements were still largely able to avoid the conservative aspects of the developing profession while at the same time utilizing other aspects to further social change programs.

How directly did the social work schools themselves influence the settlements? In 1929, twenty-nine schools were members of the Association of Professional Schools of Social Work, but of these only thirteen offered education at the graduate level, and all but four admitted students without a degree. In 1940, the number had risen to forty-one schools, all offering programs at the graduate level. However, only a handful of settlement workers held the Master of Social Work (MSW) degree.

The schools could, of course, influence the settlements indirectly through the development of social work techniques and through the public statements and speeches of leading educators. As a separate technique or discipline, group work was in the process of establishing itself while community organization had not even reached that stage. In order to guide settlement workers in acquiring the group work technique, the National Federation of Settlements invited member houses to submit some of their club reports for analysis. A sample analysis of a club leader's performance at St. Martha's House in Philadelphia reflected the influence of psychiatry and psychology in the Federation's emphasis on the individual development of the club members. The Federation then admonished the club leader to be more aware of the reactions of club members toward each other and not to try "to foist her own standards on the group," [3] in other words, to be neutral. Nowhere in the analysis did a concern with social issues appear. The emphasis was not on a technique for reforming society, but adjusting the individual to the existing society.

Among the faculties of the social work schools were social action advocates, but their advocacy of social action had little influence on the curriculum. Probably the most prominent school for group work was at Western Reserve University. Here Assistant Professor Clara A. Kaiser thought students needed not only techniques, but a knowledge "of the broader social implications of settlement work and social work as a whole." [4] Another Western

Reserve professor, Grace Coyle, won the Pugsley Award of the National Conference of Social Work in 1935 for her paper, "Group Work and Social Change," which reaffirmed the role of social action within social work.[5] However, a glance at the thesis subjects of group work students at Western Reserve shows more concern with recreation and ethnic life. Typical was "The Development of Basket Ball as a Leisure Time Sport in Greater Cleveland." [6]

Even in one of the worst years of the Depression, 1932, only one thesis at Western Reserve dealt with social conditions: "An Investigation of Existing Data on Economic Conditions in the Area of the University Neighborhood Centers and an Interpretation of the Data as They Apply to Community Organization." [7] The University Neighborhood Centers referred to was actually run by the School of Applied Social Science and financed through Western Reserve University (chiefly with Mrs. Dudley S. Blossom's contributions). This unique arrangement did not last long. With the decline of Blossom's contributions, the chief concern of the School of Applied Social Science was to transfer the settlement to the Cleveland Welfare Federation.[8] Consequently, the faculty did not use University Neighborhood Centers for social action programs. Looking back on his education at Western Reserve University, a social work graduate felt that his "biggest bone to pick with the School" was its lack of emphasis on social reform and social action.[9]

Not only were very few settlement workers holders of the MSW, but a number publicly rebelled against the value which the social work profession placed on professional education. A 1931 study of New York settlements revealed "little or no demand on the part of settlements for training in the technique of group work." [10] The headworker of Neighborhood House in New Haven, Connecticut, thought that "far more important than any amount of time spent in college or in graduate professional study is a cultural background, breeding, common sense, initiative and drive." [11] The most famous settlement leader, Jane Addams, "protested against the use of the terms 'trained' and 'untrained' workers." A worker with many years experience and whose work was comparable to that of a "trained" person "should not be considered 'untrained,'" according to Addams.[12] None of the prominent settlement workers in the 1930s had the MSW, and in some cities, no settlement worker possessed it.

Throughout the decade, settlements resisted the trend towards professionalism in terms of social work education.

Along with the schools, associations were an important agent of professionalization. The American Association of Social Work (AASW) embraced all branches of social work and was the main social work professional organization. It originally combined a concern for social problems with efforts to protect and advance the status of its membership. As time passed the requirements for membership in terms of professional education were increased, while the AASW neglected social concerns.[13] Not surprisingly, few people in the settlement world could meet the qualifications for AASW membership, and some questioned its value.[14] Helen Hall, then president of the National Federation of Settlements, refused to accept as important the criteria of AASW membership in choosing settlement staff. At Hall's Henry Street Settlement, one of the major houses in the country, not more than four workers could meet the AASW requirements. Furthermore, she pointed out that settlements needed not only social workers but experts in a variety of fields, such as workers' education, consumers' problems, art, and music.[15] Her attitude typified the resistance of settlements to the influence of professionalism in terms of AASW membership in the 1930s.

The settlements' own national, professional organization, the National Federation of Settlements, was quite different from the AASW. Although the National Federation was interested in professionalism (it did a study of personnel practices in 1936),[16] its main concern was with social issues, and it carried out projects along social action lines. Furthermore, local associations of settlements in New York and Chicago were also primarily involved with social issues. These settlement associations formed exceptions to the thesis that professional associations fostered a reversal from cause to function in social work.

The addition of a paid executive secretary to the National Federation increased the effectiveness of the national office. The first person to occupy this position on a full-time basis was Lillie Peck. She began at Boston's South End House in 1912 as a volunteer[17] and rose to the position of assistant headworker. In 1930 she moved to New York as assistant to Albert J. Kennedy, then secretary of the National Federation as well as headworker of University Settlement. However,

Kennedy was more identified with music in settlements than with social action, and he tended to lag behind other leaders in his support for social causes. By contrast, Peck had no doubts that social action was part of settlement work. Therefore, she succeeded Kennedy as secretary of the National in 1934.[18] She was not a professional in an educated sense and in the next decade had to take a lesser position in the National's office. On moving to New York, she made her home at Henry Street Settlement and remained there until her death in 1957.[19] Settlement work was more than an occupation to her; it was her life.

The amount and kind of work that Peck could do was severely limited by a small budget. Membership dues produced about $5,000 a year, out of which had to come her salary, office rent and supplies, and pay for clerical help.[20] If the National had to struggle with an inadequate budget, at least it was independent of the domination of a single large contributor or outside organization. However, lack of money also meant that many activities had to be carried on by volunteers in the various committees and divisions. The divisions primarily concerned with social issues were Housing, Old Age Security, Race Relations, and Unemployment. The Unemployment Division under Helen Hall was most active.

In the spring of 1928 when the United States was generally enjoying prosperity, the Federation's Committee on Unemployment decided to embark on a study focusing on men who were thrown out of work by a stoppage in industry or by technological change. It did not attempt a statistical study, but instead asked settlements and other agencies to write case studies of unemployed people in their neighborhoods emphasizing the economic, physical, and psychological effects of unemployment. The result was a vivid portrayal of the plight of the unemployed, as this excerpt from Hall's *Case Studies of Unemployment* shows:

> When unemployment comes, the husband and wife most often face the situation together. But this unity changes as the wife is harried by debt collectors, the rent man, the insurance man. She sees the children half fed and getting thin, often sick, and needing clothes she can't buy; and then, too, she may be working herself and adding fatigue to worry. In the first days of her husband's job-hunt she is sympathetic and fights to keep his courage up and defends him in the neighborhood. The poignancy of his struggle has not been

lost in her own discouragement. I remember when Mrs.
White came round to tell of her husband's first pay envelope
after nearly a winter's search. "You know," she said, "the
look on his face when he give it to me was like a child with a
Christmas present." But that was his first winter out. Now,
facing the third one, the Whites no longer present a united
front. She doesn't believe he tries and is bitter against him
and he no longer cares very much, for he has the gang and is
"in on the bottle as it is handed around," and only comes
home late to sleep. The strain and disappointment vent
themselves in wrangles. As Mrs. White puts it, "There were
no ugly words in our house when he was workin, but I'm so
tired now I don't know what I'm saying." And to come home
from anything as disheartening as "makin' the rounds" only
to be accused of not really trying doesn't make for harmony.
The blame the husband sometimes gets only bespeaks a
nervous strain on the part of the wife, but often she has read
in the papers of prosperous times and that adds to her distrust
of her husband's earnestness in his job-hunt. "If other men
get jobs, as the papers say, why can't he?" . . . Mrs. White's
bitterness toward her husband is aggravated by the fact that
she is no longer able to control her ten- and twelve-year old
boys and they have lost respect for their father so that he
can't help her. Then, too, she has had to take her oldest boy
out of school.[21]

By introducing the reader to actual people like the Whites, Helen Hall
hoped to arouse sympathy for the unemployed.

The study was timely, for when the Depression hit, the NFS
was one of the few organizations that had done recent research on the
effects of unemployment. A professional writer, Clinch Calkins,
popularized the study in *Some Folks Won't Work*.[22] Through the
ironic title, Calkins hoped to reach a potentially sceptical public,
describe the unemployed's often desperate efforts to get work, their
struggles to avoid going on relief, and the psychological damage of
unemployment. When interest in the study continued, Hall put
together *Case Studies of Unemployment*, a collection of 150 of the
original case studies.[23] She also utilized this study at state and federal
hearings on unemployment insurance.[24] Through her position as head
of the National's Unemployment Division, she did all she could to
stimulate public opinion in favor of welfare reform.

Like the National Federation, the United Neighborhood Houses of New York had an office and paid staff which was supported through dues and contributions, but its operational budget was about twice as large as the National's.[25] It may have been easier for United Neighborhood Houses to raise money because of the composition of its board. Whereas the National Federation board consisted almost entirely of settlement headworkers, the United Neighborhood Houses board was organized to have an equal number of representatives from three groups: headworkers, settlement board members, and "general public."[26] Not only were the last two categories likely to have more money to contribute than the salaried headworkers, but they also often had considerable influence in New York City. Probably the most influential non-settlement worker was the board president, Stanley Isaacs, who was also president of the borough of Manhattan.[27]

The Chicago Federation of Settlements resembled the United Neighborhood Houses of New York in its interest in social issues, but it lacked a paid staff and headquarters of its own during the 1930s. Its regular meetings were attended by settlement workers and often included speakers and discussion of social issues, followed by the passage of resolutions. Typical was the vote of the Chicago Federation of Settlements to endorse the Costigan-LaFollette Bill, which would have meant direct federal relief under Hoover.[28]

Other cities also had local federations of settlements, but these organizations show practically no involvement with social issues. The federations in Chicago and New York probably were social action oriented, not only because they were the two largest cities, but also because neither city had a Community Chest. The absence of a Chest meant that settlements were largely their own masters. Significantly, the social action oriented leadership of the National Federation of Settlements also came largely from New York and Chicago.

Professionalism meant more than social work schools and professional organizations. It was also an intangible set of values, attitudes, and even a life-style. Settlement workers had been the forerunners of modern social workers, and a number of the old settlement pioneers were still active. However, a heritage of reform involvement in the Progressive Era did not necessarily mean that the settlement worker would be pro-New Deal. A case in point is George Bellamy.

"We will never have prosperity under the new deal," wrote

Bellamy in 1939. Six weeks after Roosevelt's first inauguration, Bellamy had concluded that the president "did not know anything about government, democracy, and certainly about ways of creating prosperity." [29] As a progressive, Bellamy had been active in housing reform and the public playground movement. However, he failed to keep up with the times, and the New Deal found him anachronistic. Why?

Possibly the answer lies in Bellamy's background. As a young man, he worked his way through Hiram College and then founded Hiram House in 1896. Financially, it was "touch and go" these first few years, but he, like an Horatio Alger hero, worked hard and succeeded. Perhaps because the Alger myth had worked in his own life, Bellamy never relinquished it.[30] He had worked hard and succeeded, so why couldn't everybody? "The world-wide depression is, in the main, caused by a moral collapse," he argued. "The invisible, immutable laws of nature will not stand for an excess of dishonesty, exploitation and an unhampered freedom of diseases. . . ." [31]

The success of Hiram House had become assured when industrialist Samuel Mather and other prominent Clevelanders began to support it. As Bellamy associated with these men over the years, he seems to have absorbed their values and outlook. Things like salary and membership in the "right" club came to be important. At the beginning of the Depression, Bellamy was earning $7,500 a year as headworker. This salary was cut to $6,000 during the Depression.[32] Although he protested his sacrifice, a national study of salaries in settlements during 1937 showed $6,000 to be the highest.[33] By this time, he had acquired property in four communities on the outskirts of Cleveland, owned stocks with a market value of $18,837.80, and was driving a new Buick sedan.[34] He was also applying for membership in Cleveland's exclusive Union Club. Thanks to the membership of a number of his friends, two of whom took "care of the admission fee and the common stock purchase requirement," he was admitted in 1938.[35] However, as he still found the dues high, after some difficulty he arranged to have his membership transferred to the "clerical and academic" classification.[36] If his desire to associate and identify with men of wealth and social prominence appears somewhat out of place in the settlement context, his aspirations nevertheless were probably characteristic of the upper middle class.

In trying to identify with upper class Clevelanders, perhaps it was natural that Bellamy had absorbed their views. Certainly, his association with them was made easier by a common viewpoint. He still retained the nineteenth century ideas of his college years. "Progress," he wrote, "has been reached through the process of fundamental laws of evolution." Depressions were part of this progress, being "Nature's ways of cleaning away the debris of dishonesty, graft and exploitation, making possible a new start." [37]

Yet, he was aware of the suffering the Depression caused. On one occasion, he described a hungry little girl who was "hunting eagerly in garbage cans for food," observing "the joy that filled her emotions" when she "drew out a big whole potato." He found praiseworthy a little boy crying with hunger on the Hiram House playground. One of the settlement workers offered to buy the boy a glass of milk; but the boy, still crying, refused, saying, " 'No, my mama doesn't want me to take something for nothing.' " Bellamy declared, "Hiram House has endeavored to build into [its neighbors] a sense of self support and self respect, succeeding, we believe, beyond even our best of expectations." [38] Concern with upholding an outdated philosophy of "rugged individualism" seems to have taken precedence with Bellamy over the need for more adequate relief programs.

Bellamy was one of the few pioneer settlement workers never elected to the presidency of the National Federation. Quite probably his archaic views eliminated him from the leadership of this reform-oriented organization. In spite of this personal disappointment, he continued to be active in the National, serving as chairman of the finance committee and on the board. In 1938 the National made Bellamy an honorary president. At the same time, it elected a more reform-minded Clevelander, Alice Gannett, head of Goodrich House, vice-president and later president.[39]

Not all the old pioneers turned their backs on the New Deal like George Bellamy. Mary Simkhovitch still headed Greenwich House in New York, ardently supported the New Deal, and was a leading housing reformer in the 1930s.[40] Grace Abbott, in the Progressive Era a Hull-House resident and during the Depression vice-president of the Hull-House board, organized the Committee of Social Workers, which endorsed Roosevelt in 1936.[41] Lillian Wald was also a New Deal supporter,[42] but was forced to withdraw as

headworker of Henry Street Settlement early in the decade because of
ill-health. The most famous of the pioneers, Jane Addams, supported
Hoover, even in 1932. However, in spite of heart disease, she also
headed the Illinois Committee for Old Age Security,[43] remained as
head of Hull-House, and published three books.[44] Her last public act
before her death in 1935 was to visit the Cook County commissioners
to argue for a better relief program.

 While many of the old pioneers were still around, a new
generation of settlement leaders took over the leadership of the
settlement movement in the 1930s. Lea Taylor included herself when
she dubbed this group "the transitional generation." They stood
between the Progressive pioneers and the later social work school
graduates. Some might expect this "transitional generation" to have a
significant number of the sons and daughters of the newer immigrant
groups among its ranks, but this does not appear to have been the
case. What probably happened was that as the second generation
immigrants became Americanized, they had a tendency to reject
nearly everything associated with immigrant status, including settlements. Others might expect the "transitional generation" to be of a
lower social class than the pioneers. The newcomers were probably
less genteel, certainly less inclined to volunteer their services gratis,
and had less preoccupation with religion. Yet, both groups did come
from a broadly defined middle class. No significant nationality or
social class factors appear to separate one generation of settlement
workers from the other.

 Likewise, the younger generation sought to carry on the unique
lifestyle of the settlement worker. The president of the National
Federation of Settlements from 1930 to 1934, Lea Taylor, exemplified
this lifestyle. Her father, Graham Taylor, founded Chicago Commons
when she was eleven. From then until her retirement, except for four
years at Vassar, Taylor lived at Chicago Commons. A motivating
factor in her work was her lifelong admiration for her father, whom
she replaced as head of Chicago Commons. She was also representative of reform-oriented settlement workers in her extensive involvement in outside organizations. For example, in 1932 she served as
head of Chicago Commons, president of the Chicago Federation of
Settlements, and president of the National Federation. She gave
"many talks before local groups," represented the National twice at

hearings in Washington, and served on a variety of committees, including the advisory committee of the Cook County Bureau of Public Welfare.[45]

Settlement workers tended to have outgoing personalities and to be able to establish rapport with people throughout the social spectrum. Part of Taylor's charm was her self-effacement in view of all her accomplishments. For example, she maintained that her thirteen-year term as president of the Chicago Federation of Settlements "was partially because I could type, get out the notices, and do other secretarial work in addition to the presidency." In a more serious vein, she admitted, "I had a city-wide concern which every settlement didn't have and I could help identify the problems on which the Federation should work." [46] She was the sort of person who attended meetings of the unemployed while being listed in the *Chicago Social Register*. Her ability to work with people at all levels of society was remarkable.

Her female sex was also typical of settlement workers. For example, the directory of the National Federation of Settlements in 1930 listed 125 female headworkers to thirty-nine male headworkers.[47] A minor row erupted over this issue when a new head resident at Jacob Riis Settlement in New York, Henry Shiphard, took the anti-feminist position that men made better headworkers than women. His views were published in the New York *World Telegram* under the headline, "Where Men Are Superior." As luck would have it, that staunch old feminist, Jane Addams, saw the item. She clipped it out and sent it to Lea Taylor with a terse note: " 'I think that the Federation of Settlements might consider disciplining this young man. It's a voice of forty years ago.' " Taylor decided that disciplining in this case was a man's job and turned the matter over to Albert J. Kennedy, head of University Settlement in New York.[48] Kennedy excused Shiphard by saying, "He was probably misquoted in some degree." [49] To many people, male social workers carried more status, but women continued to dominate the leadership in the settlement field.

Settlements came into being at a time when the feminist movement was unusually strong and more women were seeking work outside the home. During the Progressive Era, a woman was expected to choose between marriage and a career; and settlement work, which involved living in the house or neighborhood, presented a way of life that could become an alternative to marriage. For Sina Evans, the headworker of Neighborhood House in Lorain, Ohio, the marriage versus career choice had not changed much by the 1930s. She wrote to the secretary of the National:

> I just turned down a very nice man recently widowed with two boys fifteen and twelve years. My board members sweetly encouraged our friendship, as did others, all thinking that I would stay on for good in Lorain and here—but said man had other plans—home is the woman's place. Well, Lillie M. Peck, if you can picture me centered at homemaking . . . I couldn't—and I weighed the matter very much. I was not madly in love, but what I would want in marriage did not seem to be there—and I looked around at my meagre but oh so treasured belongings and the settlement—and I thought all of what life meant to me and decided it was no use. I would be miserable and I am not so adaptable now. . . . But I wouldn't give this [settlement] up for a lovely home, a charming man and two awfully nice boys.[50]

For some women, the settlement offered independence and an alternative to marriage to someone with whom they were "not madly in love."

Not all female settlement workers were spinsters. In 1935, Lea Taylor's successor as president of the National Federation, Helen Hall, married Paul Kellogg, editor of the *Survey*. Both continued their careers. Hall retained her maiden name; and Kellogg moved into Henry Street Settlement, of which his wife was head. Lillian Wald, the spinster founder of Henry Street, commented, "Helen Hall is without doubt jubilantly happy." [51] Hall and Kellogg were a well-matched couple. Hall's quick wit, vitality, and sense of humor complemented her husband's rather sober personality. Both shared a deep interest in and commitment to social reform. Each was fiercely loyal to the other, while at the same time, each was intensely devoted to his respective job.[52] Hall's background as a career woman had included attending the New York School for Social Work, organizing a settlement in Westchester County, war work, and the leadership of University Settlement in Philadelphia for eleven years prior to her taking over Henry Street in 1933.[53] A highly energetic woman with "the capacity to accomplish an ungodly amount of work," [54] she became actively involved in a number of organizations of a reform nature. Nevertheless, settlement workers were more likely to be spinsters than married women.

A common fallacy was that the settlement lifestyle with its emphasis on residence in the settlement house precluded headworkers with families. Among those who brought up their children in settlements were Gaylord White (Union Settlement, New York), Mary Simkhovitch (Greenwich House, New York), Albert J. Kennedy (South End House, Boston), Charles Cooper (Kingsley House, Pittsburgh), Graham Taylor (Chicago Commons), and Clyde Murray (Union Settlement, New York).[55] These people made sacrifices in terms of family privacy and a more conventional lifestyle because they believed in the importance of residence. More than any other factor, it was residence that made the settlement lifestyle unique, that set off the settlement worker from other social workers, and which placed the settlement at odds with the clinical ideals of professionalism. To professionals who saw social work as a technique to be practiced in a clinical setting apart from one's home, the settlement worker's claim to expertise on the basis of neighborhood residence made settlement workers little better than amateurs. Residence was irrelevant to the rising professionals, but settlement workers still clung to the concept in the 1930s.

Outwardly, settlements had approximately the same number of residents at the beginning of the decade as at the end; but inwardly, residency often lacked meaning. The number of residents in a settlement varied widely, but two dozen was fairly typical. At the heart of residence was volunteer service to the settlement. At Henry Street this service could range from clerical duties to club leadership and was to amount to "a minimum of two periods a week." [56] In addition, Henry Street residents were expected to attend Tuesday night meetings, which often featured outside speakers and discussion of social issues.[57] Other settlements also adopted the practice of resident meethnfs, but the meetings were not always equally worthwhile. One can imagine the suppressed exasperation of a busy resident coerced into attending a meeting given over to "such practical matters as keeping the electric light bill down." [58] As settlements encountered difficulty finding residents, requirements became lax. Settlements began abandoning regular resident meetings and, in some cases, did not even require the service that was basic to the residence concept. In such cases, about all that remained to give direction and meaning to residence was dinner table conversation. Harriet Vittum, head of Northwestern University Settlement in Chicago, remarked, "Never a week goes by that we do not discuss at our dinner table some political situation in the neighborhood." For Vittum, such conversation was "very definite and a very vital part of" settlement life.[59] Nevertheless, by the 1930s, many residents seem to have regarded the settlement primarily as an economical place to live rather than as a means of working more effectively with the poor.

The number of residents remained stable during the Depression for several reasons. Harriet Vittum was only one influential leader who defended the concept of residence. The National Federation of Settlements thought that residence was necessary,[60] and many settlement boards upheld this view. For example, in spite of the shortage of money during the Depression, Alta House in Cleveland built three apartments to replace three run-down old cottages formerly used for residence.[61] Also, a certain amount of coercion was applied by some settlements to maintain the number of residents. Jobs were hard to come by in the 1930s, and some headworkers like Ruth Austin of Gads Hill Center in Chicago were able to make the offer of a position conditional on residence in the settlement.[62] To attract and hold residents, most settlements tried to keep the cost of residence as low as possible. At the University of Chicago Settlement, residents took turns preparing Sunday dinner, and they also assisted in the serving of dinners every day.[63] The charge for a single room was $8.00 a month or $6.50 each for a double plus $31.00 a month for board.[64] However, where the cost was so low that the residents had to be subsidized, residence was likely to become a "bone of contention" within the organization.[65]

Most houses just tried to break even financially in their residence program. However, at Hull-House after Jane Addams's death, the settlement capitalized on its prestige by turning residence into a money-making program. Hull-House had an unusually large physical plant (it covered two city blocks), which included twenty-six apartments and at least twenty-seven rooms for residents.[66] Rents ranged from $40 to $65 for apartments and $15 for rooms. These rentals supplied Hull-House with one-third of its income. Without Jane Addams to raise money, it became imperative to have as many people as possible living at the settlement.[67] Hull-House began to solicit residents more openly[68] and dropped the six-month probationary period.[69] These efforts were successful; residence at Hull-House increased from around sixty-five in 1935,[70] the year of Miss Addams's death, to more than 100 in 1939.[71] This businesslike approach attracted a more passive type of resident compared to those who initiated innovative programs in earlier years.

Originally, the concept of residence was tied to social change programs, but by the 1930s, residence in the settlement was often little different from residence in a small dormitory or rooming house.[72] However, the residency principle was not widely abandoned until the 1940s.[73] It was killed by the encroachment of professionalism and by lessening emphasis on reform and social action.[74]

A 1937 study of eighty-five houses showed:

Regular paid staff	23%
Students	6%
Residents other than paid staff members giving regular service	2%
WPA, NYA & others [government workers]	33%
Volunteers giving regular service	36% [75]

The largest category, volunteers, came mostly from the middle and upper classes. However, as it became increasingly difficult to get volunteers from the traditional sources during the Depression, settlements started using their neighbors in that capacity. The unemployed were a hitherto largely untapped source. Settlements found that many of these people would "offer their services for the sake of having something to do" [76] and to keep their skills, such as typing, from getting rusty.[77] It is possible that the increasing use of volunteers from the neighborhood may have lessened the desire of people outside the neighborhood to serve in the same capacity.

Volunteers were in direct opposition to the professionals on two counts. First, they were untrained; and second, they were unpaid. Some settlements complained that volunteers were often unreliable.[78] Social agencies in general responded by relegating the volunteer to "marginal or else closely supervised" activities.[79] One result was a decline in the number of volunteer workers, first evident at Godman Guild in Columbus and in other settlements during the Depression.[80] However, like residence, the decline in volunteers was not really felt until the following decade.

The main reason why settlements were able to carry on

extensive programs in spite of budget cuts was the presence of workers whose services were, in a sense, volunteered by the government. These workers were employed on various federal work relief programs, such as WPA and NYA. No money passed through the settlements since the workers were paid directly by the government. Federal control was so complete that settlements had almost no say as to whom they would get, how many they would get, when they would arrive, or how long they would stay. The federal government was in a position to influence the settlements, but the government's overriding concern was work relief, not settlement programs. For the most part, the government workers acted as recreation and club leaders or carried out routine clerical and maintenance tasks. Although in some cases neighbors comprised a majority of settlement staff, they made no significant difference in settlement policies.

The rapid and permanent withdrawal of government workers from the settlements after 1939 created severe problems. These workers had been around since 1933, and most settlements had come to depend on them. For example, one house had a total staff of ninety, only eight of whom were paid by the settlement, the other eighty-two being either WPA or NYA workers.[81] In Cleveland, every settlement took from twenty to seventy WPA and NYA workers.[82] Alta House had used these workers to reestablish its Collinwood branch. By 1939, it was apparent that WPA help would eventually be withdrawn, and an attempt was made to replace WPA workers with volunteers.[83] The attempt failed, and in 1943 the Collinwood branch was reopened as a day-care center.[84] Most settlements survived the withdrawal of the government-paid workers, but only by curtailing their activities and adding to their paid staff.

Outsiders became involved in the settlements through the categories of "resident," "volunteer," and "government worker." The residents were usually from middle and upper class backgrounds and included such people as Paul Walter of Hiram House,[85] who in the 1950s emerged as conservative Robert Taft's campaign manager and a leader in Republican politics. Ironically, Frank W. McCulloch, a volunteer at Chicago Commons, also worked as a senatorial campaign manager in the 1950s—for liberal Democrat Paul Douglas. Settlements incorporated a wide range of ideologies. They also drew in people from all classes as workers during the 1930s. Use of these people had implications for social action programs. For example,

Frank McCulloch was active in the Workers Alliance and its forerunner in Chicago. Also the WPA brought its pro-labor Workers Education program to the settlement. Because these people were not on the settlement payroll, they had in some ways greater freedom of action than the regular staff. Yet, they functioned in a decidedly subordinate capacity.

Settlement workers possessed certain attitudes, biases, and prejudices which sometimes clashed with the professional social work subculture. Casework was the central technique in social work and psychiatry at the top of the status hierarchy. However, headworker Helen Hall occasionally ridiculed this preoccupation with casework and psychiatry. Some private welfare agencies in the early days of the Depression refused to accept cases unless psychiatric help was needed. Hall confessed to emphasizing an unemployed neighbor's past sex problem in order to get her accepted for relief by such an agency.[86] Helen Hall also looked hopefully for signs that social work education would turn away from its deep absorption in casework. She was both "amused and disheartened" at attempts to elevate group work through what she called "an inclination to use big words and social work terminology in the same way that the case workers obscured from the lay mind . . . their sometimes quite simple processes." [87]

Yet, professionalism was a force that had to be accommodated. In 1937 Hull-House finally decided to put the headworker's job on a salaried basis and hired welfare administrator Charlotte Carr. Although she lacked the proper social work education, Carr immediately began to give Hull-House a more professional, more businesslike look. She replaced a number of volunteers with paid workers[88] and characteristically changed her title from "head resident" to "director." [89] In spite of their different reactions to professionalism, both Helen Hall and Charlotte Carr were ardent advocates of social action programs.

A certain amount of tension existed between settlements and social work professionals. Only a very few settlement workers possessed the MSW or qualified for AASW membership. Furthermore, settlement leaders publicly belittled the importance of social work education, casework, and psychiatry. In their own national professional organization and in the local federations in New York and Chicago, settlements placed far more emphasis on social issues than on professionalization. This emphasis on social reform was not just an outgrowth of the reform tradition in settlements, as the case of George Bellamy illustrates. Tradition, however, gave the settlement workers a unique lifestyle—that of residence in the settlement. Settlement workers sought to develop a neighborly rather than a clinical relationship with the people they tried to help. Residence made settlement work more than an occupation; it was also a way of life, as the case of Lea Taylor shows. The use of volunteers challenged the professional concept of social work as a paid occupation requiring special training. During the 1930s, settlement workers were able to take from professionalism that which was compatible with social action and minimize the rest, such as stress on individual adjustment to society. Thus, for the New Deal period, professionalism as an explanation for the decline in reform activity on the part of the settlement movement as a whole is inadequate. Furthermore, in the final analysis, the social workers did not control the settlements' policies; that prerogative belonged to those who controlled the settlements' income—the Community Chests.

3. Boards, Chests, and Funds

*I*N the Progressive Era, settlement boards had complete responsibility for raising their own funds and establishing their own policies and programs. By 1929, however, settlements outside New York and Chicago had largely lost this autonomy. No longer did board members and others give directly to an agency. Instead, they gave to a Community Chest, which then allocated money among its member agencies. The Chest weakened the policy-making power of the individual boards because it created one city-wide body with almost total control over private social agencies. Such centralization of decision-making power, which followed the centralization of charitable finances, was bound to have implications for the nature of settlements and their involvement with social action programs.

New York and Chicago, as an alternative to the Chest system, evolved a deficit fund system. Under this system, an agency only derived a small proportion of its budget from a privately raised central fund, and since this proportion was a stated percentage, no board passed judgment on agency activities. The deficit fund left the power of individual agency boards intact. While most boards were as conservative as the Chests, the deficit fund system did allow an occasional liberal board full range for social action.

In non-Chest cities, the fund-raising function of the settlement boards was vital. Membership on these boards almost always implied financial obligations. Members were chosen mainly because of their ability to give or their ability to get others to give.[1] Indeed the emphasis on fund-raising overshadowed other functions of the boards in New York and Chicago.

In Chest cities, the individual boards still retained some advisory functions. In Minneapolis, the boards were "to formulate policies, select a competent Head Worker, [and] confer and advise at regular intervals with the Head Worker on matters pertaining to the Settlement." [2] Boards in Chest cities still retained the power to hire and fire the headworker, even though the local Chest had to approve the salary paid. Consequently, it was quite necessary for the head-worker to be in agreement with the board, and many headworkers rarely made a major decision, such as the hiring or firing of a subordinate worker, without first consulting the board.[3] Therefore, even though boards in Chest cities could no longer appropriate money for specific programs, they could effectively control how programs were carried out.

Curiously, the dominant board-subordinate headworker rela-tionship was absent in some of the major settlements in the Progressive Era. Mary Simkhovitch, author of *The Settlement Primer*, explained, "In all the early Settlements the founders either had no board or else formed boards among their interested friends." [4] In some of the strongest settlements, the founding headworker doubled as president of the board—a situation which would allow for maximum freedom of action. The best example is Jane Addams, who remained both head resident and president of her board until her death in 1935.[5] At neighboring Chicago Commons, Graham Taylor served as president of the board, while his daughter, Lea, was headworker.[6] At New York's Henry Street Settlement, Lillian Wald resigned as headworker in 1933, but continued to head the settle-ment's board.[7] It is perhaps significant that these three houses were more involved with social action than any others during the Depres-sion.

Most settlement boards were drawn from the middle and upper classes. In spite of the different functions of the boards, this was true in both Chest and non-Chest cities. Some measure of the social status and professional accomplishments of the board members can be gained by checking the local *Who's Who* and *Social Register* directories. Generally, a city's occupational elite appears in local editions of *Who's Who*; a city's social elite is listed in the *Social Register*. The former could contribute special knowledge to the board, but the latter had little to offer other than time and money. One may assume that most of the social elite (particularly businessmen and A.M.A.-type physicians) held conservative views during the New Deal. Furthermore, those on a board who had not yet achieved the distinction of a *Social Register* or *Who's Who* listing could be expected to look up to those who had. Occasionally, the conservative attitudes of the majority would be overcome by a board member with a liberal outlook, skill, and influence. However, these people were rare. The majority of the boards possessed attitudes reflecting a conservative background.

In the strong Chest city of Cleveland, probably the most aristocratic settlement board belonged to George Bellamy's Hiram House. In 1936 half of this twenty-member board was listed in the *Social Register*. Eight appeared in *Who's Who in Ohio*, of which four appeared in both.[8] Bellamy claimed that these men were selected "in order to secure a Board of financially strong and capable thinking people." Francis F. Prentiss, president of the board, adopted the custom of combining luncheons with the three yearly board meetings, which were always open to guests. These luncheons cost Prentiss personally between $200 and $300 each. Bellamy remarked, "It has been said that these occasions called together more money at one time in Cleveland than any other occasion."[9] In the same city, the Alta House board carried little prestige. Only one member was in the *Social Register*, and none were in *Who's Who in Ohio*.[10]

Most cities had a pattern of social registerites outnumbering *Who's Who* listees and also showed a wide variation in the prestige of individual settlement boards. The most homogeneous board encountered in this study was that of Workman Place Neighborhood House in Philadelphia. Out of twenty-five members, twenty-three were listed in the *Social Register*. In addition, all twenty-five were women, and none apparently had husbands in *Who's Who in Philadelphia* or were listed in that directory themselves.[11] By contrast, the most famous settlement, Hull-House, had a rather small board; but it reflected Jane Addams's ability to attract well-known persons. Of the eleven members in 1936, only one failed to make either the *Social Register* or *Who's Who in Chicago*. The board included socially prominent Louise Bowen and her daughter, Mrs. William McCormick Blair; Grace Abbott, former head of the Children's Bureau; and Sewell Avery, president of Montgomery Ward.[12]

Louise Bowen was an extremely strong-willed woman who took charge of the Hull-House situation on Jane Addams's death and continued to play an active role in the daily administration of the settlement. In so doing she clashed repeatedly with Adena Miller Rich, Addams's successor as head resident, and ultimately forced

Rich's resignation.[13] Bowen eagerly welcomed Charlotte Carr as the next head resident, but conscientiously continued to involve herself in the daily affairs of the settlement. A typical day for Bowen meant arriving at Hull-House at 10:00 A.M. where she spent the next three hours on settlement affairs, then back to her town house where she devoted two hours to managing her own estate (she was an excellent manager of her own affairs).[14] Even the independent Charlotte Carr did not select new staff members without consulting Bowen.[15] Understandably, their working relationship soon deteriorated. In 1940 Carr actively supported Roosevelt whereas Bowen favored Willkie. Meanwhile, the financial situation of Hull-House went from bad to worse, and Carr resigned in 1942.[16] Headworkers were more expendable than Bowen because during these years the settlement had a great deal of difficulty raising money. Bowen was both a large contributor and active in securing money from others. She is perhaps the best example of a board member who conscientiously interfered with the administrative side of a settlement.

Examples of a liberalizing influence were Frank H. McCulloch and his wife, Catharine, both on the Chicago Commons board. The Commons board was larger than that of Hull-House, but it was still well-grounded in the *Who's Who in Chicago* and *Social Register* groups. Out of twenty-one trustees, fifteen were in the *Social Register* and nine in *Who's Who in Chicago*, four of those being listed in both. Two others were wives of *Who's Who* listees.[17] Commons headworker Lea Taylor described Frank H. McCulloch as "a very liberal Democratic lawyer." [18] His wife, Catharine, was also a lawyer and had long been active in liberal causes.[19] Their son, Frank W. McCulloch, was a Chicago Commons volunteer and a leading organizer of the unemployed in Chicago. When Graham Taylor died, the senior McCulloch became president of the board.

Frank H. McCulloch's presence was important because the Commons board had its share of conservative members. Lea Taylor recalled "one board member, fairly liberal, who thought she was doing her duty to help the unemployment situation by supporting five servants!!" Taylor explained, "She was hemmed in by Lake Forest friends. The board opened her mind." Also, the headworker was challenged on her "views in favor of Roosevelt by one board member who was very anti-Roosevelt." Ironically, at one time the board was meeting in one part of the Commons building while a meeting of the

Workers Committee and the Communist Unemployed Councils was going on in another part of the building. Taylor recalled, "Some of the board members wondered what was going on, and so they looked in on the meeting. All they saw was a committee meeting of men." The Commons was probably more involved in social action than any other settlement during the Depression. In spite of the conservative outlook of some of its members, Taylor emphasized, "The board never once said, 'You mustn't do this.'" One reason why was the influence of Frank H. McCulloch, of whom Taylor said, "I could count on him for anything." [20] The presence of a liberal board member in an influential position could outweigh a large number of conservative trustees.

With the responsibility for raising funds shifted from the individual boards to the Chests in most cities, the way was open for the inclusion of neighbors as settlement trustees. The Depression had witnessed an increase in the number of small donations to the Chests from those of modest means, including employees. Therefore, it seemed only proper to involve "the people more and more in the formulation of policies in such basic areas as administration, personnel practices, and program." [21] Educator Gaynell Hawkins noted that in the absence of neighborhood representation on the board, the headworker became the sole interpreter of the neighbors to the trustees. Furthermore, Hawkins pointed out that "boards have been known to take action inimical to the welfare of both the settlement and its clients." [22] Consequently, a number of leaders favored the addition of neighbors to settlement boards.

Neighborhood representation on boards occurred in both Chest and non-Chest cities. In New York a questionnaire revealed that nine out of thirty-four settlement boards had neighborhood representatives.[23] Alta House in Cleveland claimed forty percent neighborhood representation on its board by the end of the decade.[24] The Alta House board, which originally had almost nobody in the elite directories, deliberately decided to add members in order to "be representative of labor, the foreign groups being served, the P.T.A., the Rotary Club and other civic groups." Among those appointed were the president of the local P.T.A. and an industrial worker who lived in the community.[25] At least two settlements temporarily had boards consisting entirely of neighbors. However, on the Detroit board, one-third of the neighbors were later replaced by the usual board members because the settlement needed money for new buildings and Chests did not usually finance capital improvements during the Depression.[26] On the New York board, all the neighborhood representatives resigned because there was no Chest and the settlement could not possibly meet its financial obligations unless it had the usual board to raise money.[27] Although most settlement leaders who spoke on the subject favored neighborhood representation, most boards did not have neighborhood members; and furthermore, in no houses other than the ones mentioned in Detroit and New York did neighbors appear to have been in a majority at any time on their boards.

The fact remains that most boards were drawn from the social, business, and professional elites of their communities. Generally, these people held conservative beliefs, and through their control of the boards, they occasionally inhibited agency programs and the political activities of the staff. For example, when Grace Abbott was recruiting people to join her "Social Workers for Roosevelt" committee in 1936, she found "a good many who are for Roosevelt who feared to come out publicly for him on account of Landon board members." [28] Such reticence was more likely to occur in Chest cities than in non-Chest cities.

However, in Chicago where the boards retained control over most of the finances of their respective settlements, a conservative program could be traced to a conservative board. In Lea Taylor's estimation, Gads Hill Center was less inclined to become involved in social action than her own settlement, Chicago Commons. A look at some of the correspondence between the president of the Gads Hill board, A. E. Bryson, and Ruth Austin, the headworker, explains why. President Bryson wrote, "Staff members owe it to those who make their agency possible to reflect their view," that is, the view of the board. The board president then implied a threat:

> Employees of private agencies will do well to ask themselves before allying themselves with any movement that threatens [such things as free enterprise, low taxes, and private philanthropy], whether they believe that the government or the state can do a better job than the private agency—and whether they would prefer to continue as employees of private interests or of the government.[29]

Meanwhile, at Northwestern University Settlement, also in

Chicago, the board was quite different. Liberal settlement leader Harriet Vittum wrote about bringing neighborhood political problems to the attention of her board and getting a favorable response. She believed that "board members [were] very much interested in the political activities of the Settlement and would like to have [the settlement] do more." [30]

The advantage in Chicago not being a Chest city was that one Chest board did not control every agency funded by it. While there were conservative boards in Chicago, their effects were limited to individual agencies. Liberal social action, if blocked in one setting, might succeed in another. It was much easier for conservative interests to stifle social action in a city if they only had to control one board (the Chest board) rather than the many boards which decided agency programs in Chicago or New York.

While Chests reserved for themselves the power to pass on the programs of individual agencies, boards in Chest cities retained the power to hire and fire their own staff members. It was chiefly through this means that they made their own views felt. After a Miss Ratzlaff was removed from the Hiram House staff, board president Francis Fleury Prentiss let headworker George Bellamy know,

> I have very little patience with a radical of the type of Miss Ratzlaff or her sympathizers, and while their views might be modified to adjust them to circumstances particularly when it means a comfortable position, they don't change their inner and at times outward feelings toward the governing class, any more than the leopard can change his spots, hence I have nothing to do with them and let them flock by themselves or adjourn to some country, such as Russia or preferably an island where they will all gather and work out their theories to their hearts' content.

Prentiss ended by recommending that another employee not be rehired and stated his opposition to "employing any one who has his views." [31] After Bellamy fired a third worker, Prentiss wrote, "I am sure the Trustees join me in congratulating you on being particularly free of the charge of carrying Socialists and Communists on your staff." By this time, Prentiss was having doubts as to the prevalence of the views of his conservative class among social workers, but he was fully prepared to continue exercising the prerogatives of the board. He

said, "Perhaps this material [meaning college girls] is not as workable
as it used to be and more apt to have radical views that might be
embarrassing," but he cautioned Bellamy to "anticipate trouble of this
kind and weed out those whose views are too advanced for your
Board of Trustees." [32] Sharing the political views of his trustees,
Bellamy readily complied.

A board could do much to set the tone of the individual
settlement. Generally, the boards consisted of people drawn from the
social, business, and professional elites of their communities, who
possessed a conservative outlook. Consequently, boards did at times
inhibit tendencies toward social action within their agencies. On the
other hand, an occasional liberal board member in an influential
position could do much to smooth the way for social action on the
part of the staff. If such a board were in a non-Chest city, it enjoyed
comparative autonomy; and the social action programs it sanctioned
had maximum freedom to develop.

The financial stringencies of the Depression prompted settlements in New York and Chicago to develop the deficit fund system
for raising money. Chicago began in the early thirties, and New York
had established one by 1939. In place of a Chest assuming full
responsibility for meeting member agency budgets, the deficit fund
met just a certain percentage. In 1939, Gads Hill Center in Chicago
drew $6,136 out of a total income of $19,114 from the Community
Fund.[33] In New York the percentage was even lower. Hartley House
in 1939 received only $1,040 out of $16,887 in income from the
Greater New York Fund.[34] In the deficit fund system, the main
responsibility for raising money remained with the individual agencies. But, unlike Chest agencies, the fund agencies retained their
autonomy.

The fund did not come into being without some significant
people raising objections. Jane Addams kept Hull-House out of any
system of joint financing while she lived. Were Hull-House to join
even in a deficit fund system, she believed that it "would lose its
individuality and the right to guide its own destiny." [35] She was an
excellent fund-raiser, and during her lifetime either "obtained from
friends or gave from her own resources about $30,000 a year." [36] After
her death, Hull-House almost immediately began taking steps to join
the fund.

The worst feature of the Community Chest from a social action standpoint was that it could exert pressure to curtail programs; the deficit fund was devised to avoid this evil. The originators of the deficit fund did not want "a general board of control which alone would be responsible for maintaining and developing the best in social service," nor did they want "the opportunity to be of service . . . limited to the few who may control a chest." [37] However, the deficit fund board had its share (perhaps more than its share) of upper class wealth as represented by such names as Armour, Blair, Cudahy, Insull, and Ryerson. On the other hand, Lea Taylor was also a member.[38] Nevertheless, the deficit fund did get involved in the aftermath of Elizabeth Dilling's *The Red Network*. Dilling accused a number of people connected with the Chicago settlements of Communist sympathies. To quiet an outraged follower of Dilling, the executive secretary of the deficit fund wrote, "If in any case there is any tendency on the part of any settlement to engage in political activities whatsoever, the directors of the Fund will be most eager to put a stop to it." [39] However, the difference between such pressure coming from a deficit fund as opposed to a Community Chest was that the individual agency, being dependent on the deficit fund for only a fraction of its budget, was in a much better position to resist.

The Chicago plan influenced New York to adopt a similar one. The New York deficit fund was designed to solicit from both corporations and employee groups. Yet, as Helen Hall pointed out, the board of directors of the fund provided no representation for labor although the board automatically included the heads of the five Chambers of Commerce. Also, there was "no plan for general community participation in this controlling group." Hall, who at the beginning of the decade headed University House in Philadelphia, a settlement almost entirely dependent on the Philadelphia Community Chest, called the New York deficit fund plan "something . . . being imposed by a small group of Wall Street businessmen and forced on the community." Stanley Isaacs, president of the United Neighborhood Houses board, concurred that "the big givers will try to control the [deficit fund];" but he did not think they would "have much success." However, it was really too late to block the new plan. On a motion made by veteran settlement leader Mary Simkhovitch, the United Neighborhood Houses agreed to join the deficit fund plan for one year, meanwhile making clear its objections and trying to get safeguards for agency autonomy.[40] Settlements in New York and

Chicago clearly did not want their funds to evolve into Community Chests.

Just why this antagonism towards Chests centered in New York and Chicago is open to speculation. They were, of course, the two largest American cities. Also, their social workers had a distinguished history of involvement in reform. Whatever the reason, New York and Chicago failed to develop a Chest and that fact perhaps attracted other settlement reformers who sensed a less repressed atmosphere for their activities.

Almost all cities of any size had adopted the Community Chest system by 1929. Cleveland was the first in 1913, followed by other cities with settlements, such as New Orleans in 1914, Louisville, Buffalo, Des Moines, and Detroit in 1917, Rochester in 1918, and the Twin Cities in 1919.[41] By 1934, 385 cities had Community Chests.[42]

Events during the decade had a certain effect on the source of donations. During the first three years of the Depression, in spite of declining personal income, the amount of donations to the Chests rose. Then, with the election of Roosevelt and the inauguration of the New Deal, Chest income fell.[43] Settlements survived though "more and more the solicitor of funds was hearing, 'Why doesn't the government do this?' "[44] The 1933, 1934, and 1935 Chest campaigns exploited anti-New Deal sentiment among the conservative business class by laying particular stress upon private philanthropy, individual responsibility, and local control. The Chests repeatedly conjured up an image of federal domination to arouse Americans to new heights of private effort.[45]

Most of the money continued to come from rich individuals. This dependence on wealthy contributors was true also in the absence of the Chest. Isabel Taylor, of the executive committee of the National Federation of Settlements, described certain people with "established habits of giving" as "jaded givers. . . . They prefer to give to established undertakings, association with which will add to their prestige and provide them with pleasant social contacts." [46]

An important difference between the Progressive Era and the New Deal, particularly relating to wealthy givers and social action programs, was the tax laws. Donations to charity were relatively unhampered during the Progressive Era, while during the New Deal they came to be influenced by tax incentives. For example, the personal income tax in 1930 allowed a fifteen percent exemption for gifts to charity.[47] A law allowing corporations a five percent exemption for charity passed in 1935. Thereafter, business became an increasing factor in fund raising. However, to qualify for this exemption, a corporation could not give to an agency whose major function was legislation. As early as 1937, Lea Taylor, head of Chicago Commons, stated that tax exemption provisions "had been used by the Council of Social Agencies as a means of preventing action on social legislation." [48] Hence, the granting of tax exemptions for charitable contributions served to restrict the social action programs of private organizations. These restrictions were not present during the Progressive Era and may partially explain why settlements were more involved in reform in the early 1900s.

In addition to increasing corporate contributions, the Chests sought to broaden the base of contributors. Consequently, shortly after the stockmarket crash in 1929, four staff members of North East Neighborhood House in Minneapolis accompanied two Chest volunteers to the Northern Pacific Round House "to solicit the employees." In two hours they secured $175 from people who had never given to the Chest before.[49] This scene became more common as the Depression continued.

Even though the base of giving may have become more democratic during the Depression, the actual organization of the Community Chests appears to have remained just as much in control of the elite givers. An excellent example is the budget committee of the Philadelphia Welfare Federation in 1939. The committee claimed thirty-four members. Of these, twenty-five were listed in the *Social Register* for 1938. They included the president and chairman of the Council of Social Agencies and the chairman of the budget committee. Only eleven of the thirty-four were listed in *Who's Who in Philadelphia* for 1939. Clearly, the budget committee was dominated by the upper class as represented by the *Social Register* rather than the occupational elite included in *Who's Who in Philadelphia*. Furthermore, every one of the eleven members listed in *Who's Who in Philadelphia* was also listed in the *Social Register*. Of the nine not listed in either directory, one was the wife of a pathologist and another the wife of a realtor, both husbands being listed in *Who's Who in Philadelphia*. A social elite resting on money and membership in the "right" clubs, not an occupational elite based on expertise and knowledge, ran the budget committee of the welfare federation.[50]

Centralizing the approval of budgets in a Community Chest committee tended to have a leveling influence on the agencies of a particular city, for what one institution was granted, another was likely to request. As a result, settlements in Chest cities tended to be largely homogeneous. On the other hand, the deficit fund cities of Chicago and New York possessed the strongest settlements in the country along with the greatest number of small, weak houses. In neither city was the leveling influence of the Community Chest present.

Most Chests held tight control over the budgets of member agencies. For example, North East Neighborhood House in Minneapolis suddenly discovered that it needed $406 for a new roof. The headworker went to the Chest where $300 was squeezed out of North East's original budget. Among other items, the Chest forced a $52 reduction on the food for the settlement's nursery school.[51] In addition to closely regulating all expenses of individual agencies, Chests also established rules regarding the solicitation of funds outside of the Chest system. For instance, in Cleveland the Chest placed a moratorium on capital fund drives of member agencies during much of the Depression, probably because it felt that such drives would cut into its own revenue.[52] With its absolute control over the budgets of member agencies, the Chests controlled their programs and put pressure on settlements to curtail social action programs.

Settlement leaders felt that Chests pressured them "to stress recreational and institutional activities rather than interpretation of neighborhood needs or efforts to change bad living conditions."[53] To cope with "the tension in Chest cities over the support of agencies in which discussion of economic and political issues is a part of the program," the National Federation of Settlements suggested that perhaps its representatives could meet with certain Chest executives and also the national organization of Chests could do "educational work" with local Chest personnel.[54] However, the Chests continued to inhibit settlements involved in controversial social action programs.

A National Federation of Settlements conference in 1939 heard complaints regarding Chest interference in the presentation of a play and in a discussion of consumer problems. In Cleveland a group at University Settlement had written and produced a play dealing with controversial issues such as relief and unemployment conditions.[55] After reading the script, the director of the Cleveland Chest "asked that the performance not be repeated." In this case the settlement board, which included faculty from the School of Applied Social Science at Western Reserve University, opposed the Chest. They emphasized "the effect on the young people of cancelling their play," and consequently the Chest allowed the play to continue.[56] At the same conference, Helen Hall, president of the National Federation of Settlements, told about attending a meeting on consumers' problems in Providence. There a social worker told her that they would like to do more, but "the local Community Chest would not permit them to be actively interested." Miss Hall commented, "This kind of a thing is a warning to settlements. They must not sink into being little recreation centers and have no influence on the community." [57]

Because of the business domination of the Chests, they were more likely to clash over labor issues than anything else. Helen Hall described a group of girls, dissatisfied with working conditions in a small factory, who walked out. They took their problems to a settlement where they were "given a place to meet," and they eventually joined a trade union. "Sometime afterward the community chest of that city had notice that the industry to which that small factory belonged would not give money to the chest if that agency were in it." In this instance the Chest stood by the settlement in question. On the other hand, "in another city a trade group threatened" to "withdraw their contributions to the Chest . . . if one of its agencies did not withhold all education directed towards the passage of the Child Labor Amendment." The agency quit working for the passage of that amendment.[58] In still another case, "a manufacturer threatened to cut off his contribution" to a Chest if a "settlement continued to provide a meeting room for a trade union group." [59] Added to these overt, recorded examples must be many unreported instances of intimidation as well as more subtle methods of influencing settlements to avoid controversy by eschewing social action programs. In fact, the repressive atmosphere generated by the Chests may have been more important in stifling the traditional settlement commitment to reform than was direct confrontation between agencies and the Chest.

For these reasons, many leading settlement workers expressed grave doubts as to the value of the Chests. Charles C. Cooper, headworker of Kingsley House in Pittsburgh, a Chest city, wrote, "It is inevitable that the free spirit of the settlement house will come into conflict with the rigidity of the Chest control." The Chest, he thought, had "a tendency in some cities, like Cleveland, to force" the settlements "to become recreation centers." He predicted "that certain elements in the communities will sooner or later endeavor to control things, through the large funds of the Chest." [60] The head-worker of University Settlement in New York, Albert J. Kennedy, had reservations regarding the Chests because "the limitations on freedom of experiment seem to be too great." [61]

Another New Yorker, Mary Simkhovitch, observed, "When the final division and appropriation rests with a board not deeply informed in regards to the purposes, methods and proven values of the various claimants, injustice is sure to ensue." She warned, "If the Neighborhood House enters a chest, it must see that its fundamentally educational character is understood." [62] In Cleveland, the city that originated the Chest, George Bellamy of Hiram House declared "that the chest stifles initiative and change in organization." [63] Finally, a leading social work educator, Wilbur Newstetter, stated flatly, "Any agency which allows itself to be dictated to by any Chest has sold out." [64] Unfortunately, many did "sell out."

4. Unemployment, Relief, and the Settlements: The Hoover Approach

*H*ERBERT HOOVER'S approach to the Depression was to stress private philanthropy and voluntary effort to solve social and economic problems. In past depressions, the relief and unemployment problems had been met largely through private charity. Hoover clung to the idea that greater efforts along these lines would get the United States through the Great Depression. Furthermore, many of Hoover's wealthy supporters were reluctant to establish extensive government relief agencies out of fear that once established, they would become permanent. Even when Hoover made some token government money available to the states, they often distributed it to the poor through existing *private* relief agencies. However, Hoover's preference was for relief money to be privately raised. It was as though many of the wealthier people supporting Hoover thought that by clinging more firmly to the old way of doing things, by more strongly dedicating themselves to traditional values and institutions, their former prosperity would somehow return. These people did all they could to strengthen the Community Chest and private philanthropy in general. They were joined in the early years of the Depression by many who favored extensive government relief programs, but who, given the political realities of the Hoover years, recognized private philanthropy as the most immediate way to help those in need.

As the Depression deepened, life for the poor surrounding the settlements became desperate. Many were dependent on public or private relief, but the archaic relief machinery in the early 1930s kept breaking down. City after city blundered from one relief crisis to another, lowering relief standards and imposing undue havoc on an increasing number of relief recipients.

Settlements could not help being drawn into the twin problems of unemployment and relief. Nearly all houses gave relief themselves, although relief and welfare were not normally considered a settlement function. Nevertheless, the settlement workers not only gave such services, but saw themselves as experimenters on a small scale in quest of solutions to social problems; and so within the established framework, they cast around rather pathetically for programs or projects that might mitigate the growing Depression. In these ways, the settlements were caught up in the conservative response to the depression of the Hoover years.

The welfare organization in Cleveland, Ohio, was indicative of the archaic relief machinery common at the time. Since 1922, the city had appropriated nothing for direct relief. The county supported certain kinds of relief, such as pensions for the blind and for mothers. All the state did was to provide "institutions for the feeble-minded, insane, and epileptic." [1] This situation meant that the growing numbers of unemployed had no place to turn for relief but the private agencies. Instead of yielding to pressure to grant relief of a general nature, the city of Cleveland chose to bolster the private agencies by turning over to them for distribution what relief funds it was able to raise.[2] This refusal to establish public relief machinery lasted until August 1933 when, under mounting pressure from the New Deal, the county finally organized an agency for general relief.[3] Ill-equipped to handle large numbers of people and with limited resources, the private agencies struggled from crisis to crisis during these years. Relief standards dropped, necessities were not always met, and the nagging uncertainty existed—what would happen when the relief funds were exhausted?

In Chicago, the settlement houses were among the private agencies charged with dispensing relief. Money for this purpose was supplied through the Joint Emergency Relief Fund, which raised $10,500,000 from both public and private sources in the winter of 1931–32. The Chicago socialite and treasurer of the Hull-House board, Louise Bowen, originally thought this was "enough money to care adequately for the poor"; and charities gave relief in cash so that clients might do their own purchasing. However, Bowen complained that the relief recipients "spent their money for chickens and ducks and even cigarettes and candy, and turned up again at the end of about three days to say they had nothing." When the welfare offices were deluged with more clients than they had anticipated, it was necessary to economize on the amount of relief given. Therefore, charities switched to "grocery orders on the neighborhood grocer," until they discovered that clients were using the orders to get some cash from the grocers. Not because of abuses but because of increasing numbers of recipients, relief funds continued to dwindle; and so the charities stopped paying rent unless the family was on the verge of eviction. About this time, charities also discovered that they could feed twice as many people for the same amount of money by switching from grocery orders to food boxes. Relief agencies obtained food directly from wholesale grocers, which the agencies then put up in seven different kinds of boxes. "There was the box [for] the normal family with children, the box of Kosher food, the box for the unorthodox Jew, the box for the diabetic family and one or two others." Bowen admitted,

> We felt that to ration and not pay rent was a terrible thing to do, but it meant if we did pay rent and we did give adequate grocery orders that at least half the people who were coming to us would not have anything at all to eat and would starve to death.[4]

Like Chicago, Philadelphia gave food in kind, but no cash. Helen Hall, then headworker of University House, described a neighbor who had gone without cash month after month, except for what she was able to get by begging from friends. The woman received a basket of groceries every week, but said, "There's times I could have screamed at the sight of it." The baskets often contained cocoa, but her children would not drink it. The cocoa boxes piles up in her cupboard, and she was tempted to sell them; she did not because she was afraid her neighbors would report the incident, causing her to be cut off relief.[5] Other clients, out of desperation, may have been less timid.

New York utilized one of the cruelest devices for making food relief go farther. Headworker Helen Hall said that the Department of Public Welfare began arbitrarily refusing a monthly food order for every tenth family, a practice dubbed "Skip the Feed." The "tenth" families in her neighborhood, hungry, frightened, and distressed, often turned to the settlement for help.[6]

Chicago's policy of withholding rent was also fairly common in many other settlement cities. Philadelphia's Committee for Unemployment Relief, which handled most general relief cases caused by unemployment, had a flat ruling not to pay rents under any circumstances. In Cleveland, fifty percent of the rent would be paid once a family had received an eviction notice. A family forced to move received enough money to pay one month's rent in another place. Cleveland reported 5,000 evictions in 1931. In Toledo, Pittsburgh, and New York, rents were also paid sporadically. Landlords could often be induced to let the non-paying tenants remain because in many city neighborhoods, a vacant unit was a target for vandalism. However, as Helen Hall pointed out, undoubtedly the tenants' sense of responsibility was weakened.[7]

The people who were the real victims of this widespread failure to pay rent were the landlords. Helen Hall told about a Mr. Lazar who "had worked all his life at unskilled labor, part of the time in the sewers of Cleveland," and somehow had managed to buy two two-family houses, one of which he divided into four apartments. He had saved a thousand dollars when he lost his job. Since then, his tenants had only paid rents sporadically; he had used up his savings, and had borrowed all he could against his property. Meanwhile, his two oldest girls had dropped out of school in order to save money on carefare and shoes, but the youngest children were refused milk in school because their father owned property.[8] Refusal to pay rents only added to the relief rolls.

In exasperation, some landlords did evict their tenants. In such cases, the parents might leave the children on the sidewalk to watch their furniture while the hunt for new quarters began. At that point, the relief office would usually step in with one month's rent for the new landlord; but landlords, knowing that they were unlikely to get any more rent beyond the first month, were reluctant to rent to people on relief. If a family was unsuccessful in finding new quarters, its furniture might be sent to a city warehouse and the members parceled out among relatives or neighbors or sent to institutions. Even if this ultimate disaster could be avoided, the threat of eviction played on the nerves of destitute tenants. After she became headworker at Henry Street, Helen Hall was visited by a hysterical woman, who kept repeating: " 'Don't let them do it! Don't let them do it!' " Hall learned that the woman "was to be evicted for the second time in three months." During the first eviction, the family's "furniture had been broken and left out in the rain while the . . . four children had been scattered in finding shelter for the night. This time her two babies were sick and she was afraid." [9]

Confronted by people needing help, it was natural for the settlements to do all they could to get these people in touch with the proper relief agencies and to see that they were given the necessary assistance. Headworker Lea Taylor recalled that the entire first floor of Chicago Commons was used for interviewing, and that "most of the problems discussed related to relief or some crisis in the home." Often the settlement worker's solution was to call the relief office. Relief office personnel were at one point so tired of the constant pressure being put on them by the settlement in this manner that they refused to accept calls from the workers. The settlement's solution was to dial the number and then let the client talk.[10] Chicago Commons tried to aid its neighbors further by "acting as a clearing house of information as to sources of relief." [11] In New York, this information function of the settlements was formalized. There the Home Relief Bureau assigned workers to thirteen settlements two evenings a week "for the purpose of clarifying Home Relief Bureau policies and giving information directly to communities through these" settlements.[12] Nearly all settlements, formally or informally, functioned as liaisons between relief recipients and their local relief offices.

Often the relief offices could do little or nothing for the needy because the offices lacked resources. In order to raise money, public and private emergency committees sprang into being in the early years of the Depression. In New York, veteran settlement leader Lillian Wald went on the radio to urge listeners to contribute to the emergency relief organization under the direction of Harvey Dow Gibson.[13] Lea Taylor also supported Chicago's emergency relief measures when she urged radio listeners to buy tax warrants for the relief program and to give to social agencies and private relief.[14] Although these emergency committees were of a stopgap nature, settlement leaders supported them while urging better relief for their clients.

Even conservative headworkers such as Ruth Austin of Gads Hill Center, Chicago, occasionally found themselves protesting the current relief practices. In 1930 Austin could remark, "There is a very pleasant side to all this unemployment situation. . . . Those who have jobs certainly are going to try to hold them and those who have been out of work for a long time are going to value any kind of a job when they get one." [15] However, by 1932 Austin was complaining that the boxes of food distributed by the United Charities lacked flour, sugar, and condensed milk and that the rations were in very small quantities.[16] Letters of complaint by settlement leaders were common.

These letters carried more force when they were backed by an organization. The city settlement federations were in an ideal position to express themselves. For example, a worse alternative to giving boxes of food to clients was the Chicago proposal to feed unemployed adults in the public schools. The Chicago Federation of Settlements voted against this plan, thus contributing to its defeat.[17] In New York, Lillian Wald served with Harry Hopkins on the Welfare Council. Wald got the Coordinating Committee to send a letter to the Board of Estimate stressing the necessity for relief during August and September 1932 and the need for an appropriation of $3,250,000 for home and work relief during those two months.[18] Other New York settlement leaders served on a Committee on Hearings on Unemployment in 1933. After due investigation, the committee sent a letter calling the attention of the Board of Estimate to delays in the granting of relief amounting to "weeks or even months." The committee further complained that rent was not paid until dependent families were "actually evicted and their furniture put on the street." The letter urged that additional sums be appropriated for relief.

When letters failed to produce the desired results, the next step was to pass resolutions. In 1931 the Chicago Federation of Settlements resolved that its member houses write or telegraph their state representatives to vote in favor of emergency relief in Cook County.[19] The following year this same federation passed a resolution urging the Illinois Relief Commission to prevent curtailment in the amount of relief given individual families, particularly in the food budget.[20] United Neighborhood Houses of New York was also active in passing resolutions. For example, in 1934 it recommended cash relief in place of grocery orders, a recommendation that apparently was adopted by the state.[21] However, resolutions did not always produce the desired results.

Additional pressure could be exerted for better relief programs through publicity. Karl Borders, assistant head resident of Chicago Commons, published a sweeping denunciation of the American system of charity and relief in the periodical the *Unemployed*. To be eligible for relief, an unemployed man was obliged to sell his property, often at a loss. If he could possibly mortgage his furniture or borrow a few dollars, he had to do that. "Finally," wrote Borders, "when completely investigated, cataloged, and generally broken on the rack, he is given a 'special job' or a direct charity dole." Borders did not say that social workers enjoyed this process or were proud of it. He did say that "this is the way the system works, that our great industrialists do take pride in it and defend it against the 'dole of unemployment insurance' as the American plan of local self help." In Borders's opinion, "At its best it is a damnable system!" [22]

The woman for whom Karl Borders worked at Chicago Commons, Lea Taylor, published a more detailed criticism of the relief system the following year. Taylor noted that relief agencies in some places refused to pay utilities with the result that candles and oil lamps were reappearing in the tenements. Meager food allowances meant malnutrition, a lowered resistance to disease, and premature death. The refusal to pay rents except on eviction did nothing for a family's self-respect. Taylor concluded by urging "social workers all over the country, singly and in groups [to] stand together and boldly demand that minimum relief must include more than a bare subsistence ration of food." [23] The month before, Helen Hall, then head of University Settlement in Philadelphia, had published an article arguing for the inclusion of rents in relief budgets.[24] Settlement workers did their best to publicize the plight of relief recipients in the hope that the programs would be improved.

Helen Hall was one settlement leader who personally carried her publicity efforts to the federal government. During the first winter of the Depression, Hall spent several days in Washington talking to congressmen and administration officials. Years later she recalled her exasperation:

> I tried to make the men on Capitol Hill see, as I did, my neighbor with her baby in her arms showing me that the baby had gone from 11 pounds to 9 or hear her voice as she told me that she would steal milk before her baby starved to death. Or to see the family of young children across the street living on bread and tea for three months before we discovered their plight. And to see babies of three lying inert, not able to use their legs because of malnutrition. These real people were by that time multiplied by millions and yet the mild unemployment bills *were not to be allowed even to come up for a vote.*[25]

Hall made other trips to Washington during the Hoover years to help build up support for the massive federal relief programs that finally came with the New Deal.

Looking back on the nine months from October 1933 to June 1934, Albert J. Kennedy of University Settlement in New York summarized the efforts of United Neighborhood Houses to improve the existing system. During this time, the group protested the inadequate relief, delays, and evictions "in the press and to those in authority." It conferred with the head of the Home Relief Bureau on difficulties and formed with the bureau the Joint Home Relief and Settlement Committee. The federation sent a statement to the state authorities urging cash relief instead of relief in kind. It also made proposals for the reorganization of the Emergency Home and Relief Bureaus and recommendations as to the "amount of relief which should be demanded in order for each family . . . to have the necessary budget." This list of activities was typical of settlements which sought to make the best of an inadequate system. The federations which were most active in this sense were those in Chicago and New York, the two major non-Chest cities.

However, putting pressure on the authorities was only one approach to the problem. Nearly all settlements, whether liberal or conservative, in Chest cities or not, took a more direct approach to the problems of unemployment and relief. Although not relief-giving agencies in normal times, virtually all settlements gave some sort of relief during these years. They also experimented with various programs from employment bureaus to made-work projects. Although the amount of relief given was insignificant compared to the regular relief-giving agencies, settlements did what they could with the resources they had.

Because of their limited resources, settlement relief was often given in conjunction with or subordinate to the regular relief programs. In 1931 Union Settlement in New York City served as one of the registration centers for the Emergency Work Bureau. It offered unemployed heads of families "made work" for a three-day week at five dollars a day.[26] The bureau was jammed. On the third day, a man arrived at 9:30 P.M. in order to be the first in line when the office opened the next morning. "In spite of a steady rain, about" fifty others had joined him by midnight. According to the Union Settlement headworker, the sight of this line of "tired, wet and hungry men," all unemployed and "with wives and children dependent on them," disturbed the settlement residents. They began the practice of serving coffee and rolls to the crowds of unemployed, as well as helping with the registration procedure.[27] The settlement also managed to raise a small relief fund to help the unemployed directly.[28]

During the Hoover years, the unemployed had no federally sponsored public employment bureau to turn to in their search for jobs. Therefore, some settlements tried to carry on a free employment bureau for their neighbors. The settlement employment bureaus in Minneapolis specialized in finding domestic work for women. With the sudden laying off of men in the fall of 1929, the number of women seeking employment sharply increased. In November 1929 North East Neighborhood House reported that it was only able to find employment for about one-fourth of the applicants.[29] One of the lucky ones to find employment was an Indian woman who had left her reservation "because of the terrible conditions—no coal or wood or clothes." [30] In February 1932 the settlement was only able to place one in six applicants. The jobs available paid little. In return for doing "all the washing, ironing, scrubbing, housecleaning, cooking and baking, besides taking care of four children," one girl was paid three dollars a week.[31] By the summer of 1932 only nine percent were being placed.[32]

Because they hated to see girl after girl go away empty-handed, the settlement workers instituted vocational education classes and a special activities group. The classes stressed cooking and serving meals and child care and were designed to help the students secure jobs as maids and waitresses.[33] The club formed was called the "Putter Class" because they puttered around "mending or altering their dresses . . . making new clothes," and doing craft work.[34] Although this activity must have seemed rather aimless at times to the girls, nevertheless it helped to fill their days when a job was not forthcoming.

If their employment bureaus could not come up with sufficient jobs, some enterprising settlements turned to creating jobs themselves through various made-work projects. Roadside Settlement in Des Moines worked out a system whereby the unemployed repaired donated furniture, shoes, and clothing and did some janitorial work in return for so much per hour in credit toward the "purchase" of any of the repaired items.[35] Although some projects of this nature involved payment in scrip, Roadside's project was of a more elementary nature. In New Orleans, Kingsley House was fortunate enough to acquire the use of a gift shop in the French Quarter with which to sell items made or repaired by the unemployed neighborhood women.[36] However, the Minneapolis settlements put made-work on a definite wage basis. For example, North East Neighborhood House employed around seventeen women for four to six days per week to can donated vegetables and fruit and repair garments.[37] The regular relief agencies, including the Public Welfare Department, handled the distribution of the finished products. Altogether 188 different women received a total of $6,518.97 through this project.

Another popular made-work project in the early years of the Depression was the community garden, whose prototype was run by Godman Guild in Columbus. The idea was to put the unemployed to work raising their own food. The Columbus Council of Social Agencies furnished "seed and supervised the plowing of the gardens, which under depression conditions were offered to the worker free of all charges." The public relief department furnished night watchmen.[38] President Hoover's Emergency Committee for Employment publicized Godman Guild's gardens in their seventh bulletin, entitled *The Godman Guild Community Gardens, A Permanent Food-Garden Project Applied to Emergency Needs*, published in May 1931.[39] In Pittsburgh, Soho Community House distributed seeds and registered applicants for garden plots.[40] Hiram House of Cleveland lent camp facilities to house men who were assigned to a nearby community garden for ten-day work relief assignments.[41] Even in the highly urbanized area of Chicago, the local Federation of Settlements voted to recommend that the Illinois Relief Commission continue the backyard garden project as "a general garden project." [42] The idea of having the poor grow their own food had wide appeal as a simple solution to depression problems during the Hoover years. However, after communities had paid the transportation of workers to the outlying gardens and supplied night watchmen, they found themselves little farther ahead financially. Sometimes it was simpler and more efficient to give relief directly.

Direct relief could hinder the pride of the recipient, depending particularly on how it was handled. The headworker of the North East Neighborhood House of Minneapolis described an incident in which a worker asked a group of girls to bring items for Thanksgiving baskets. Most of the girls contributed canned goods. However, one girl brought only a potato, explaining that it was all her family could afford to give. The settlement "saw that her family got a basket but none of the other girls knew it." [43]

At Hiram House in Cleveland the giving of direct relief called to mind visions of "Lady Bountiful" and "only the worthy poor need apply." In a note thanking the Cleveland financiers M. J. and O. P. Van Sweringen for a shipment of apples, headworker George Bellamy explained, "They have been very carefully distributed in the places where we feel they are the most needed and will be the most appreciated—two factors which do not always go together." [44] Although the social work profession might disapprove of the tone of Bellamy's note, it was effective in extricating a second shipment of apples from two men whose companies were about to go bankrupt. [45] Bellamy kept a file of stories about the "worthy poor" which he probably used in letters, speeches, and personal contacts to solicit donations for relief. The following account of the "very thrifty" L. family probably elicited sympathy from wealthy conservatives:

> Mr. L. has worked hard and Mrs. L. has helped by saving money and keeping the house clean and the children well dressed. The money carefully saved was invested in property until they had eight or nine apartments to rent. At present all of the apartments are filled with families dependent on the A.C. [Associated Charities] and as the A.C. is not paying rent, the L's are left without income. They are a superior family, maintaining a high standard of living and so much pride that they would rather starve than go to the A.C. for food.
>
> On frequent calls to the home, the visitor found them without fire except for the gas range in the kitchen. The visitor suggested that they come for some wood and while it was being loaded on a small pusch [sic] cart, one of the older girls remarked that they have had no wood or coal for their heating stove all winter, and this would mean the first fire in it. [46]

Hard work, savings carefully invested, so proud that they would rather starve than seek charity, and circumstances beyond their control combined to certainly make this family one of the "worthy poor."

In some cities, settlements assumed the role of providing

emergency assistance until a family was accepted for relief by a regular agency. The United Campaign in Philadelphia provided settlements with money for this purpose.[47] At Henry Street in New York, the McCann Relief Fund was used to help people until other means could be found. For example, the Home Relief Bureau had dropped the Price family because they believed that Mr. Price had some income which he was not admitting. Henry Street supplied the family with coal and food tickets which could be exchanged for butter, bread, and beans, and put pressure on the bureau to reinvestigate the family. After the bureau investigator arrived, Mrs. Price was still doubtful they would be accepted because the "investigator remarked that she had worn a new outfit which consisted of a dress which was torn in places" the "investigator could not see, shoes she claims are her daughters which she wears when she goes out and a coat which was given to her by an aunt who lives out of town." It required more pressure from Henry Street and another investigation before the family was finally accepted. Mrs. Charles E. F. McCann made possible the McCann Fund, which covered relief costs for about ten families at a time during 1932 and 1933.[48] The availability of such funds meant that the regular relief agencies could afford to neglect the needs of such people as the Prices, at least for a time. Yet, the humanitarian impulse of the settlement was to meet the immediate need.

The Chicago settlements had the most extensive relief program. Chicago Commons board member Edward L. Ryerson, Jr. served as director of the Illinois Emergency Relief Commission from September 1930 to March 1933.[49] Ryerson firmly believed that private agencies had a role to play in the distribution of relief,[50] and he channeled some of the state funds into private agencies, including settlements. For example, from October 1, 1930, to October 1, 1931, Chicago Commons received $3,092.90 from the Governor's commission for relief.[51] The Commons solicited additional funds on its own to supplement this money, which it used to supply clients with food, coal, carfare and lunch money (high school students only), clothing, and utilities (when some other relief agencies refused to pay utility bills).[52] However, by the fall of 1932, Illinois decided to discontinue using federal or state funds for private agencies.[53] This action cut back on the settlement relief programs, but they continued to raise funds on their own for relief purposes throughout the Depression.

By the spring of 1933, some settlement projects anticipated the New Deal programs soon to be put into·operation. Henry Street Settlement in New York recruited fifteen unemployed boys whom it sent to its camp to clear trees, work on the athletic field, and repair roads. This miniature Civilian Conservation Corps, the Henry Street boys' worker thought, would "have some advantages over the President's plan by providing facilities for building the morale of the boys." [54] The Provident Associated Bureau for Homeless Men and the Citizens Committee of Relief in St. Louis paid the wages of men who served as club leaders and teachers at Neighborhood Association.[55] Soon identical programs would be run in most settlements, except the wages would be paid by federal work relief programs rather than local agencies.

During the early years of the Depression, the settlements tried to cope with growing unemployment and relief problems by staying within the established framework. They put pressure on existing agencies to maintain decent standards of relief. The settlements also sought to supplement the regular relief agencies with small relief programs of their own. They, too, joined the ranks of Americans baffled by the Depression, who sought solutions in such elementary ideas as having the unemployed grow their own food in community gardens. But every year the Depression worsened. By 1933 it was clear that private philanthropy, the Community Chest, and local relief were not enough.

From a radical viewpoint, it might be tempting to criticize the settlements for their support of Community Chest and other private fund drives because the handouts took the revolutionary edge off the protests of the poor. However, the meager handouts of the Hoover years did not retard the New Deal. While virtually all settlements were involved in such conservative "solutions" to the Depression as private philanthropy, settlements outside Chest cities at the same time worked for basic reforms of the relief structure. By 1933, they were ready to welcome the New Deal.

5. Unemployment, Relief, and the Settlements: The New Deal

*V*IRTUALLY all settlements participated in the conservative attempts to cope with the Depression during the Hoover years. Yet some also sought solutions outside the old framework by enthusiastically supporting federal work relief programs and working for the passage and then the implementation of programs under the Social Security Act. Forward-looking settlements also favored large-scale federal experimentation, such as TVA (Tennessee Valley Authority).

However, in spite of the massive involvement of the federal government in relief programs, local relief programs continued. Although there was no open split in the settlement movement over the issue of local vs. federal relief, the New Deal programs served to separate the liberal from the conservative settlements. Significantly, those settlements which were most strongly in favor of the New Deal were also those settlements which were outside of Community Chest control.

The National Recovery Administration (NRA) was one of the first major New Deal agencies, and the attitudes of settlement workers toward it reflected the divided opinion of the country towards the NRA. Jane Addams was outspokenly in favor of the NRA. In November 1933 she declared that the economic "situation seems to demand a managed credit system, high wages, shorter hours that more people may share these wages, and a huge public works program." She pointed to the laborer who had "lost his house and lot through his unpaid mortgage, and his savings through the closing of his local bank," and said, "That the NRA has come to his rescue fills many of us with sincere gratitude." [1]

Lea Taylor's opinion of the NRA was somewhat qualified. She

believed that it had raised some wages, standardized hours, and perhaps contributed to a slight upturn in employment; but when she looked at the immediate Chicago Commons neighborhood, she could see little effect. "Neighborhood stores report a little increase in money circulation and larger pay checks cashed"; but she also complained that some firms "while displaying the NRA signs, are flagrantly violating its pledge." Fear of losing their jobs deterred the employed from making direct complaints.[2] Taylor did not condemn the NRA, although she doubted its effectiveness.

In Cleveland, the director of Hiram House, George Bellamy, openly condemned the NRA. He thought the NRA codes might "retard progress for a generation." Harking back to nineteenth century beliefs in progress and individualism, Bellamy proclaimed: "Labor and Capital must recognize the merit system, the profit system. They level up, not down. They create a code of ethics. They punish inefficiency, they stir imagination and desire for expanding achievement." [3] In Bellamy's opinion, the United States had learned a lesson from the NRA. In 1936 he wrote, "Just as Germany, accustomed to mass control, could not function as a republic, so America, accustomed to freedom, could not function under the NRA." [4] Thus, the strongest support among settlement workers for the NRA came from the non-Chest city of Chicago. The most vociferous opposition came out of Cleveland, the original Chest city.

Even before the National Industrial Recovery Act became law, Congress created the Federal Emergency Relief Administration (FERA or ERA), which was under the direction of Harry Hopkins. In July 1933 Hopkins decreed that all federal money given to the states to be used for relief had to be distributed by public agencies. Cleveland was one of the cities which, up to then, had been distributing all relief funds, including federal money, through private agencies. Hopkins's order resulted in the creation of the Cuyahoga County Relief Administration.[5]

The creation of the FERA also meant that private relief programs, including the very minor settlement ones, retreated into the background. For example, in her study of Boston's settlements, University of Chicago professor Edith Abbott pointed out that once the extensive ERA programs got under way, the settlements "played a smaller part in the relief work." In place of the former relief activities, settlements made space available for sewing projects, organized training classes, helped with choral organizations and ERA orchestras, sponsored classes in nutrition, and provided special activities for the unemployed.[6]

Because neither the FERA nor the Public Works Administration generated enough work relief, Roosevelt created the Civil Works Administration (CWA) in November 1933. The CWA was the most massive work relief program which had ever been undertaken by the federal government. In the winter of 1933–34, it furnished employment for 4,000,000 people, half of whom were taken from the relief rolls, and half of whom were referred by their public employment offices.[7]

Settlement workers cooperated with and endorsed the CWA for a variety of reasons. The headworker of Shaw House in Boston used his position as a member of the State Advisory Council for the Public Employment Service to see "that a large number of worthy people from this neighborhood and other neighborhoods similarly situated received employment under the Civil Works Administration, not only in the laboring and menial positions but many in the highest paid ranks." [8] Because the CWA was organized very rapidly and was intended only for short-term projects, officials were open to suggestions like headworker Alice Gannett's that CWA workers be used to scrape the swimming pool at the Goodrich House camp.[9] Thus, settlements benefited from maintenance services provided through work relief programs. In addition, the black headworker of Phyllis Wheatley House in Minneapolis, W. Gertrude Brown, thought that "the CWA was a 'God-Send' to the Negro in Minneapolis." Blacks placed on projects in Minneapolis included the first black file clerk at General Hospital, and the first black book binder in the public library system. Brown predicted, "These placements will go a long way in conquering prejudice." [10] Help for their neighbors, benefits in terms of services to their houses under work relief projects, and the social ideals of the CWA were among the reasons why settlement workers eagerly endorsed the program.

Nevertheless, from other quarters in the nation, criticisms of waste and "boondoggling" were heaped on the CWA. Roosevelt bowed to the critics and discontinued the program in the spring of 1934.[11] The National Federation of Settlements opposed the closing down of the CWA "until some more orderly scheme of protection against unemployment takes its place." Settlement workers admonished, "To get up the hopes of hundreds of thousands of harassed incomeless families and then dash them is as short-sighted as it is cruel." With reference to the millions of workers to be dropped, the National rhetorically asked, "What is to happen . . . if Civil Works are tapered off in the next three months faster than any rise in employment?" [12]

Fortunately for some people, smaller projects were continued under the FERA. The following winter the National Federation of Settlements requested the federal government to grant money to the states for cultural, educational, and social projects on a year-round basis. Specifically, the suggestions of the National Federation included federal nursery schools, vocational training, concerts, centers for teaching music, professional theatre groups, and amateur dramatics.[13] The National Federation of Settlements believed the FERA would be receptive to its suggestions because the FERA had already sponsored " 'white collar' work projects." [14] Many of these projects were later incorporated under the WPA (Works Progress Administration).

Another work relief project in operation between the time of the demise of the CWA and the rise of the WPA was the Civilian Conservation Corp (CCC). The head of the Boys' Work Division of the National Federation, Mark McCloskey, urged that the CCC be extended to include "the boy whose family is not on relief rolls." [15] South End House in Boston numbered among its residents the educational supervisor for the CCC camps in New England.[16] However, probably because the CCC usually carried on its projects in rural areas, most settlement leaders were more interested in other programs.

The WPA program was of major concern to the settlements after its organization in June 1935, both because some of its projects helped bolster the settlements' programs and because the WPA took on many settlement neighbors. The WPA program was originally designed to take some of the relief load off the states. As the WPA program got under way, grants to the states for direct relief under FERA were discontinued. To underscore the fact that WPA was replacing direct relief, the federal government initially ruled that WPA wages could not be supplemented by direct relief. Lea Taylor and others on the Advisory Committee of the Cook County Bureau of Public Welfare opposed this regulation. In a letter to Federal Relief

Administrator Harry Hopkins, they pointed out that WPA wages for
unskilled labor in Cook County were set as low as fifty-five dollars per
month, although "many, many of the casual labor group have been
getting relief at a higher figure." [17] Yet the regulation stood.

Through the Current Discussion Group, some of the neighbors
of the Chicago Commons came together to discuss the situation. The
men compared the fifty-five dollar wage with the relief payments for
families of different sizes. A Mr. Rocco, "who was trained for a trade"
but had been assigned to dig ditches, was particularly incensed. He
said that "he had talked to other workers on the job concerning the
need for more pay but had been told by the foremen he was hired to
work and not talk." The "members of the group recommended . . .
that he talk to the others before and after work but not on the job."
The discussion then turned "to what could be done to improve the
WPA situation. Some said to strike. . . . Others said to refuse WPA
jobs—stay on relief until WPA pay was adequate for one's family." [18]
Through their close contacts with people on WPA, settlement workers
were well aware of the program's shortcomings.

Nevertheless, settlement leaders worked to see that the program succeeded and, to that end, offered suggestions for projects. The
Chicago Federation of Settlements urged the WPA to take over the
local Emergency Education Program and to approve the Chicago
Leisure Time Service. The former project was concerned with adult
education. The Chicago Recreation Service had worked out all the
details for the latter, which only needed approval from Washington to
begin.[19] The WPA accepted both projects, which greatly benefited the
education and recreation programs in the settlements. In Cleveland,
staff member and resident of Hiram House, Paul Walter, was
secretary to the Mayor's Board of Suggestions for WPA Projects.
Among the suggestions approved was "the organization of a Juvenile
City" as a traditional summer recreation program of Hiram House.[20]
Later on, the settlements urged that certain WPA projects be retained.
Yet in spite of the protest of the Chicago settlements, the WPA
discontinued its Chicago Rat Extermination project in 1938.[21] In the
early days of the WPA when projects were being organized, the WPA
was receptive to ideas coming from the settlements.

Liberal settlement leaders also supported the WPA by serving
on various advisory committees. In 1934 Lea Taylor mentioned "the
wide public service now being rendered by settlement staff or board

members" on committees "for co-ordinating relief activities." [22] Taylor herself was active on Chicago's WPA committees.[23] In Philadelphia settlement workers formed a committee to meet with WPA officials to iron out problems resulting from WPA programs carried on inside the settlements.[24] New York settlement leader Helen Hall served on the advisory board of the WPA's controversial Federal Theater Project.[25] That settlement workers like Hall and Helen Harris of New York very much wanted to keep the WPA programs in their houses is evident from their trip to Washington to protest a proposal to withdraw WPA workers from private agencies.[26] No total withdrawal occurred until the end of the WPA program.

During the early years of the WPA, the settlement attitude toward it was generally favorable. The conference of the National Federation of Settlements in June 1936 pronounced, "Work relief carries three distinct advantages over direct relief: It preserves the morale of the worker; it enables him to maintain his skill which is often his only capital; and, properly organized, it results in substantial community projects." The conference went on to urge that public works projects be expanded.[27] Six months later, the Federation board passed a resolution endorsing the WPA and expressing the hope that some of the cultural projects would prove to be permanent.[28] Later on headworker Mary Simkhovitch conceded, "Many of the projects may have been foolish or wasteful"; but she thought, "The difference in spirit and attitude towards life which work brings to the unemployed as contrasted with receiving public money as charity" made all of the projects worthwhile.[29]

However, because the economy had seemed to improve during 1936, Congress had cut WPA funds in 1937 in hopes that those consequently dismissed from WPA would find regular jobs. Instead, the economy took a downturn. A study of workers dismissed from the Chicago Leisure Time Service in mid-1937 showed that only 34.3 percent secured either part- or full-time private employment. The remaining 65.6 percent were forced to find other alternatives, such as local relief. Furthermore, the liberal settlements questioned whether it was "necessary to dismiss people from WPA to get them to look for, find and accept private employment." [30]

Meanwhile, in Minneapolis, North East Neighborhood House was beginning to resent "the extra expense incurred by having the WPA Sewing Unit in [the] basement." The settlement asked the WPA to pay twenty-five dollars per month rent to cover the cost of utilities used by the unit. The WPA refused, closing out the unit instead.[31] Settlements of a conservative bent tended to make an issue of incidental expenses incurred in housing WPA programs.

Whereas in 1935 the National Federation of Settlements had wholeheartedly endorsed the WPA, in a 1937 board meeting of the National opinion was divided. Professor Wilbur I. Newsletter of Western Reserve's School of Applied Social Science "emphasized the importance of WPA as a backlog of security." At the same meeting, conservative George Bellamy "maintained that now is the time to get going projects to put people on the land surrounding our cities where they can grow much of their food, so that the relief investment would have something to show for it in health and subsistence homesteads." Charlotte Carr, recently appointed head resident of Hull-House, shot back that "out of her experience as Relief Administrator in New York we should have no illusions as to the inadequacy of emergency relief activities in the early years of the depression." She added, "It has been our new standards of public relief that have not only safeguarded homes but have held up industry through creating a bottom buying power among great masses of people." [32] Coincidentally both Minneapolis, where the WPA sewing unit was forced out of the settlement, and Cleveland, home of anti-New Dealer George Bellamy, were strong Chest cities. By contrast, non-Chest Chicago welcomed the New Deal advocate, Charlotte Carr.

When the WPA began to be curtailed, some of the strongest protests came from the National Federation of Settlements and from Chicago settlements. In 1939 the National Federation adopted resolutions which urged the restoration of the recently abolished Federal Theatre Project and which condemned WPA's arbitrary dismissal of people it had carried more than eighteen months, and "that there be no limitation of funds which would cripple the WPA effort." [33] At a 1939 dinner conference in Chicago, Lea Taylor urged organizations to "testify in favor of projects" and to "make sure information gets to places of importance." She advised that "boards might be educated because some of them need it." [34] A couple months later, Taylor and Harriet Vittum, another Chicago settlement leader, organized a rally in connection with the National Conference of Social Work convention to protest WPA cutbacks.[35] At the University of Chicago Settlement, neighbors wrote letters to congressmen protesting the cuts.[36] Yet the protests were to no avail. By 1940, Marcy Center in Chicago, which at one time had sixty-five WPA workers, was down to two, and it expected to lose those soon.[37]

Generally, settlement attitudes toward the National Youth Administration (NYA) paralleled their attitudes toward the WPA. Both programs were organized about the same time. The NYA concentrated on providing part-time work for students and vocational training for young people out of school and unemployed.

The director of Hiram House might be anti-New Deal but he still cooperated with the federal programs. At one point, Hiram House had eighty-five WPA and NYA people on its staff. The NYA lavished praise on the house for instilling good work attitudes in these workers[38] and for running a model summer recreation program.[39] Neither the large number of workers nor the praise from the NYA won the director of Hiram House over to the New Deal. However, the characteristic response of the settlements to federal work relief was basically to cooperate with and support government programs.

Yet, the Depression gave conservatives more to denounce than the New Deal. In 1935, Hiram House was busy satirizing the Townsend Plan. Dr. Francis E. Townsend had "proposed that government . . . pay a pension of $200 a month" to "every person over sixty who agreed to stop work and spend the money within thirty days." [40] This simplistic scheme for ending the Depression won wide support, but not among settlements. A Hiram House skit began with Iban A. Washoutsky meeting Dr. Townsend, then singing:

> He made me discern
> How to get, yet not earn
> 200 a month as a stipend.

The Townsend Planners entered and to the tune of "Happy Days Are Here Again" sang "Our Townsend checks are here again." They were soon followed by the Tax Payers' parody of "How Dry I Am." Inflation crept in and five years later the Townsendites sang to the tune of the "Old Gray Mare":

> Oh, the Townsend plan, she ain't what
> she used to be, Ain't what she used
> to be. . . .[41]

The moral of the story was clear—the Townsend Plan would never work. Probably the lasting significance of the Townsend Plan is that it served to deflect criticism from the Social Security Act.

The Social Security Act signified a turning point in the relief structure of the United States. Prior to its passage in August 1935, relief and welfare were the responsibility of state and local governments. Up to that point, the New Deal relief programs had been temporary and formed in response to emergency conditions. The Social Security Act marked the federal government's permanent assumption of responsibility for certain relief and welfare programs. Specifically, the act included Old Age, Survivor's and Dependent's Insurance (popularly known as Social Security), and unemployment insurance. Also included were the categorical aids: Old Age Assistance, Aid to Dependent Children, and Aid to the Blind; plus some support for state medical programs, particularly for crippled children. The categorical aids required state legislation before they could be established locally. They were administered by state and local governments, and need determined an applicant's eligibility. Subsequent federal relief and welfare legislation has been built on the framework established by the 1935 Social Security Act.

In the early years of the Depression, the organization which worked the hardest to secure passage of such legislation was the American Association for Social Security under the leadership of Abraham Epstein. On the board of this association was Mary Simkhovitch, head of Greenwich House in New York. Jane Addams was one of the vice-presidents; and Helen Hall joined the socialist, Norman Thomas, on the association's Advisory Committee on Social Insurance.[42] Initially, the strategy of the association was to work for state laws. Late in 1930, Epstein formally approached the National Federation of Settlements with the request "that settlement workers in states where Committees to agitate for Old Age Pensions were organized be asked to assist such committees, and in states where there are no such committees, to form them." [43] The next issue of the National Federation of Settlements publication, *Neighborhood*, contained a list of some dozen states with Old Age Pension Laws and urged settlement leaders in the remaining states to campaign for these laws.[44] Some of the settlement workers did so.

In Cleveland, Alice Gannett, president of the Ohio Consumers' League, was already working for unemployment insurance. Wilbur I. Newstetter, head of University Neighborhood Centers and a professor at SASS, joined her on the Ohio Consumers' League's Cleveland Committee for Unemployment Insurance.[45] The latter organization sponsored a bill on unemployment insurance in the Ohio legislature, but the bill was killed after being opposed by the Cleveland Chamber of Commerce.[46] When it was revived, Helen Hall, the settlements' chief authority on unemployment, testified before a commission in Columbus.[47] Other Cleveland settlement workers joined the fight. Helen Phelan, head of Merrick House, spoke at an unemployment insurance rally.[48] Even George Bellamy wrote to the governor of Ohio, "There must be security given to the factory city worker." [49] Yet, the involvement of these workers in agitation for unemployment insurance seems to have taken place largely through the Consumers' League and outside the context of the settlement.

Such was not the case in Chicago. There the settlement workers used their organization, the Chicago Federation of Settlements, to lend weight to their position. In 1931 they sent Lea Taylor, their president, to Springfield to attend a hearing on Old Age Pensions.[50] Apparently the trip was unsuccessful for two years later the Chicago Federation of Settlements formally endorsed another unemployment insurance and old age security bill.[51] In addition, the adult education director of Chicago Commons, Glenford Lawrence, was instrumental in forming the Committee on Economic Security, later the Illinois Committee on Unemployment Insurance.[52] Lawrence drew the unemployed settlement neighbors into the campaign for unemployment insurance. These men "contributed most of the physical labor that went into the printing and distribution of bulletins, the major means of letting loose the thunder." Illinois passed an unemployment insurance bill in 1937.[53]

In 1932 the National Federation had advocated that the states institute a compulsory unemployment insurance system and endorsed "the principle . . . of federal encouragement of state legislation to this end," advocated by Senator Robert F. Wagner.[54] As the Depression wore on, the National became increasingly receptive to the principle of federal involvement. In 1934 it urged the use of "the federal taxing power as a leverage for instituting state systems of unemployment insurance," plus "a system of federal aid for old age pensions." [55] However, the pronouncements of the Federation lagged behind those of individual leaders. In 1931 Jane Addams pointed out that Detroit, which accounted for six percent of the nation's unemployed, had more than its share of relief problems. She did not think "it just that their maintenance should depend" entirely upon the property owners of Detroit. Instead, "the stockholders living in various parts of the country," but "whose incomes have been derived from the industries centered in Detroit" had an obligation to help meet the relief costs there. Jane Addams concluded, "In proportion as our great industries have become nation-wide in ownership, it would seem a normal process to support our unemployed by national taxation." [56] Advocacy of *national* unemployment insurance was also implicit in the studies done on the German and British systems by University of Chicago Settlement head, Mollie Ray Carroll, and Henry Street's Helen Hall.[57]

However, the most direct connection between settlements and the Social Security Act was the presence of several people associated with settlements on the Advisory Council of the President's Committee on Economic Security. Among the twenty-three who served were Helen Hall, president of the National Federation of Settlements; Grace Abbott, vice-president of the Hull-House board; Gerard Swope, president of the Greenwich House board; and Paul Kellogg, Hall's husband, editor of the *Survey*, and resident at Henry Street.[58] Kellogg, Hall, and half a dozen others were dissatisfied with the recommendations submitted by a majority of the council and formulated a minority statement advocating a larger tax on payrolls.[59] Kellogg reported, "The weak points of the [Wagner-Lewis] bill are that the federal aid principle is not applied, no standards are included, and the benefits are frightfully inadequate." [60] Those who hoped that the Social Security Act would bring about a basic income redistribution were disappointed.

Unlike Hall and Kellogg, Grace Abbott stayed with the majority of the advisory committee and with the bill in Congress. According to the secretary of the President's Council on Economic Security, Edwin E. Witte, Grace Abbott was "above everyone else . . . responsible for the child welfare provisions which occur in the Social Security Act." While many members of the committee said "that such matters as infant and maternity services, crippled children's services and even dependent children's services had nothing to do with social insurance," Abbott insisted that they be included. They were, and Abbott then gave the congressional bill her full support. Meanwhile, criticism of the bill from Townsendites and liberals such as Kellogg and Hall mounted. Witte claimed that the House Ways and Means Committee came "very near . . . to ditching the entire bill." Realizing how critical the situation was, Abbott "took the lead in organizing a small committee to contact leaders of public opinion in all walks of life, who joined in a statement presented to Congress urging action upon the pending social security bill and expressing the idea that it was necessary to make a start if social security was ever to be improved." Witte thought that "that statement helped a great deal." He also thought "that the Congressional Session of 1935 was the last for several years in which the Social Security Act could have been passed." [61] In other words, had liberals succeeded in blocking the 1935 bill, they might have had no bill at all.

In June 1935 the National Federation gave qualified endorsement to the Social Security Act. The Federation was still hopeful that national minimum standards for relief would be included.[62] However, even when they were left out of the act passed that August, the Federation went on to urge states to pass the necessary enabling legislation. Their immediate concern was to make the act operational; it could be improved later.[63]

Almost immediately the National sought to build on the 1935 Social Security Act, which offered only minimal health services to needy children and in connection with the categorical aids. For years many settlements had offered private health services on a small scale. These services illustrate the type of care that was sometimes offered to the poor who had to depend on charity to meet their medical needs. North East Neighborhood House in Minneapolis ran a dental clinic, which employed a dentist seven and a half hours per week.[64] The equipment in this clinic deteriorated to the point where it was beyond repair. For example, a patient might be sitting in the settlement dental chair and it would suddenly drop. In addition the machine operating the drill was also worn beyond permanent repair. The dentist was afraid of a serious accident. The only reason the clinic had a gas machine was because a staff member donated one.[65] Yet, the clinic, whose services were offered to the poor of the neighborhood without charge or for a small fee, scheduled appointments months in advance. Although they were fully aware of the problems of this dental clinic, Minneapolis settlement workers argued that a settlement clinic was better than a public one "because of the close contact the settlement has with the patient and generally with his family." [66]

Poorly equipped dental clinics were only part of the substandard medical services offered by private charity. The University of Chicago Settlement had a physician come regularly to examine club members, neighbors, and unemployed persons. For this doctor to prescribe drugs was often futile, for her patients had no means with which to buy them. Instead, this doctor acquired large quantities of drug samples. She did her best, occasionally substituting the drugs she had on hand for the proper drugs which her patients could not obtain.[67] In many cases, physical ailments were just not brought to the attention of a doctor. Eventually these people would suffer from the lack of a healthful diet, sound dental care, and proper medical attention. Private charity was not the answer to the medical needs of the poor.

While some settlements clung to their clinics, the National Federation campaigned for national health insurance. In 1936 the National sent a young doctor and his wife to Britain to study that country's health insurance program. As a result, Dr. Douglas W. Orr and his wife, Jean, wrote *Health Insurance with Medical Care: The British Experience*. The Federation hoped that this book would reach a wide audience and generate support for the upcoming battle for health insurance.[68] Also in 1938 the National Federation passed a resolution endorsing "medical care through the insurance principle" and approving Senator Wagner's governmental inquiry into health insurance.[69] In February 1939 Senator Wagner introduced a bill to expand the Social Security Act to include some form of national health insurance.[70] The National Federation had gathered material to be used at hearings in favor of the measure,[71] and National president Helen Hall was urging social workers to do all they could in their local communities to create support for the bill.[72] Then World War II broke out. National medical insurance failed to be enacted due to preoccupation with foreign affairs and the implacable opposition of the American Medical Association.[73] Within the settlement movement, the fight for national medical insurance was largely limited to the National Federation.

Aside from relief programs, probably the foremost New Deal experiment in social and economic planning on a regional scale was the Tennessee Valley Authority. The National Federation endorsed the principle behind the TVA in 1934 when the settlements passed a resolution urging "the public trusteeship of the sources of energy in the United States: waterpower, coal, oil, gas, and their operation under democratic and cooperative control." [74] The National demonstrated its imagination and pioneering heritage when it held its 1936 conference on the site of TVA at Norris, Tennessee. Delegates occupied dorms and cabins previously "used by the construction force when the great dam building was on" and became familiar at first-hand with the project. The National Federation of Settlements was the first national organization to hold a conference on the site.[75] In so doing, it gave unique and dramatic support to the TVA.

Even though he was active in the National Federation, George Bellamy, of Hiram House, retained his conservatism. In order to counteract the spirit of the New Deal ("The Federal Government is giving away so much money, encouraging indolence and a care-free spirit, as well as a feeling that society owes everybody a living" [76]), Bellamy instituted the "Industrial Projects Department" at Hiram House in the fall of 1938. This department attempted to involve the neighborhood teenagers in setting up actual businesses, such as a bake shop.[77] The idea was to teach capitalist values.

By 1939 the worst of the Depression was over. The New Deal had served to separate the liberal from the conservative settlements. While no other settlement leader was as outspoken against the New Deal as Bellamy, leaders such as Robbins Gilman in Minneapolis occasionally took anti-New Deal positions. Others simply remained silent, denying support to liberal programs that was often vital to their passage. What active backing existed for the New Deal relief and welfare measures tended to center among settlement workers in New York and Chicago and in the leadership of the National Federation. When these leaders criticized the New Deal, it was usually because it did not go far enough. Some were even willing to align themselves openly with groups more radical than the New Deal.

As businessmen began to recover economically, they generally saw the New Deal with its major welfare programs as a threat to free enterprise. By the end of Roosevelt's first term, they were in strong opposition to his programs. Since the Chests were largely controlled by businessmen and other well-to-do people and since the Chest system allowed maximum control over member agencies, the lack of vocal support for the New Deal among settlement workers in Chest cities is therefore significant.

6. Unemployment, Relief, and the Settlements: A Radical Alternative

*T*HE New Deal raised questions about unemployment and welfare on which some settlements took liberal positions while others were outspokenly conservative or significantly silent. For the militant among the unemployed, the New Deal did not go far enough; consequently, groups of unemployed formed in the early years of the Depression to work for a more radical alternative to the New Deal. They campaigned for better welfare programs and became connected with socialist organizations. Many of these groups were rooted in settlement neighborhoods and desperately needed financial support, supplies, meeting places, and leadership. Settlements were in a position to help them, and some did. But because of the radical political connections of these groups, their presence most severely tested the independence of settlements from Community Chest and conservative giver control.

The settlements which helped radical groups of unemployed, such as the Workers Committee on Unemployment and the Workers Alliance, were largely limited to houses in New York and Chicago—the non-Chest cities. Except for an occasional token group, settlements outside these two cities shunned organizations of the unemployed which had radical political affiliations. In spite of fairly extensive sources on Minneapolis settlements in the thirties, the only mention of the Workers Alliance is that it met at North East Neighborhood House in October 1938.[1] In Boston, which had an extremely weak Chest system, the South End House group was moved over to Lincoln House, where the board then endorsed its presence.[2]

In other cities, settlements refused to have anything to do with radical groups of unemployed. Columbus's Gladden Community House went the merry way of recreation, explaining:

> The youth of this neighborhood want social life and entertainment in their leisure time. Most of all they want legitimate

jobs. They are not keen about talking seriously about their problems. This we think is fortunate so long as we provide an outlet for their energy. Radicalism is just that far away from them. Social dancing has been the most popular activity. . . .[3]

Baden Street Settlement in Rochester would not even organize recreational groups for the unemployed only, reasoning that "the more the unemployed continue their association with the employed the better the morale of the unemployed remains." Furthermore, "grouping of the unemployed is not a particularly safe arrangement."[4]

Perhaps the most significant reason for avoiding the radical groups of unemployed was expressed by a person from Detroit who declared that "he would not contribute his dollar to the Community Chest if he knew Communists were allowed to meet in a settlement."[5] Most of these groups were not Communist. Yet, Community Chests were highly sensitive to this sort of criticism. The result was a totally different attitude toward the groups of unemployed in Chest and non-Chest cities.

Given the almost complete absence of the radical groups of unemployed in Chest city settlements, the involvement of New York and Chicago settlements with radical organizations of unemployed was that much more remarkable. Of the two cities, Chicago was the more active. The Chicago settlements provided such groups with leadership, meeting space, and some financial support.

The Chicago Workers Committee on Unemployment (CWCOU) owed its inception in the summer of 1931 to a group of fifteen or twenty members of the League for Industrial Democracy (LID), an off-shoot of the Socialist party.[6] Among this group were Karl Borders, a Chicago Commons resident; Frank W. McCulloch, a volunteer at the Commons and son of Commons board members Frank H. and Catharine Waugh McCulloch; and Lea Taylor, headworker at the Commons and president of the Chicago Federation of Settlements.[7] Borders had resigned as assistant head of the Commons the year before to become the executive secretary of the Chicago chapter of the LID.[8] Although he received a Bachelor of Divinity degree from Union Theological Seminary in 1916, Borders had quickly abandoned the religious field to work for secular, humanitarian causes.[9] A contemporary noted that Borders's "leadership was never spectacular and his manner lacked fireworks and he had no political shrewdness," but this contemporary also praised his "sincerity, level-headedness, and infinite patience." [10] Apparently, Borders had an aptitude for administration since he went on to become chief of the Bureau of Supply of the United Nations Relief and Rehabilitation Administration in 1944 and was head of the United Nations International Children's Emergency Fund when he died in 1953. Until 1934 when he joined the Works Progress Administration,[11] Borders was chairman of the CWCOU and headed the Chicago branch of the LID. In the judgment of a member of the CWCOU in 1934, it was largely due to Borders's "personal prestige that audiences were obtained with the authorities, that the cooperation of various liberal civic groups was at times secured, and that settlements and churches allowed locals to meet in their quarters." [12]

When Borders left Chicago in 1934, Frank W. McCulloch replaced him as chairman of the CWCOU. The reform tradition was strong in the McCulloch family. Frank W. McCulloch's mother, Catharine Waugh McCulloch, was a noted suffragist, a lawyer, and "the first woman elected to a judicial office in the United States (Justice of the Peace in Illinois)." [13] She managed both a family and a career at a time when a woman was expected to do either one or the other. Her son Frank graduated from Harvard Law School in 1929. He explained, "My volunteer work at the Commons and my association with the LID and Karl Borders led to my helping him and the Commons in the early stages of the CWCOU." These associations also introduced McCulloch to Paul Douglas, then a professor of economics at the University of Chicago and active in the LID. From 1949 to 1961, McCulloch served as an assistant to Senator Douglas and then served as chairman of the National Labor Relations Board from 1961 to 1970. In the early days of the CWCOU, McCulloch wrote the group's constitution and was its first treasurer.[14]

Motivated by the sufferings of the unemployed and a loss of faith in capitalism, the original group of fifteen or twenty professionals formulated a platform calling "for a planned economy in which social security and the right to work would be placed above private profit in industry and agriculture." [15] The next step was to mobilize sentiment behind the platform. The group issued a formal call to organized action to the unemployed workers of Chicago. In September 1931 the pastor of Humboldt Park Methodist Church, the Reverend W. B. Waltmire, first organized a local of unemployed workers. Meeting in his church basement with forty to fifty jobless men of the immediate neighborhood, he explained the group's platform. The men wanted to know more, so the following Monday the chairman of the newly established Workers' Committee on Unemployment, Karl Borders, addressed them.[16] As the group continued to meet, attendance rose to around 300 members.[17]

Meanwhile, other groups called "locals" were organized, mostly in settlement houses. Settlements were probably chosen because of their affiliations with a number of the leaders, the availability of meeting rooms near the homes of the unemployed, and the favorable attitude of the Chicago houses toward social action programs. These locals sent representatives to the House of Delegates, which met first in Association House[18] and later at Chicago Commons. The original group of professionals became the Advisory Committee and included, besides the settlement workers already mentioned, the Reverend Norman Barr, head of Olivet Institute; Glenford Lawrence, assistant head of Chicago Commons; Harriet Vittum, head of Northwestern University Settlement; and Hull-House residents Jessie Binford, Florence Jennison, and Robert Morss Lovett.[19] In addition to rendering assistance during certain crises, these individuals allowed the CWCOU to use their names in order to gain entry for the unemployed into all sorts of meetings and meeting-places. These settlement workers also made themselves available as speakers on behalf of the CWCOU. The original committee turned over the actual direction of the CWCOU to the House of Delegates and to the officers,[20] who included, besides Borders and McCulloch, Glenford Lawrence as a committee chairman.[21]

The CWCOU existed on a financial shoestring. Its official source of income was a ten-cent initiation fee and monthly dues of five cents.[22] At its peak, the organization claimed around 20,000 members in fifty-two locals,[23] but only a minority actually paid dues. However, the CWCOU was fortunate in that its chairman and treasurer doubled as the chairman and treasurer of the Chicago office of the LID. Consequently, the Workers' Committee had the use of the office of the LID. The LID also paid Karl Borders a salary, although Borders was "devoting about nine-tenths of his time to guiding and building the Workers' Committee." [24] The settlements had little money to spare, but in November 1932 Curtis Reese, head of Abraham Lincoln Center and a vice-president of the Chicago LID, moved that the Chicago Federation of Settlements donate one hundred dollars to the CWCOU and that each settlement contribute an additional five dollars or more. The motion carried.[25] In spite of settlement support, insufficient funds still hampered the growth and effectiveness of the CWCOU.

Nevertheless, the hearings sponsored by the CWCOU in January 1932 to publicize the living conditions of the unemployed "gave great impetus to the growth of the unemployed locals." [26] The hearings were organized by Karl Borders; Esther Loeb Kohn, a resident of Hull-House; Graham Taylor and daughter Lea Taylor; and Harriet Vittum, head of Northwestern University Settlement.[27] Their purpose was to publicize the plight of those on relief and to mobilize public opinion to back state aid for the unemployed. The first of the series of six hearings was held at Chicago Commons. Among those giving first-hand reports of the effects of the inadequate relief system were "social workers, landlords, milkmen, nurses, real estate people and businessmen, and many of the unemployed themselves." [28] One jobless person, after telling how he had been forced to move four times because the charities paid only one month's rent in a place, confessed:

> I didn't have anything to eat this morning. I went to the National Tea and took a loaf of bread, went to another grocery store and got a jar of jam and that is what I had for breakfast this morning. I am not ashamed to say it. As long as I have to have something to eat, I will get it if I have to rob.[29]

A school principal described the alternative to stealing:

> We were practicing for a chorus and a little boy about twelve years old was in the front line. He was clean in his overrralls, but didn't have very much on under them. . . . All at once he pitched forward in a dead faint. This was two o'clock in the afternoon. When he was revived, I tried to find the cause and he said he was hungry. He had not had anything to eat since the day before.[30]

The CWCOU hearings dramatized the fact that more relief funds were needed.

The hearings were a success. Reporters from the Chicago *Daily News* and *Daily Times* attended them and gave them some publicity. Mimeographed copies of the testimony were also distributed to interested people and institutions in the Chicago area. The CWCOU thought that the hearings were a factor in arousing the public sentiment which was necessary to get the state legislature to appropriate $18,750,000 for relief the following month. The hearings also increased the prominence of Karl Borders and added weight to his testimony in Washington on behalf of the Costigan-La Follette bill which would have enacted a federal relief program. As it was, Illinois did receive a $9,000,000 Reconstruction Finance Corporation loan due in part to Borders' statements and the urgent postcards sent to Washington by rank-and-file CWCOU members.[31] By giving the unemployed "a chance to tell their story to a group of sympathetic persons who would try to do something to help," the hearings alleviated some of their sense of hopelessness and stimulated morale. They also contributed to "better understanding within the community between various groups: the grocer and the landlord had a chance to tell their side of the story."[32] A second set of hearings in June 1933 resulted in the welfare board's decision to finally include rent in relief budgets.[33] Further indication of the success of the hearings occurred when settlement leaders Mary Simkhovitch, John Lovejoy Elliott, Karl Hesley, and Grace Gosselin followed the Chicago example and held similar hearings in New York City the same year.[34]

The money wrested from the state of Illinois for relief following the first set of hearings lasted until the end of May 1932. Cook County then attempted to keep the relief stations open by selling $6,250,000 in tax-anticipation warrants.[35] However, few people would buy them, so "the relief stations were going to be closed for two weeks as one way of saving money."[36] The CWCOU attacked the situation in three ways. It sent a delegation to Mayor Cermak; it sent another delegation to the newspapers and radio stations and got thirteen short periods of radio time;[37] and it sent a third delegation, composed of Lea Taylor, Frank McCulloch, and some of the unemployed men themselves, to call on the bankers. Taylor recalled their visits to three or four banks. "In most cases we didn't get beyond the secretary, but we let the president of the bank know we had been there and that something must be done by the banks of the city to advance money . . . for it was criminal to consider closing relief stations." [38] The day before the stations were scheduled to close, eighty Chicago bankers and industrialists met and arranged to buy enough tax warrants to keep the relief stations open. [39]

The next crisis came in October of that year when "the Chicago Emergency Relief Commission announced that grocery orders which had been intended to cover two weeks must be made to last a month." In cooperation with other groups of unemployed, including the Commission of Unemployed Councils, the CWCOU decided to stage a march to protest the cut. [40] To make the final plans, the Unemployed Councils and the CWCOU divided the chairmanship [41] of a general conference attended by some 700 delegates. The Communists managed to pack the meeting, and their chairman opened the gathering by calling Borders a " 'betrayer of the working-class'. . . . The Communists jeered and booed, demanded that political banners be carried." [42] Lea Taylor recalled, "The Workers Committee delegates got excited and wanted to pull the chairman off the platform." However, "Karl Borders said it would cause a melee and as he was scheduled to be the second chairman to conduct the meeting, he took control of the tense situation." [43] A reporter at the time described Borders as "a short, gentle, stubborn man, with a clear gray eye and small mustache—the kind of serious middle-class radical who especially infuriates Communists." Borders "urged the superior importance of getting relief over the quarrels of political factions, and persuaded most of the groups to stick." The meeting voted against the carrying of political banners. [44]

In spite of the cold and the pouring rain, 20,000 people took part in the march through Chicago's Loop on October 31st. At one point "they were halted by a cordon of police who . . . tried to drive them [back onto the sidewalk as specified in the city permit,] but the Communist leaders locked arms and led the column against the police, who gave way without resistance." [45] Among settlement workers taking part in the march were those from Chicago Commons, who "marched with their local Workers Committee group." Lea Taylor remembered a woman who spotted a "Foster for President" sign. The woman shouted to a policeman, "Get that man." Instead, "the policeman calmed her down." [46] In reasonable order, the marchers proceeded on to Grant Park, where they heard speeches. The handbills proclaimed:

All Out Against Starvation. No cut in food! No evictions! Cash Relief! (Minimum of 7.50 per week for families; 5.00

per week for single workers). Gas, water, and electricity! Medical and dental care! Clothing for all! Lunch and carfare for school children! [47]

Illinois borrowed another sum of money from the Reconstruction Finance Corporation, and the relief cut was withdrawn.[48]

In spite of its apparent success, the hunger march left a bitter aftertaste. The disruptive tactics of the Communists, their display of political banners when the majority voted against them, "the effrontery with which the Communists broke faith with the other marchers," and "the brazen way they made a red-flag day out of a hunger march . . . proved almost fatal for the future of the unemployed movement." A CWCOU leader remarked, "It was the end of the Workers' Committee's headlong plunge to the left." [49] The CWCOU avoided further participation in united front activities.

In addition to the demonstrations, the CWCOU sustained a number of regular activities. The CWCOU constitution required each local to hold at least one meeting a month,[50] and many held weekly meetings. These gatherings gave the unemployed an opportunity to discuss common problems. The meetings also helped to consume time which hung heavily on the unemployed. A contemporary student of the unemployed thought that the Workers' Committee "served as an outlet for discouragement, bitterness, and unconsumed energy." It served, also, "as a bolsterer of egos. It gave a man a sense of importance to stand in front of a crowd and to shout, to be on the organization committee, to tell other people what to do." To some extent, feelings of aimlessness gave way to a sense of direction,[51] and the on-going activities of the CWCOU probably helped to maintain the morale of its members.

Nearly every member of the CWCOU was on relief, and partly as a result of the emergency nature of the relief organization, many had been the victims of countless administrative errors, conflicts, and oversights. Therefore, the locals set up grievance committees to investigate the complaints of dissatisfied members and then discuss these complaints with the District Administrators of Emergency Relief.[52] Settlement workers, such as Lea Taylor and Harriet Vittum, helped the grievance committees gain access to the relief authorities. The settlements also organized conferences among social workers, the unemployed, relief supervisors, and others which met monthly and acted in an advisory capacity to the relief stations.[53] At one such conference chaired by Lea Taylor, Harriet Vittum said that North-western University Settlement "repeatedly housed evicted families over night." A relief official "stated that if a family was evicted it was partly the fault of the family because it waited too long before notifying the relief station." In an eviction case, the relief station would first call the bailiff's office to get a twenty-four hour postpone-ment of the eviction. The relief authorities then contacted the evicting landlord and asked him to apply the money he would have to spend for the eviction fee toward the family's rent in a new place instead.[54] If successful, this technique meant the relief authorities could avoid paying even the first month's rent. The settlements as well as the unemployed protested against such practices.

When they could not budge the relief authorities, the grievance committees turned to direct action. If someone's gas, water, or electricity had been shut off, a skilled member of the organization would turn it back on. The Gas Company reacted at times by not just removing meters but also disconnecting the gas at the street so that unemployed mechanics could not turn it on again.[55] At a number of settlements the Workers' Committee kept "a squad of ten men on duty all day, shock troops, to pop into any emergency" which arose. For example, if somebody needed help to bring home a load of relief coal, these men would spring into action.[56] They also kept a list of vacant flats available, and immediately on hearing of an eviction the men were on their way with a list of vacancies and sturdy backs for moving furniture. Sometimes the landlord would try to avoid the expense of eviction by harassing a tenant. For example, he might remove the door to a flat or knock a hole in the water pipe, flooding the kitchen. Then, the Workers' Committee would send carpenters to make another door or a "plumber, doing his tour of duty on the emergency squad," would fix the hole in the water pipe.[57] The activities of the grievance committees did much to win support for the CWCOU among the unemployed.

The unemployed had found that the best method for building locals was hanging around the relief "stations and interceding for people in difficulty." Consequently, when the relief authorities estab-lished a central Public Relations Bureau to deal with complaints, the CWCOU protested.[58] The protests had no effect, and the Workers' Committee was forced "to centralize its own activities" with a resultant loss in local autonomy.[59] No longer were members of individual locals able to intercede for clients at neighborhood relief offices since to settle a complaint meant a trip or a phone call to a centralized bureau, something few unemployed could afford very often. Consequently, the organization declined in both numbers and spirit as a result of the centralized Public Relations Bureau.[60]

Another activity, which lasted for six months, was the publication of the CWCOU's fortnightly paper, the *New Frontier*. The Chicago newspapers actually gave very little coverage to the CWCOU, and the *Chicago Tribune* even took the position that those on relief "have failed to make the grade." [61] The *New Frontier* presented the viewpoint of the unemployed and served to tie the fifty or more locals together. The paper was published at LID headquarters and edited by Robert Eller Asher. Karl Borders, Chicago Commons resident, and Glenford Lawrence, assistant head of the Commons, served on the editorial board.[62]

Among the most disturbing articles published in the *New Frontier* was a series on garbage dumps and the people who frequented them for food. The *New Frontier* asked locals "to visit the dumps, interview any people who are eating the food scraps," and send in their reports. Thus the paper obtained the following description of the Roseland Garbage Dump:

> About twenty-five men and boys and one woman stood in two rows all day, all the way down to the garbage hill waiting for that load to come down. And then, like a flock of chickens, they started to scratch in that smelly pile, and pick out certain things, which they deposited in baskets they had with them. Apples seemed most popular even when half rotted away. Carrots, potatoes, and bread also found their way into the baskets. . . . Some claimed they were taking the stuff for rabbits and chickens, but I noticed that a pile of lettuce and spinach leaves, which would have been ideal feed, were left untouched. Most of them admitted that it was for their supper.[63]

Why did they not go to the relief station? Some were too proud, and others did not or would not meet the eligibility requirements. An unemployed housemaid was an example of the latter. Because she was single, she could only get relief by selling what little furniture she had and moving into a county shelter. She chose instead to work for her room, but was dependent for food on Ohlsen's dump:

> When asked what kind of food she got there she replied, "Sometimes good, sometimes not fit to eat. Those greedy men sometimes get into the trucks before they are dumped and get the things away from us women without us getting a fair chance." [64]

The announced intention of the *New Frontier* "to print these interviews and continue printing them—sickening as they are—until the abuse is entirely corrected" [65] was largely rhetoric. Even at two cents a copy,[66] the paper only lasted four more months.

Besides publicity, the CWCOU responded more directly to the need for food and other items by attempting to set up commissaries, but this activity was not popular. For example, a local at Chicago's Association House once hauled in 10,000 cabbages from a Wisconsin farm. "It took days for the House to dig itself out of what it still calls 'case-work cabbages.' " [67] At University of Chicago Settlement, the unemployed pooled their skills and ran a barber shop and did shoe and furniture repairing in addition to securing farm produce for its members.[68] Yet compared to other cities, such as Seattle and Los Angeles, self-help projects made little headway in Chicago.[69] Commissaries were "short lived . . . partly because of the difficulty of any equitable distribution of the goods," but also "because of the feeling that full energies should be devoted to pressure for increased relief budgets, not to supplementing inadequate rations with hit-or-miss barter methods." [70]

In Chicago, political action dominated the organizations of unemployed. On March 4, 1933, coinciding with Roosevelt's inauguration, the CWCOU joined socialist and labor groups in holding a mass meeting to demand "legislation for the millions of unemployed workers." [71] Another mass meeting on October 31, 1933, held to commemorate the march of the previous year, featured Norman Thomas as guest speaker.[72] A rally on March 2, 1934 protested the demise of the CWA.[73] The CWCOU participated in May Day parades in 1933 and 1935.[74] And a number of settlement residents joined a march on November 24, 1934 demanding more adequate relief budgets.[75]

The unemployed also used more traditional means of political pressure. They wrote their congressmen,[76] ran candidates (unsuccessfully) in the aldermanic elections,[77] and testified before the state legislature.[78] When the *Chicago Tribune* advocated the "disfranchisement of the unemployed," the CWCOU picketed the Loop offices of that paper.[79] The unemployed valued their political rights, and they used them.

The CWCOU experienced its greatest successes in 1932. Its efforts to put pressure on the authorities had maximum impact in a crisis atmosphere. However, by 1933 the county relief office had established a Public Relations Bureau, which mitigated the effect of the grievance committees. Also, the New Deal began to meet the demands of the CWCOU for better relief programs. Yet, the Workers' Committee continued to agitate. Although never significantly large in numbers, it was a vocal group to the left of the New Deal supporters. By making its presence felt, the radical CWCOU may have influenced conservatives to be more receptive to the less radical New Deal program. Certainly its members must have felt that the Workers' Committee was having some effect or they would not have continued to agitate year after year.

In some of the settlements and churches of New York City, the New York branch of the LID organized a Workers' Committee on Unemployment (similar to the Chicago Workers' Committee). The settlement leadership was not quite so much in evidence as in Chicago, but the advisory committee of the New York group included New York settlement workers John Lovejoy Elliott, Grace Gosselin, Karl Hesley, Helen Harris, and Mark McCloskey. By April 1933, eight locals had been organized in seven settlements. Later on, the organization was reconstituted as the Workers' Unemployed Union. By 1935, New York had around thirty locals, half of which met in settlement houses.[80]

Although not as strong as the Chicago organization, the New York group carried on similar activities. At Henry Street, the local held "weekly mass meetings with prominent speakers on problems of relief and unemployment and general social conditions"; it had a Grievance Committee; it sent representatives to Albany to lobby in favor of the Unemployment Insurance bill, and it took part in relief demonstrations.[81] Also in New York, the settlements joined the Workers Unemployed Union and other organizations to form the Citizens Conference on Unemployment, whose purpose was to oppose the sales tax and "to insist on a higher standard of relief." The New York group was hampered by the lack of a permanent office and asked the settlements to provide quarters "for their exclusive use." However, when it came to a choice between meeting in the settlements where facilities were limited and groups could only use rooms for an allotted time or meeting in permanent quarters outside the settlements, the Workers Unemployed Union chose the settlements. The members thought that "there was much mutual benefit to be derived from the joint activity of the Settlements and the Unions" and "that it was the Settlement's task to provide good leadership until that which was latent in the membership of the Local could be developed." [82] In both New York and Chicago, a close relationship existed between the groups of unemployed and the settlements.

Around 1934 the Chicago and New York Workers' Committees on Unemployment helped to form the Workers Alliance. This new organization continued to hold mass meetings, demonstrations, and marches. On at least one occasion, a settlement leader was instrumental in securing a permit for a march. Graham Taylor wrote to one of Mayor Kelly's officials that if the city would grant permission to the Workers Alliance to demonstrate for more adequate relief, it would aid the Chicago relief administration "to win cooperation and avoid needless conflict" with the unemployed.[83] The resulting demonstration only numbered about 1,500 people,[84] which was fairly typical in the latter years of the Depression. However, the Workers Alliance added two other weapons to the arsenal of the unemployed. Because it had a viable national organization, it could put pressure directly on Congress, as when seven hundred delegates marched on the White House and Capitol in April 1936.[85] Also, because many members were on WPA and dissatisfied with the low pay, the Workers Alliance or its affiliates could encourage those on WPA to strike.[86] The Workers Alliance remained the major organization of the unemployed until 1939 when its ranks split over the question of Communist control.

The national organization of the Workers Alliance admitted the Communist Unemployed Councils in March 1936 and established proportional representation on its executive board: Workers Alliance, fifteen; Unemployed Councils, seven; and independent groups, three.[87] The local branches were directed to follow suit, and so the Cook County Workers Alliance admitted the Unemployed Councils.

Glenford Lawrence, head of the Adult Education Department at Chicago Commons, noted that three of the four locals meeting at the Commons "had voted against the amalgamation" because they feared radicalism. After the amalgamation, "the character of the meeting of the House of Delegates (the body of representatives of the individual locals) changed . . . to such an extent that" the "conservative locals felt less and less at home." The Greek local at the Commons disintegrated; "the Polish local wanted to split off from the Workers Alliance when the communists were admitted"; and the Mexican local was largely "weakened by radical-conservative conflict." [88] By 1939 only one tiny, struggling local remained at the Commons.[89]

The weakening of the non-Communist forces changed the balance of power within the Alliance. In February 1939, Norman Thomas, Socialist candidate for President in 1936, charged "that Communists were seeking to 'control or destroy' the Workers Alliance and to drive from its ranks members of the Socialist party." Specifically, Thomas cited the refusal of the national board "to renew the charter of the Illinois Workers Alliance" and what amounted to the ouster of Frank McCulloch, a Socialist, from the national executive board and leadership of the Illinois organization. Since "it was Frank McCulloch's practice to 'lean over backward' to avoid friction between Socialist and Communist forces," Thomas termed the situation "most regrettable." [90] Lea Taylor backed McCulloch and denied the use of the Commons to the Communist-controlled segments of the Workers Alliance.[91] Many of the non-Communist forces withdrew from the Alliance and formed the Workers Security Federation,[92] still under the chairmanship of Frank McCulloch in Illinois.[93] Probably the single biggest mistake the Workers Alliance made was to admit the Communist Unemployed Councils in 1936. The subsequent internal dissension did much to weaken and eventually kill the organization.

A favorite weapon of conservative groups is to charge their opponents with communism. In supporting the groups of unemployed, settlements risked these allegations. For example, in 1933 the American Legion's Illinois branch accused thirty prominent Chicago teachers, clergymen, and social workers of "having succumbed knowingly or unwittingly to the wiles of Communism." [94] Among those singled out were two settlement residents, Karl Borders (Chicago Commons) and Robert Morss Lovett (Hull-House), and three headworkers, Norman Barr (Olivet Institute), Mary McDowell (University of Chicago Settlement), and Jane Addams (Hull-House). The following year these people and others connected with Chicago settlements, particularly Curtis Reese of Abraham Lincoln Centre, were again charged with harboring Communist sympathies, if not outright communism, by Elizabeth Dilling, in *The Red Network*.[95] In 1935 the executive secretary of the Chicago Community Fund, Frank D. Loomis, received a series of letters from a right wing Chicago manufacturer regarding Communist infiltration of these settlements.[96] On one occasion Loomis asked Reese to answer the charge that the headworker was among the main speakers at a Communist meeting.[97] Reese, who described himself as an "independent liberal," said that he used the occasion to get "a communist and radical gathering to applaud a capitalistic president," [98] Franklin Roosevelt.

On the surface, the Chicago settlements refused to be intimidated. For instance, in January 1937, Hull-House entertained Earl Browder, then head of the Communist party.[99] Generally, settlements met accusations of Communist activity by publicly proclaiming their belief in free speech. The real danger in such allegations was that they could influence a settlement privately to tone down a liberal program in order to avoid suspicion.

Yet, New York and Chicago settlements gave qualified support to groups of the unemployed. When an affiliate of the Workers Alliance endorsed a strike against the WPA, the United Neighborhood Houses of New York took the opposite view "that one can not strike against the Federal government." [100] The Communist issue caused further problems. New York headworker Mary Simkhovitch thought settlements should open their doors to Communists as well as non-Communists, but "no settlement should allow any group which is planning to engage in unlawful acts to meet in its building." [101] Helen Hall asked the locals at Henry Street to convey in their resolutions and banners that they spoke for themselves and not for the settlement.[102] In 1937 Curtis Reese of Abraham Lincoln Centre got the Chicago Federation of Settlements to contribute five dollars toward the expenses of a state-wide Workers Alliance conference at Hull-House, but the Federation refused to be represented at the conference, although individual houses were free to participate on their own.[103] The following year a Chicago settlement, Hyde Park Neighborhood Club, refused meeting space to groups of the unemployed, but the refusal was based more on the fact that the Alliance had some black members than on the group's radical politics.[104] With these qualifications, the Workers Alliance was welcomed in the New York and Chicago settlements up to 1939.

Why were radical groups so strong in New York and Chicago settlements, while scarcely present in settlements elsewhere? New York and Chicago were, of course, the two largest cities and had local federations of thirty or more settlements. Yet, Philadelphia had twenty-two settlements in the National Federation and Boston twenty-eight.[105] Also, both New York and Chicago had offices of the LID, but the LID organized groups in other cities as well. In Cleveland, the delegations from the Council of the Unemployed persistently harassed welfare officials and city politicians for better relief programs, particularly for relief in cash. On some occasions, crowds of 300 to 400 gathered outside Cleveland's Associated Charities office, but were prevented from entering by the police.[106] Yet, Cleveland's settlements would have nothing to do with radical groups of unemployed.

The important difference is that both New York and Chicago settlements housed leaders with radical political philosophies. In addition there was no Chest or welfare federation to regulate the activities of these settlements, thus radicals were free to organize. As a rule, the boards of the major settlements in these two cities did not interfere with settlement activities. Consequently, settlements in New York and Chicago functioned in a political and social environment which allowed them to give freely of themselves in order to strengthen the organizations of the unemployed. That these settlements did make a vital contribution towards organizing the unemployed may be seen in the words of Frank W. McCulloch:

> The cooperation of the Commons was so constant, its leadership so central a factor in the establishment and maintenance of the CWCOU (and successors), its interpretation of the true needs of the unemployed and encouragement of their joint action for jobs and adequate relief so effective that I suspect many of us took the Commons—and other settlements—too much for granted.[107]

7. The Settlements and Labor

NOT all settlement neighbors were unemployed during the Depression. For the fortunate ones with jobs, the Depression brought about a political climate favorable to labor unions. However, the scarcity of jobs meant that workers outside unions were prone to exploitation. As a result, the settlements were occasionally drawn into the labor disputes of their neighbors. The settlements in the liberal, non-Chest strongholds of New York and Chicago were also drawn into the New Deal's controversial, pro-labor Workers Education program. Since labor issues were often class related, pitting the employer against the employed, the involvement of settlements in labor disputes was a good clue to their general political and social orientation and an index of Chest involvement.

Pittsburgh was a strong Chest city, and also a city in which the settlements abstained from significant involvement in social action, including labor issues. This does not mean that Chest officials frequently said no to settlements who proposed activities of a liberal nature. Rather, an atmosphere was created which discouraged those who might propose such activities. In *A Social Study of Pittsburgh*, published in 1938, New York School of Social Work professor Philip Klein observed, "the question is not merely how much pressure has in fact been applied to discourage participation in liberal activities but also to what extent has the discretion and caution deemed necessary to avoid potential pressure throttled [social workers'] freedom of expression and action." Klein added, "Issues do not usually become public." He cited as evidence the following excerpt from an interview with the anonymous head of a Pittsburgh settlement:

We [social workers] have all felt under pressure at this time to discontinue activities with the liberal groups. . . . The pressure here is of a different, more terrifying type on account of the big steel interests which control the town. Most people are afraid to call their souls their own. Few of those who have liberal inclinations will take an active part for fear they may be branded as instigators. . . . In my opinion, you can talk about anything in Pittsburgh except conditions which affect the local situation.[1]

Another settlement head commented, "The monied people . . . don't criticize as long as the liberal or radical groups use hotels, and therefore should not criticize when they use settlement houses, community centers and schools." The latter headworker ignored the fact that by forcing liberal groups to use hotels, the opposition forced them also to dip into their usually slender financial resources for rent. As a center of heavy industry, Pittsburgh had labor problems; but the settlements did not become involved in them.

The situation was similar in another strong Chest city, Minneapolis. There headworker Robbins Gilman was unable to recall that North East Neighborhood House had "ever had any definite connection with Union Labor in any way." He claimed the settlement "would be very glad to [accommodate] any local group of Union members providing we had rooms"; but added, "I would feel that before doing so I should receive assurances not only from my Board but from the Community Fund that allowing Unions to meet here would be an acceptable policy." He then noted that the anti-union "open shop" policy had "generally prevailed in Minneapolis, due to the activities and support [of] the big contributors to the Community Fund." Personally, Gilman would have liked to see the Minneapolis settlements show "a friendly attitude toward" unions;[2] but apparently he did nothing about it.

Although North East Neighborhood House avoided unions, the settlement did show concern for working conditions. Through its employment bureau, North East became aware of low wages and unsanitary working conditions; and it reported violations of the state laws to the Minnesota Industrial Commission. For example, the settlement unearthed a sweat shop where sixteen-year-old girls worked six days a week, ten hours a day, for $2.00 to $2.50 a week. The Industrial Commission recovered $186 in unpaid wages, which was turned over to the girls, and punished the manufacturer.[3] Gilman referred to the State Industrial Commission as "the type of machinery set up largely through the efforts of social workers ten, twenty, or even twenty-five years ago." [4] He was willing to utilize existing laws for the protection of workers, but unwilling to involve the settlement more directly in union activities.

Indeed the legislative approach enjoyed wide settlement support. During the Depression, the Child Labor Amendment attracted much attention. Settlement workers also worked for the passage of minimum wage and maximum hour legislation.

When the Supreme Court ruled previous attempts on the part of Congress to regulate child labor unconstitutional, Congress passed the Child Labor Amendment in 1929. It then went to the states for ratification and the issue soon became bound up with the Depression. In a speech before the Women's City Club in Cleveland, headworker Alice Gannett called attention to the fact that the better factories which had refused to hire anyone under eighteen were abandoning this policy. "They are hiring children," said Gannett, "because it costs less." Furthermore, children were often forced to work when their elders were unemployed.[5] On the other hand, some people, including President Roosevelt, thought that more jobs would be available for adults if children were excluded from the labor market.[6] These were basically the reasons why settlement workers favored the amendment.

Yet, the settlement movement was not solidly behind the amendment. A board member of Denison House in Boston predicted that Massachusetts would not ratify the amendment because of opposition by the textile interests. He recommended a "lie low policy." [7] George Bellamy attacked the proposed amendment directly. He thought it would give children the impression "that work is bad, there is something wrong about it and that they should be shielded from it." The child's ambition for work should be encouraged. Children who do poorly in school should be allowed to work. Farm children, who work and assume responsibilities while young, become good citizens. Bellamy clinched his argument by saying, "A child labor law might have prevented the making of a Lincoln and a Washington." [8] However, such outspokenness against the Child Labor Amendment within the settlement movement was unusual.

The fight to secure passage of the amendment involved individually Jane Addams, Lillian Wald, and Lea Taylor, plus the National Federation of Settlements. At the request of the National Child Labor Committee, Jane Addams spoke over the radio on "Child

Laborers Who Need Protection Now." [9] Addams also served on the board of the National Child Labor Committee along with Lillian Wald. A long convalescence gave Wald ample time to write. "The Child and the Law" urged ratification of the Child Labor Amendment,[10] and "The Race Marches Forward on the Feet of Little Children" called attention to the plight of children employed as migrant farm laborers.[11] Lillian Wald also personally wrote to a number of prominent people regarding the amendment. A 1933 letter to Governor Herbert Lehman of New York asked him to try to make room for ratification on the agenda of the Special Session of the legislature.[12] Later, Wald wrote to inform Katherine Lenroot, head of the Children's Bureau, of his support.[13] A letter to General Hugh S. Johnson, NRA administrator, commended him for eliminating child labor in the code regulating the cotton industry.[14] Lea Taylor functioned on a different plane. As head worker of Chicago Commons, she asked the staff to incorporate child labor material into the programs of the women's groups and to remain informed regarding state legislation.[15] As individuals, these women lent their prestige to the Child Labor Amendment.

The National Federation became involved with the amendment in 1936. At its June convention, the Federation voted "to send telegrams to both political parties asking them to include a plank favoring passage of the Child Labor Amendment in their platforms." [16] After the November 1936 elections, half the states had ratified. With only twelve states to go, the National urged "every settlement in every state that" had not yet ratified "to make the passage of the Amendment their first order of business for 1937." [17]

The amendment never passed. Instead, Congress passed the Fair Labor Standards Act in 1938. This law made the shipment of goods in interstate commerce illegal if "manufactured by children under sixteen," thus ending the exploitation of children by industry.[18] When the Supreme Court upheld this law, most people felt there was no longer any need for the Child Labor Amendment; and it ceased to be an issue.[19] Along with other groups, the settlement workers could claim some credit for ending child labor, as a result of the activities of some of the more liberal leaders plus the actions of the National Federation of Settlements.

The Fair Labor Standards Act also included minimum wage and maximum hour provisions. Settlement workers were more united behind these provisions than they were in favor of the Child Labor Amendment. The National Federation supported the state approach first and in 1933 pledged "its efforts to secure in the various states minimum wage legislation." [20] However, by 1936 the New York Supreme Court ruled that a state could not pass minimum wage legislation while at the same time the United States Supreme Court struck down a federal minimum wage law. The National declared, "A way must be found to permit both the states and the nation to regulate maximum hours and minimum wages for men, women and minors" if it meant a Constitutional amendment.[21]

For once George Bellamy and Hiram House of Cleveland were in harmony with the liberal settlement leaders. A Hiram House staff worker had discovered a nineteen-year-old girl working in a hotel food department from 6:00 A.M. to 10:00 or 12:00 P.M. seven days per week for a dollar per day. The girl did it because she came from a large family that had "been on the Associated Charities for several years and the money was very much needed in the home." [22] Bellamy responded to this situation by writing to Grace Abbott, then head of the Children's Bureau. He suggested that the government get "a minimum wage law to apply to all—men, women and children" and asked Abbott to present his arguments to Frances Perkins, Secretary of Labor. Grace Abbott replied that Perkins agreed with him.[23]

Until passage of the Fair Labor Standards Act, settlements worked to gain and implement state minimum wage laws. In Cleveland the Consumers League of Ohio, whose president was the headworker of Goodrich House, Alice Gannett, spearheaded the fight for a state minimum wage law.[24] Among those organizations which joined the Consumers' League in pressing for this legislation were the Settlement Union of Cleveland, Goodrich House Women's Club, and Neighborhood House of Lorain, Ohio.[25] After passage of the law, settlements continued their support and cooperated in a study on the wages of food handlers in hospitals, drug stores, hotels, and restaurants, which was presented to the recently established State Minimum Wage Board.[26] Also, in Illinois Lea Taylor of Chicago Commons served as chairman of the Minimum Wage Board for the Wash Dress Industry. She arranged hearings, did research,[27] and recommended a minimum wage of thirty-seven cents per hour[28] which was approved by the state.[29] Such activity was very much in the reform tradition of the settlements.

From their experience with state laws, settlements knew that enforcement did not automatically follow passage of a bill. Chicago Commons was aware that "the state ten-hour law [was] violated again and again . . . yet there [was] little complaint because jobs [were] so scarce and so eagerly taken, whatever the conditions." [30] After the passage of the Fair Labor Standards Act, settlements were determined that it be effective. The National Federation urged member settlements to "use every opportunity to interpret" the labor laws to both their boards and adult groups. The National also supplied blanks which houses could use to report violations as well as instances where the law brought about more employment or better wages. [31] Although settlements did their part, a major factor in securing better working conditions was the improving economic situation.

Unionization was more controversial than laws regulating wages, hours, and factory conditions. In 1934 the National Federation of Settlements urged the rigorous safeguarding of the right of workers to organize as the first step in creating a healthy balance of power under the code system of the NRA. [32] Following the wave of strikes in 1937, the National Federation conducted a symposium on "The Place of the Settlement in Industrial Relations" under the direction of Chicago Commons worker Glenford Lawrence. Lawrence recommended four ways in which settlements could help labor. First, they should know labor history and be able to relate it to the current situation. Second, they should have first-hand knowledge of present labor disputes, rather than a reliance on the press. Third, they should be familiar with the activities of labor unions and legislation that affects unions. Finally, settlements should do everything they could "to unite with other groups in pushing for better labor relations." [33] Lawrence practiced what he preached, but not all settlements followed his example.

As previously noted, Robbins Gilman expressed some personal sympathy with unions, but this sympathy did not carry over into the program of his Minneapolis settlement. When the Twin Cities chapter of the AASW sponsored a series of discussion sessions on labor relations, Gilman was invited to send some staff members. He gave this assignment to two part-time workers, both of whom had conflicting commitments for about half the meetings. [34] Thus the AASW effort had no impact on the program of Gilman's North East Neighborhood House.

The situation was quite different in Chicago, largely due to the leadership of a number of liberal settlement leaders, the lack of interference on the part of the boards of the major settlements, and the absence of a Chest which could control individual settlement programs. For example, Abraham Lincoln Centre invited a black, Frank Crosswaith, to speak. Crosswaith was a "special organizer for the Brotherhood of Sleeping Car Porters," the Elevator Operators Union, and other unions in which blacks were represented. In addition, Crosswaith edited the *Negro Labor News Service* and had run for various offices as a Socialist.[35]

Settlements could also aid unions in more informal ways. For example, during a lull in the Chicago Commons game room, staff member George Myers joined two settlement neighbors, Joe and Nick, in a discussion about union efforts to organize the leather-goods factory where both worked. Joe reported that about half the workers had joined with the union, but he was undecided. He said that he still owed a day's pay, two dollars, on his union membership and wondered if the dues were worth it, although the union was promising a thirty percent raise. To forestall trouble, the boss had stationed nine policemen in the factory, but Joe was worried about getting safely to and from work. He was also worried about losing his job. His friend, Nick, had just been fired by the boss after spreading "the word around about the union meetings." Joe was also peeved because most of the girls were too timid to sign up; yet if he risked his job, they would benefit. Finally, Joe thought he might be fired, even if the union managed a successful strike. The Commons worker, George Myers, discussed with Joe the need for and advantages of unionization. Myers said "that all progress in the labor movement had come because someone was willing to stick his neck—and his job—out." Also, Myers contacted Glenford Lawrence about Nick being fired for pro-union activities. Lawrence decided to refer Nick's case to the National Labor Relations Board.[36] Because settlements were in contact with people whom the unions were trying to reach, they were in a position to aid union efforts to recruit new members.

The pro-union efforts of some settlements were formalized when these settlements became part of the federal government's Workers Education program. The essence of Workers Education is best conveyed by an anecdote concerning a cooking class for working women. The lesson was on soups, and the teacher placed a lot of emphasis on the uses of bones and their nutritional value. When she asked for questions at the end of the class, one woman finally "stood up and said, 'Could you please tell us who had the meat off those bones?' Workers education . . . is that branch of adult education that asks ugly questions." [37]

Workers Education sought to provide educational opportunities for the working class. It tried to arouse a sense of community among workers and "to reach unorganized workers . . . to stimulate social action." It also encouraged unionization.[38] A major goal was to get the workers to think for themselves and to develop in the neighborhood groups spokesmen and leaders "who are the products of local situations and therefore most qualified to speak and to represent them." [39]

From 1934 to 1939, the National Federation of Settlements supported the Workers Education program. The National's 1934 resolution applauding the program was followed by the establishment of a Workers Education Committee under the chairmanship of Glenford Lawrence of Chicago Commons. The rest of the committee consisted of New York settlement workers, a reflection that settlement classes in Workers Education centered in these two cities. However, an occasional settlement elsewhere took part in the program. Resolutions supporting Workers Education were passed again in 1935,[40] 1936,[41] and 1937.[42] Workers Education was one of the more controversial New Deal programs and it needed all the support it could get. Shortly after the National Federation passed the 1937 resolution, the federal government announced that funds for the program would be cut, and the program ended in the states where it was weakest.[43] In 1939, Workers Education faced another crisis. Federal administrator Hilda Smith wrote to the National Federation asking that individual settlements express their appreciation of the program and request its continuation and expansion.[44] Nevertheless, it was soon phased out along with other WPA programs.

While it existed, individual settlements made important contributions to Workers Education. They made it possible for the program to go beyond labor groups and unions to reach large numbers of unorganized workers. Settlements also contributed their facilities, their knowledge of neighborhood conditions, and their group work and community organization skills.[45] In addition, settlements were often well located in relation to where workers lived, and the houses had some tradition which could lend prestige to Workers Education.[46] In 1936 nine New York settlements participated in the program— Greenwich House, Hartley House, Henry Street, Hudson Guild, Union Settlement, Church of All Nations, Goddard Neighborhood Center, Hamilton House, and Riis House. Chicago had seven settlements involved—Chicago Commons, Association House, Northwestern University Settlement, University of Chicago Settlement, Bethlehem Community Center, New Marcy Center, and Goodwill Center. However, only one settlement each in Philadelphia, Toledo, and Cleveland had Workers Education classes in 1936.[47] Except for an occasional settlement outside New York and Chicago, such as Brashear in Pittsburgh,[48] most houses never became active in the program. In other words, Workers Education was yet another example of the tendency for social action to characterize New York and Chicago settlements, while such action was largely absent in settlements elsewhere.

Workers Education officially began in New York and Chicago in 1935 although both cities had active adult education programs in settlements before that date. Many of the workers attending classes were unemployed. "M.S." was characteristic of them. He was a twenty-six-year-old shipping clerk, recently married, who had been fired after participating in a strike. He wanted a better understanding of why he had lost his job, and he brought his wife to the classes also so that she could better understand his unemployment.[49]

Hull-House, under Charlotte Carr, placed a great deal of emphasis on Workers Education. In addition to English classes, Carr added more specialized classes in labor laws, labor problems, and "training for union leadership." [50] However, with Charlotte Carr's resignation in 1943, a strong advocate of unionization and labor left the settlement field.[51]

Both New York and Chicago settlements suffered from charges of communism as a result of the Workers Education programs. In New York the Hearst press accused the Workers Education School at Henry Street of "using Government funds to overthrow the Government." The newspaper gave only one-sided reports of the classes, stressing "the relatively few references to Communism and giving a completely false impression." [52] Later on, Glenford Lawrence complained that the Workers Education program at Chicago Commons had "been termed 'red,' " causing work at the settlement in general to suffer. The classes had this reputation partly because many members were also members of the Workers Alliance, but also because the anti-Fascist stand of most of the teachers had alienated conservative elements within the neighborhood.[53] Therefore, it was not surprising when settlements became concerned over the possibility that boards might limit the discussion of controversial issues.[54]

Loose charges of communism were not the only factors in hampering Workers Education or in keeping the program from officially involving settlements in more conservative cities. A federal official in the Workers Education program noted that school officials in Massachusetts opposed Workers Education. The problem was basically the pro-union stance of the program. This official warned, "If settlements go into workers education, they will have to recognize collective bargaining for which workers' education stands." [55] Robbins Gilman of Minneapolis admitted that his settlement was not actively engaged in Workers Education as such, although it was trying to develop an adult education program as fast as possible.[56] While settlements in New York and Chicago plus a scattered few elsewhere were active in Workers Education, a National Federation of Settlements survey revealed "the failure of the majority of settlements to report on any vital piece of social education with either young people or adults." In other words, most settlements showed a significant absence of "activity along the social problem lines." [57]

When settlements did become involved in specific labor disputes, the scene of involvement was likely to be Chicago. In response to a wave of strikes hitting the nation in 1937, Chicago settlement workers formed the Citizens' Emergency Committee on Industrial Relations. Members included such well-known Chicago leaders as Harriett E. Vittum, Glenford Lawrence, and Lea Taylor, in addition to Marguerite K. Sylla, head of University of Chicago Settlement; Dr. Curtis W. Reese, head of Abraham Lincoln Centre; and Frank W. McCulloch, then a volunteer at Chicago Commons and several decades later to be chairman of the National Labor Relations Board.[58] The purpose of the committee was to gain accurate information about industrial disputes and present this information to the public. The committee was particularly interested in reaching a middle class audience.[59]

The Citizens' Emergency Committee had already been formed when the 1937 steel strike erupted in Chicago. In the ensuing violence over the issue of union recognition, the Chicago police killed ten strikers.[60] Members of the committee were present when this "Memorial Day Massacre" occurred. They got testimony from those who were hurt in the melee, then tried without results to talk to the chief of police. The committee then went to the mayor, to be given only vague promises. While taking notes at the coroner's inquest, three members of the committee were arrested. Accused of being "Communists because they had papers bearing the letterhead of the Council of Social Agencies" (the coordinating body for private social agencies in Chicago) on them, the "men were grilled for hours" before being released. The committee testified in Washington, but the press gave it little notice. The committee also obtained a newsreel of the massacre but had great difficulty getting it shown in Chicago. It did manage to arrange a few private showings, the first of which was at Hull-House.[61] Hull-House board member Louise Bowen supported the showing of this film. She commented, "I suppose we will get a good deal of criticism of this [showing] but at any rate if the police acted badly they ought to be shown up." [62]

Not all board members were as receptive to the Citizens' Emergency Committee as Bowen. In one agency some board members objected when two social workers and a club leader joined the committee. These board members thought those who joined should be asked to resign. Fortunately, the majority of the board did not agree. Although conservative elements were present on the boards of Chicago settlements, the boards of some of the leading settlements possessed influential liberals who apparently managed to curb attempts to limit social action activities in the settlements. Also, the leading Chicago settlements were strongly liberal and set the tone for the rest to follow if they so chose.

Even though Chicago had only a deficit fund system, settlements were not immune from pressure applied by large givers. Chicago Commons learned this when it became involved with a group of girls who were dissatisfied with wages in the small candy factory where they worked. The girls desired to form a union and strike, but they did not know how to begin. Chicago Commons taught the girls how to run a meeting and also referred them to the NRA, which insisted that their wages be raised to the code level. Nothing came of the girls' efforts to hold a mass meeting for the purpose of forming a union, but Lea Taylor was summoned to see the head of the deficit fund. The latter had been told that the Commons "was trying to stir up candy workers." Taylor recalled, "I said, 'Look here, what would you do?' He said that he had to interpret our actions to a city wide industrial group involved in raising" the money for the deficit fund.[63] Although the pro-labor activities of the Commons jeopardized a potential source of contributions, the fund in this case stood by the settlement.

However, that was not always the case in other cities. Without naming names, Helen Hall, then president of the National Federation of Settlements, told how "a trade group threatened a community chest with a boycott during a drive if one of its agencies did not withhold all education directed toward the passage of the Child Labor Amendment." In the words of Hall, "The action in this case was not so courageous." [64] A group of large contributors were able to use the Community Chest to stifle social action on a specific issue in all the member agencies of that city.

If one were to gauge the political and social orientation of settlements by their attitudes toward labor, a general division would appear. While most settlements favored the Child Labor Amendment and other regulatory legislation, not all worked openly to further unionization. Settlement participation in the pro-union Workers Education program was centered almost entirely in New York and Chicago. These were also the two cities where settlements were most favorably disposed toward assisting unions and becoming involved in labor disputes. However, even in Chicago, such involvement could lead to the threatened firing of a staff member by the board or an attempt to put pressure on an agency through denial of contributions to the deficit fund. That Chicago settlements withstood such pressures and continued their pro-labor activities is a tribute to the dedication and ability of the staff workers and volunteers as well as to the presence of some influential and liberal board members coupled with a weak deficit fund. Chicago settlements raised most of their money themselves. Therefore, the Chicago fund could only pass along a *request* that the settlement discontinue a certain activity, and the activity continued.

Economically related issues tended to split settlements into two camps—those of the liberal deficit fund cities of New York and Chicago and the conservative Chest cities elsewhere. Yet not all social action of the thirties was related as directly to economic issues as unemployment, relief, and labor problems. Better housing for low income people had strong advocates in both political camps. Also, both groups occasionally worked for better race relations. However the issues of housing and race relations during the New Deal are worth examining in more detail because, although the greatest progress in these two areas was made after World War II, it was the decade of the 1930s that helped to lay the groundwork. What is distressing for settlements is that these efforts did not provide firmer foundations for the post-war housing and civil rights movements.

8. The Settlements and Housing

*H*OUSING occupies a somewhat anomalous position in twentieth century social reform. On the surface, laws to provide public housing and to regulate slum dwellings seem to infringe on private enterprise and so to be anathema to conservatives. Yet private enterprise has a lucrative source of profits through urban renewal programs. If slum areas are to be cleared for new developments, slum-dwellers must be housed elsewhere. Thus, paradoxically, conservatives (especially if they are real estate operators) find it in their own best interests to support public housing. This type of "pseudo" social reform was also true of the housing movement during the New Deal; economics and altruism melded into a viable program of social innovation—public housing. Therefore housing was the one area of reform in the thirties that left little room for controversy over settlement roles. Indeed there were no sharp differences in attitude toward housing problems in Chest-supported settlements and non-Chest-supported settlements. Both housing reformers and certain groups of conservatives saw it was to their advantage to support public housing.

Initially, the New Deal had taken a fresh approach to housing and city planning—areas which had been a major concern of settlements from the time of the Progressive Era. Prior to the Depression, settlements and other interested groups had sought solutions to housing problems through building regulations and zoning laws. Such measures were upheld during the 1930s, when attention shifted to the development of large-scale public housing due first to the need to find suitable projects for the PWA and then to a concern for low income housing.

What role did the settlements play in the housing movement? In a sharply critical letter to New York settlement leader Albert J.

Kennedy, Edith Elmer Wood, a noted housing reformer, charged that the settlements "have no philosophy of housing, no program," and so could not "provide real leadership to their friends in the tenements." Instead, she said that the settlements were showing "a timid opportunist leadership, advocating or opposing this or that as it comes up." [1] While the charge may have been somewhat justified at the time, afterwards the settlement movement did make a stronger effort to provide leadership in the battle to improve housing for the poor.

The oldest means of dealing with the problem of substandard housing was through building regulations. Although New York had had building regulations since the Tenement House Law of 1867, a Hamilton House club leader, visiting a tenement home (built according to pre-1901 building regulations) to find out why a boy had been absent for two successive weeks noted "the narrow dark stairs, the stench from the hall toilets, [and] the peeling plaster." The plaster was so bad that in places the laths could be seen. There was a hole in the floor of one room which extended through the ceiling of the apartment below. The club leader discovered that the boy's "absence was due to the fact that his foot had been badly bitten by a rat while he was asleep!" Rather than comply with the 1936 regulation that old-law tenements be renovated to include a private toilet for each apartment, many owners simply allowed their buildings to deteriorate.[2] The persistence of such conditions raised doubts as to the effectiveness of building regulations, but settlement workers continued to utilize whatever weapons they had, including existing laws, in the fight for better housing.

The United Neighborhood Houses of New York was in the forefront of the battle for better building regulation laws. In 1929 New York passed a law calling for the "renovation of 'old Laws' and converted dwellings to bring them closer to standards set by the tenement house act of 1901." [3] In the same year the secretary of the New York State Board of Housing asked Lillian Wald to submit a summary statement to be used with the state legislature, covering such questions as, "Is the Tenement House Law being enforced?" [4] Another New Yorker prominent in the fight for better housing was Stanley Isaacs, president of the board of United Neighborhood Houses and chairman of its Housing Committee. In his successful campaign for borough president of Manhattan, Isaacs claimed,

> I have fought in Albany year after year to place upon the statute books laws which would compel the owners of old-law

tenements to make them fit to live in, as safe as possible from
the fire hazard, equipped with adequate sanitary conven-
iences, and to prohibit the occupancy of damp and unwhole-
some cellars and rooms without windows to the open air.

In spite of such conditions as those he described, Isaacs thought the
lawmakers had achieved all they could for the tenants without being
unfair to the owners.[5] Eventually, in some buildings the cost of
rehabilitation to meet the requirements of the new housing regulations
got to be more than the cost of a new structure;[6] but many tenants
could not afford rents in new or rehabilitated buildings unless
somehow subsidized.

By 1935 federal funds were "available for use in the demolition
of . . . structurally defective buildings." [7] In Chicago this availability
of funds spurred the settlements to work for rigorous enforcement of
existing building regulations. Lea Taylor was among those strongly
pushing the Chicago Federation of Settlements' "project of reporting
violations of housing conditions." [8] A pamphlet, "Minimum Standards for Multiple Family Houses in Chicago," was made available to
settlement workers, who were also supplied with blanks for reporting
violations.[9] Some settlement boards joined the campaign for better
housing through building regulations. The board of University of
Chicago Settlement endorsed a petition urging the City Council to
eliminate substandard housing.[10] Eleven days later when a city
ordinance was proposed "setting up minimum standards for habitable
houses," the measure won the endorsement of the board of Chicago
Commons.[11] However, in the first eight months of the settlement
campaign to report housing violations, social workers only turned in
fifteen such complaints.[12] Obviously, it would take more than building
regulations to eliminate substandard housing in Chicago and other
cities as well.

During the preceding decade, hundreds of cities had turned to
zoning in order to improve the urban environment.[13] Robbins Gilman
actively invoked Minneapolis zoning laws in the 1930s to protect his
neighborhood. The settlement was largely responsible for barring a
pickle factory from its vicinity, and for getting a railroad to abolish its
switching yards next to a local playground. After being appointed a
court arbiter, Gilman was able to prevent the rebuilding of a factory
which had burned. He also developed excellent connections with the

ward alderman, who refused to grant a license to an open-air carnival at his asking.[14] Gilman's connections were even more useful when he sought to have the request of a neighborhood bar for reinstatement of its liquor license denied (the previous one had been revoked). The alderman suggested that Gilman circulate a petition, which he did, securing sixty-one signatures. During the hearing, the alderman also arranged to have a worker at North East Neighborhood House testify. Meanwhile, the owner of the bar made a fruitless appeal to Gilman for his support by promising to "run a 'clean joint!' " Gilman also claimed that his life had been threatened, "anyone able to keep a license for a beer saloon from being granted in the First Ward [being] potentially a marked man." [15] Through effective political connections, Gilman was able to defend the moral tone and residential character of his neighborhood. He claimed that when he told Charlotte Carr about his successes with zoning, Carr said, " 'I wish we had that much influence with the Alderman of our Ward in Chicago.' " [16]

Settlements could not openly campaign for building regulations and zoning laws without alienating certain segments of the community. Gilman's wife found that slum "properties [were] tangled up in the manipulation of the control of property values, the limitation on real estate development, and tax exemptions or evasions." The situation involved politics, which "occasionally prevented or delayed legal action." Without giving specific examples, she charged, "Opposition was strong enough at times to stifle social action, or action by agencies which had Board members concerned in some unaccountable even mysterious way with the network." "Fortunately," she thought, "the North East Neighborhood House was singularly free from such an alliance and did take the leadership in follow-up action against offenders." Yet "the settlement did not escape retaliation." Early in its history, opposition to the settlement housing efforts developed "and continued throughout the years. It had a limiting influence on phases of its work and was the cause of certain parts of the programs never being allowed to develop." [17] This inability of settlements to bring about effective enforcement partially explains why building regulations and zoning failed to solve the housing problem.

By the 1930s, if not before, settlements became aware of the need for a more direct approach to the problem of housing—the actual construction of homes and communities for people with low and moderate incomes. In the early years of the Depression, some settlement leaders had hopes that this goal could be reached through limited dividend companies, private landlords who agreed to limit themselves to a reasonable profit such as six percent. The forty-nine member advisory board of City Housing Corporation, the company that sponsored the Sunnyside and Radburn housing developments, included New York headworkers Lillian Wald, John Lovejoy Elliott, and Mary Simkhovitch.[18] As experiments in low income housing, these communities were failures. Urban historians have explained, "Even though the dividends of the City Housing Corporation were limited to six per cent and certain economies in efficient site planning were realized," the end result was housing out of the reach of the low income group.[19] However, these communities did incorporate novel planning ideas, which led New York head worker Albert J. Kennedy to praise Sunnyside for being "a true neighborhood."[20]

The federal government first entered the housing field through the Reconstruction Finance Corporation (RFC), which made loans available to limited dividend companies.[21] Neighborhood Association helped to initiate one of these projects in St. Louis. As early as 1931, board members of this settlement indicated an interest in forming a limited dividend company (to pay five and a half percent or six percent) to clear two or three blocks of slum housing and build in its place housing for low income groups. Recognizing that these men needed help to raise the estimated $1,000,000 needed for the project,[22] Neighborhood Association pressured the state legislature for "an Enabling Act which will permit cities of 100,000 and over to approach the RFC."[23] Eventually, the project, Neighborhood Gardens, got a $500,000 federal loan. Rent amounted to $9.67 per room.[24] In 1938 the judgment of the National Federation of Settlements was that "while successful for people two or three degrees above slum dwellers economically," Neighborhood Gardens "did not meet the needs of the people for whom it was originally intended."[25]

As early as 1933, settlements called attention to the displacement of low income tenants by those who could afford the higher rents charged by the limited dividend projects. Hamilton House did a study of tenants displaced by the Knickerbocker Village project on New York's Lower East Side. After being displaced from the notorious "lung block," so called because of the prevalence of tuberculosis, eighty-three percent of the tenants had moved into "Old

Law Tenements, declared to be unfit for human habitation by the Tenement House Commission" in 1900.[26] Limited dividend projects, no matter how highly motivated, did little to improve the housing of the poor.

Jane Addams was among those settlement leaders quickly disillusioned with the limited dividend projects of the RFC. She was once asked to look over the plans for what "was, in fact, a limited dividend project, with all the characteristics of a private enterprise, but put forth in the interest of people of moderate income." Miss Addams soon "realized that all that was wanted of her was a good word for it to Washington." The rents in the project were to be rather high; and so she refused to give her endorsement.[27]

Several New York settlements tried to rehabilitate tenements on their own. However, in order to recover expenses, they had to charge rents which placed the apartments "out of reach of the lowest income group." [28] The private enterprise approach, even on a limited dividend basis, could not solve the housing problem.

Settlement workers then looked to outright grants from the federal government for the construction of low income housing. In 1933 the Housing Division of PWA was organized. At first it tried to continue the limited dividend approach, but as Lea Taylor remarked, "Nothing develops from the limited dividend company projects." When the Housing Division decided to discontinue loans to limited dividend companies and build the projects itself, she commented, "It is a marvelous opportunity to get new housing." [29]

Phyllis Wheatley Settlement House in Minneapolis tried to make the most of this opportunity for the blacks living in its neighborhood. In 1933 representatives from Phyllis Wheatley and the Urban League met with the city planning commissioner to call attention to "the very great need" for better housing in the neighborhood. A special committee grew out of this meeting, chaired by W. Gertrude Brown, headworker of Phyllis Wheatley House, and charged with the responsibility for making a survey of the district to "determine the need and present same to the government." The resulting survey showed that the neighborhood consisted of 530 Jews, 672 Negroes, and 309 "other." Sixteen families had no toilet or had to use an outside one, and ninety-seven occupied premises which should be razed.[30] By 1935 the federally sponsored Sumner Field Project was being built.[31]

Phyllis Wheatley's interest in the project continued after the approval of the federal program. W. Gertrude Brown, a black, served on the Advisory Committee of the project[32] and actively worked to protect the interests of blacks in connection with Sumner Field. In March 1936, Brown requested that the Phyllis Wheatley board appoint a special committee "to work with a similar committee of the Urban League to look into the matter of the employment of [Negroes] on the administrative personnel of the new housing project." [33] The following month, Brown announced that the Advisory Committee had selected one black and one Jew as administrative personnel.[34] Even though this was only token representation, Phyllis Wheatley helped to establish the principle that the administration of the project was to be integrated.

However, its major concern was that the former residents of the area, many of whom were black, be admitted to live in the new project. In April 1936 the settlement board passed a resolution "that former residents of the area involved . . . be given priority when applications to occupy the new buildings are considered," [35] and the project went along. The Phyllis Wheatley board went further, taking two steps to implement this policy. The first was to recommend that the government keep the rents within range of as many black families as possible, "even at the cost of eliminating some of the modern improvements." The second step was to urge as many former black residents as possible to register in order to be eligible to return to the project. The board discovered in February 1937 that only twenty-eight of the 269 families registered were black. Many blacks failed to realize that they had to register if they wanted to come back once the houses were built.[36] Therefore, Phyllis Wheatley employed a woman "to contact the families who have not registered and endeavor to get them interested in the necessity of" doing so.[37] In one month's time, this woman "secured 106 applications to return."

Since it still appeared that there might be vacant space in the project, the Phyllis Wheatley board also decided "to contact Negro families new to the district." [38] A year later, the settlement tried to stimulate interest among blacks in the project by calling a mass meeting. "Several hundred interested and enthusiastic citizens" came to watch motion pictures of the project and hear talks on such subjects as " 'What the Negroes Have Done to Participate in the Housing Project.' " [39] Finally, the settlement conferred with project officials regarding "the large number of rejections which Negro people had brought to our attention" in order "that adjustments . . . be made as far as possible." [40] In other words, Phyllis Wheatley Settlement House was determined that the project be integrated, not only in principle, but also in practice.

From the standpoint of the federal government, the main purpose of the PWA projects was to provide work and stimulate the economy. Low income housing was of secondary consideration. Thus, much of the opposition to the PWA projects sprang from the fact that the rents charged were higher than those of the housing the projects replaced. With the passage of the Wagner-Steagall Federal Housing bill in 1937, the federal government began building projects whose primary purpose was to provide low income housing. Yet, some opposition and distrust remained.

Following the passage of the Wagner-Steagall bill, Ernest Bohn, director of the Cleveland Metropolitan Housing Authority, talked to some board members of Goodrich House about the possibility of building a project in the settlement neighborhood. The headworker of Goodrich House, Alice Gannett, called a mass meeting in order to give the people of the neighborhood a chance to express their opinions.[41] Seventy-five people attended. However, even when Ernest Bohn explained that the rents in the proposed project under the Wagner-Steagall law would be truly low and within reach of people already living in the neighborhood, they protested. They wanted to continue living near the downtown area; their husbands could walk to work; there were many churches and schools with substantial buildings; and they were "near places of good entertainment." A Parent-Teacher Association representative added that this neighborhood of small houses "was a good place in which to bring up children . . . and that they liked the cottages with their individual gardens." The Workers' Alliance sent a representative who thought that the Goodrich House neighborhood, "more than any other . . . in the city, has a feeling of community consciousness." [42] Opposition to the proposed project was based largely on fear that the neighborhood would be disrupted.

Later on, the Goodrich House board became concerned about the probable effect of the project on the settlement. They believed that the proposed rents could bring about a change in the "character of the neighborhood by as much as [a] 30% rise in the economic level." They also thought that "there was no certainty the occupants of the area in the future would be the same people and types of families which now live there." The project was to be built around three sides of the settlement and the area rezoned as residential, all of which meant that should Goodrich wish to sell its land in the future, its opportunities "would be greatly restricted." Therefore, the board decided to make its approval of the project contingent on the Housing Authority's willingness to purchase Goodrich House.[43] Bohn "very decidedly would not give any guarantee" that the Authority would purchase Goodrich.[44]

The project was never built. Part of the reason for considering the Goodrich House neighborhood was the presence of the settlement house, which could have contributed needed recreational facilities to the project. However, with Goodrich House talking about selling out, the project lost attractiveness in the eyes of the Housing Authority. Neighborhood resistance was another factor. The Goodrich House board observed, "A large number of home owners . . . had no intentions of moving . . . and the authority" was "reluctant to start condemnation proceedings." [45] The settlement contributed to the dropping of the project by providing neighbors with a platform to make their opinions known and by threatening to withdraw from the area if the project were built.

Using the hindsight of the 1970s, one may speculate on whether the settlement acted wisely. Certainly, the fears voiced by the neighbors that the project would disrupt or destroy the cohesiveness of their present community would have come true. Other projects have experienced this disruption, partly because the delay in clearing land and construction means that former residents must find other quarters; the residents and board members thought disruption would occur because the project would change the economic level of their neighborhood. This fear was largely the result of past experience with PWA projects. In the late 1930s they failed to put much faith in the main purpose of the Wagner-Steagall act, low income housing. Eventually, the project probably would have brought an influx of blacks into the neighborhood; but if this prospect was in the minds of the people at that time, it went unrecorded. Nevertheless, the neighborhood and settlement feared change and blocked the project. No other plans to save the neighborhood were forthcoming and the area has languished. The housing has deteriorated even more while the settlement has had to close its gymnasium due to lack of funds.

The settlement movement, as a whole, was hardly as reluctant as Goodrich House to support public housing, nor was its leadership as opportunistic as Edith Elmer Wood charged. However, the key organization in obtaining housing legislation was the Public Housing Conference. The president of this group was Mary Simkhovitch and its secretary was "a settlement associate of Mrs. Simkhovitch's," Helen Alfred.[46] Settlement workers serving on the group's advisory committee in 1937 included Helen Hall from New York, and Albert Stoneman and Eva Whiting White, both of Boston.[47] The Public Housing Conference was influential in securing a housing division as part of the PWA, and worked with Senator Wagner's assistant, Leon Keyserling, on the detailed legislative work which finally culminated in the 1937 Wagner-Steagall Act and other housing legislation.[48]

The National Federation of Settlements lacked means for lobbying in Washington, but it could pass resolutions and urge its members to pressure their congressmen. In 1931, National president Lea Taylor accompanied her father, Graham, to the White House Conference on Housing.[49] The following year, a National Federation resolution endorsed the program of the RFC in making loans to limited dividend companies.[50] In 1934 the Federation passed a resolution specifically advocating "the aggressive use of the federal aid principle in promoting a country-wide housing program," which would include "modern accommodations . . . at rates which . . . low income families" could pay.[51] Prior to 1933 when Wood voiced her criticism of the settlements, the National Federation was not in the forefront of the housing movement. Apparently the settlement workers took Wood's criticism seriously, since the strong advocacy of the National Federation of Settlements for public housing dates from 1934.

However, the settlements were in a position to make a more unique contribution to the housing and city planning movement than the mere advocacy of legislation. They could, and they did, organize their neighbors in order that the people most affected by public housing and urban renewal could make their opinions heard. Boston and New York pioneered in this type of community organization, and settlements in a few other cities followed suit.

New York had set a precedent for involving neighbors in the fight for better housing when United Neighborhood Houses organized the individual settlement mothers' clubs into the League of Mothers Clubs before the Depression. The League was active in testifying as to tenement conditions in Albany and Washington. It did several studies on housing conditions,[52] petitioned Congress,[53] and held a mass meeting in 1935 to publicize the need for "better housing at no more than $6.00 per room." [54] Settlements also fostered the development of other community organizations concerned with housing, including the Lower East Side Community Council,[55] the Tenants Complaints Bureau of the Henry Street Housing Conference,[56] the Lower East Side Housing Council,[57] the Kips Bay Tenants' League,[58] and the Kips Bay Community Council.[59] However, it was in Boston that the settlement-sponsored movement to organize inner-city neighborhoods around housing and city planning issues achieved its highest development.

The Boston movement was Depression-born. In the winter of 1931-32, a group of unemployed architects and engineers formed the Emergency Planning and Research Bureau of Greater Boston in order to study "buildings and physical conditions in the various districts of Boston, make drawings and maps and recommendations for changes." The group felt the necessity "of finding out exactly what improvements the people who were living or doing business in 'the South End' believed were most needed" so they asked the headworker of South End House "to get together . . . a truly representative group." [60] The South End Men's Club appointed a representative committee to which were added delegates from other organizations such as the Syrian Ladies Aid Society and "the Negro section at the South-West corner of the district." [61] This committee called itself the South End Joint Planning Committee. This group was "officially affiliated with the City Planning Board." [62] Later the movement spread to other parts of Boston. Elizabeth Peabody House actively worked with the West End Joint Planning Committee[63] while other settlements helped organize the North End[64] and Eagle Hill sections.[65] Representatives of the various neighborhood-based committees also formed a Central Planning Board.[66]

These committees could point to concrete accomplishments. Most of their work was done by the standing committees of Streets and Alleys, Obsolete Buildings, Yards and Open Spaces, Housing, and Undesirable Influences.[67] Liquor licenses were of particular concern. In 1936 the South End committee voted unanimously against granting a hard-liquor license for a certain bar.[68] Again in 1938 "this Committee mobilized the apparently unprecedented number of from twenty-five to thirty citizens on each of three occasions to appear at Licensing Board hearings, and in each instance . . . was successful" in having liquor licenses denied.[69] The South End committee also got the WPA to finance a Housing Consultation Bureau which "gave advice to neighbors on" how to improve their homes.[70] Another project was to survey the neighborhood, note decadent buildings, and urge their demolition.[71] Rather than increase the density of the neighborhood, the South End group worked to make the vacant lots resulting from demolition into parks and playgrounds. In at least one case they were successful in getting the city to make construction of a playground a work relief project and in getting South End House to assign a recreation director to the area.[72] The presence of a member of the City Licensing Board on the South End Joint Planning Committee plus the attendance of representatives from government departments, such as Public Works, Police, and Health in an advisory capacity lent weight to the decisions of the committee.[73]

If Boston demonstrated the strength of neighborhood-based planning committees, Chicago demonstrated their weaknesses. Hull-House's Italian, Greek, Mexican, and Negro neighbors were in the habit of going their separate ways, but the settlement under Charlotte Carr tried to get them to work together. The various races and ethnic groups did cooperate in "a successful campaign to clean up the neighborhood alleys," [74] but such cooperation did not last. Hull-House's failure to bring about "more trust between nationality and racial groups" fatally weakened "the neighborhood planning efforts of the 1940's and 1950's." [75]

However, more than ethnic and racial rivalry was at fault. The housing in many settlement neighborhoods was primitive. In the neighborhood surrounding Woods Run Settlement in Pittsburgh, 74 percent of the dwellings had "no bath tubs or showers," and 90.5 percent had no central heating system.[76] With some reluctant financial assistance from the city, Woods Run housed a public shower room. The room was not sanitary, and Woods Run appealed unsuccessfully to the Community Chest of Allegheny County for money to overhaul the facility.[77] Meanwhile, "no public housing project has been initiated or proposed for this area, whereby a better standard of living might be available." [78] Even so, Woods Run had a Community

Council with a Housing Committee, but about all this group did in the face of deplorable housing conditions was to cooperate "with the Pittsburgh Housing Association and the prominent landlords" to forestall evictions[79] and distribute grass seeds and geraniums. In this strong Chest city, the problem was not entirely due to the apathy of the neighbors. A Woods Run worker reported the following encounter "with a self-appointed leader" on a neighborhood street corner. The man on the corner thought something more fundamental should be done about housing conditions than a clean-up-your-yard campaign, but the settlement worker was more concerned with grass seeds and geraniums.[80] This incident illustrates why some neighbors would tend to think of the settlement in terms of superficial recreation rather than a place to which they could take serious problems and get help in trying to solve them.

If these groups failed to make significant contributions to the city planning efforts of the 1940s and 1950s, at least part of the blame must be aimed at settlement leaders who directed neighborhood-based planning groups into ephemeral projects. Had these groups attacked more basic problems, such as inadequate housing, and had they developed more political expertise or acquired more power and responsibility, some of the public housing and planning mistakes of the ensuing decades might have been avoided. The idea of neighborhood involvement in community planning was revived and given emphasis within the Model Cities program of the 1960s. As it was, settlements of the 1930s took advantage of an opportunity to make a unique contribution to housing and city planning by organizing their neighbors, but they lacked enough faith in what they were doing to make these organizations significant. The settlements as centers for community planning based on neighborhood participation soon dropped by the wayside. However, in defense of the settlements it should be pointed out that the thrust of the New Deal was toward more centralized government; local control was something to avoid.

The settlements' involvement in housing problems was natural, since all served neighbors from slum areas. Throughout the Depression, the settlements continued to utilize the older approaches of building regulations and zoning to try to insure adequate housing for the poor. However, it was not always economically feasible for landlords to carry out these regulations without raising rents. Not only was decent housing needed, but it was needed at the low-income level. Settlements then thought limited dividend projects would provide a solution. They were soon disillusioned, and so openly endorsed government-subsidized housing in 1934. In spite of the influence of settlement leaders like Mary Simkhovitch, who served as president of the National Public Housing Conference, the settlement movement as a whole was relatively late in making a commitment to government-subsidized housing. However, having made this commitment, the settlements remained in the forefront of existing legislation until the passage of the Wagner-Steagall Act in 1937. Even then, relatively few public housing units were built prior to World War II. The most original contribution made by the settlements in relation to housing and city-planning was to organize their neighbors into advisory groups. Unfortunately, neighborhood-based planning organizations went against the New Deal trend toward increasing federal control. Had the settlements really tried to gain significant power and recognition for neighborhood-based planning groups, the settlement contribution to housing would have been that much more significant. Also, had planners paid more attention to the housing groups and forums the settlements did organize, maybe subsequent mistakes in the housing field could have been avoided. However, given the temper of the times, perhaps the settlements should be commended for doing as much with neighborhood-based planning as they did.

While the settlements could have shown more foresight in housing by placing more emphasis on neighborhood involvement in the planning process, their major lack of foresight came in the area of race relations.

9. The Settlements and Race Relations

SETTLEMENTS did not recognize race relations as a major problem during the 1930s. For the most part, black migration northward had come to a temporary halt. Also, most people were occupied with problems of economic hardship, and gave priority to such issues as unemployment, relief, and labor problems. The presence or absence of a Community Chest made little difference in whether or not settlement activity occurred on behalf of blacks. Supposedly, one of the advantages of joint funding is that it makes planning for the future possible and sees that gaps in a community's social services are minimized. However, the Chests did not supply blacks with the same level of services available to whites, did nothing to pressure their member agencies into dropping discriminatory policies, and failed to plan for the subsequent inundation of many settlement neighborhoods by blacks. At best, the settlement house record in race relations during the 1930s is mixed; but part of the blame lies with the lack of leadership by joint funding agencies.

Racial problems existed during the Depression, and made their presence felt within the settlement movement. For example, in searching for convention sites, the National Federation had to deal with the problem of segregated hotels. In individual settlements, the racial issue might be as near as a group of black families across the street in need of recreational facilities. The settlements had to take positions, one way or another, on these issues. The National had to choose whether it would meet in integrated facilities or not, and the local settlement had to decide if it would encourage black families to come to the house or ignore them. The groundwork laid by the settlements in race relations during the 1930s is important in view of the heavy Negro migration northward into settlement neighborhoods in the 1940s and 1950s.

The regional National Federation of Settlements conference at Unity Farm near Kansas City in 1934 gave settlement workers a dramatic opportunity to express their attitudes on Jim Crow segregation of public facilities. A committee of Kansas City settlement workers made the arrangements for the conference. They chose Unity Farm because it was willing to make facilities available to both blacks and whites on an equal basis, with the exception of overnight accommodations. The Kansas City Urban League was to arrange housing for black delegates in Kansas City and supposedly the black delegates were informed accordingly. The Kansas City committee claimed that these arrangements were the best that were possible.[1]

However, all did not go as the Kansas City settlements had planned. Downtown hotels dropped their Jim Crow policy for the National Conference of Social Work convention, which was meeting in Kansas City at the same time. Meanwhile, black delegates had made reservations in advance for Unity Farm. When they appeared, the management refused to accommodate them, saying "Negroes are not permitted to stay overnight at the farm under any circumstances." Lea Taylor, then president of the National Federation of Settlements, offered to take the black delegates (about half a dozen) into her suite, but the Unity management even refused to allow that. One of the black delegates, W. Gertrude Brown, was stung by the discriminatory treatment. She discarded her prepared speech for a conference luncheon and "flayed the policy of the managers of" Unity Farm instead. That done, the blacks walked out of the conference.[2]

The white delegates vacillated in their response. Some thought the matter should be "hushed up." They "pointed out that Unity had come a long way in permitting Negroes to even eat in the dining rooms for the concession had been granted only recently." Others disagreed.[3] In the end the official protest came, not from the National Federation of Settlements, but from the National Conference of Social Work. In a resolution, the latter organization endorsed the black delegates' walk-out and deplored the failure of the white delegates at the settlement conference to join their black comrades in withdrawing from the meeting place.[4]

The incident did, however, help to clarify and strengthen the convention policies of the National Federation. The Twin Cities settlement headworkers demanded a public apology for the insult to the black race and to their fellow headworker, W. Gertrude Brown.

Should this apology not be forthcoming, the settlement headworkers threatened to withdraw from the National.[5] Lea Taylor responded to the Twin Cities group with a resolution making arrangements for local federation meetings contingent on the approval of the national office.[6] At subsequent conferences, the National went to great lengths to avoid segregation.

One of the feats of the National Federation of Settlements during these years was to hold an integrated convention in a southern state. The federation accomplished this by selecting as the location the TVA building site at Norris, Tennessee. Delegates were assigned without regard to race to dormitories used by the building crew and were asked "to bear in mind that we are in a construction camp, and that due consideration must be given to the regular conduct of work." [7] Privately, National Federation of Settlements secretary Lillie Peck commented, "I don't think it will hurt any of us to live a little less luxuriously for a few days, and we may get something of the spirit of the less highly organized days of the movement." [8] The conference went as planned, and the federation achieved its objective of an integrated meeting in the South.

After the Unity Farm fiasco, National president Lea Taylor expressed the hope that the federation's Interracial Committee would do some work.[9] In 1931 Grace Gosselin, who headed this committee, admitted "feeling extremely guilty because I have done so little for the Interracial Committee of the National Federation." She wanted to do something, but seemed at a loss as to how to proceed and resigned.[10] The Federation never did have an active Interracial Committee during the 1930s. Although the organization passed resolutions on a variety of social issues, it was noticeably silent on racial matters. National conferences also tended to side-step the issue when it came to scheduling topics for sessions. Finally in 1939, 120 settlement members sixteen to twenty-five years old participated in a session on "America's Minority Problems." [11] Part of the reason why the National did not do more for race relations probably lay in the diversity of practices among settlements on racial issues, which ranged from strict segregation to deliberate integration.

One of the surprising facts about the settlements with respect to race relations was the paucity of houses in black areas serving blacks. Blacks formed a sizable population on Chicago's South Side by the 1930s, and although they desperately needed social and recreational services, settlements hardly filled the need. Basically, only two Chicago settlements served substantial numbers of blacks throughout the Depression, the all-black Ada McKinley Center and the ultra-liberal Abraham Lincoln Centre. In New York, the situation was the same. A survey revealed only two settlements serving a sizable number of blacks, the Brooklyn Urban League's Lincoln Settlement and the New York Colored Mission in Harlem. One settlement near an area of dense black population increased its membership fee considerably in order to ward off potential black members. Another settlement in the same neighborhood said that no blacks had applied for membership, but reported "that if they did, they would be referred elsewhere." [12]

The situation was no better in Pittsburgh. In *A Social Study of Pittsburgh*, social work professor Philip Klein stated, "To discriminate . . . seems subversive of the very foundations of the settlement idea." Yet, discriminate the Pittsburgh settlements did. Kingsley House excluded blacks from its facilities entirely. Irene Kaufmann Settlement served blacks, but did "not freely admit them on equal terms." Rankin Christian Center had "had separate rooms for Negro activities" until budget cuts forced it to abandon the black facilities. Rankin then allowed blacks in boys' and small children's clubs, but drew the line when it came to older girls' clubs and adults. One exception in Pittsburgh was Brashear Settlement, which had "no policy with respect to segregation" and which "worked closely with the Urban League in the development of its program for Negroes." [13] Mary Simkhovitch's statement, "The neighborhood finds the Neighborhood House open to all, irrespective of creed and color, race and economic position," [14] must have seemed a mockery to many blacks.

The picture was not totally negative. Chicago's Abraham Lincoln Centre was an outstanding example of an integrated settlement. Although the director, Curtis Reese, was white, the staff and residents represented both races. Furthermore, the settlement was ideally situated for an integrated program, located as it was fairly near the dividing line between the black and white communities.[15] Reese carefully controlled the membership to achieve approximately a fifty percent balance between black and white, although the balance was weighted slightly on the black side. The settlement featured interracial activities all the way from the nursery school to the adult program.[16] Among the more noteworthy events was a series of six lectures by

Melville J. Herskovitz, author of *The Myth of the Negro Past.* Herskovitz spoke to a black and white audience on such topics as the African origin of the American Negro. The lectures were preceded by dinners which gave black and white alike an opportunity to come together socially.[17] Integration was the hallmark of Abraham Lincoln Centre.

Unfortunately, for every Abraham Lincoln Centre there seems to have been an Eli Bates House. The immediate neighborhood around Chicago's Bates House was chiefly Italian. However, within four blocks of the settlement, the black area began. By 1938 it was obvious that this black area was growing.[18] The settlement board of trustees had to decide whether it would serve the changing population or close. The board soon chose to close.[19]

A third Chicago settlement, Marcy Center, followed a contradictory course, first taking action reminiscent of Eli Bates House, then trying to adopt the spirit of integrated Abraham Lincoln Centre. By the late 1920s, it had become obvious to the people running Marcy Center that the neighborhood was changing. In 1930 Marcy decided to run two Bible schools, one for the whites and one for the blacks.[20] Service to the blacks was only granted grudgingly, for Marcy Center wished to go on serving Jewish families. However, as the blacks moved into the neighborhood, the Jewish families moved out to the Lawndale section of Chicago. Marcy Center decided to follow them. Late in 1930 it transferred its operations to a new building in Lawndale.[21] Ironically, black migration to Chicago subsequently engulfed the new Marcy Center in Lawndale. However, this time (1949), Marcy Center decided to remain in the neighborhood and serve blacks.[22]

Meanwhile, the move to Lawndale in 1930 only temporarily deprived the blacks in the vicinity of the old Marcy Center of a settlement. By the mid-1930s, Marcy had reopened its former building as Newberry Avenue Center. With some difficulty, Newberry tried to serve a population of both blacks and Mexicans. The settlement gave both races the opportunity to mix socially in the gymnasium, boxing room, and game room. The boxing club elected a black as president and a Mexican as treasurer. The girls, however, were less receptive to integrated activities. A staff member noted that in the girls' clubs, as soon as the blacks became a majority, the Mexicans stopped coming.[23] Further problems (probably in maintaining order) developed in connection with the game room. The staff closed the game room for a while, then "re-opened it, at first allowing Colored and Mexican groups to use it on alternate nights." [24] A glance at a list of groups at Newberry a couple years later showed that they had coalesced along racial lines. A number were specifically labeled "Mexican" or "Colored," such as "Mexican Community Council," "Negro Community Council," and "Social dancing, colored boys and girls." [25] Yet, the staff at Newberry prized any signs of interracial fellowship. After describing an informal singing session with Mexicans around the piano during which a black boy quietly joined the group and was accepted, a staff worker cited the incident as "a tremendous step forward in carrying out that inter-racial policy adopted by our board of directors." [26] Nevertheless, Newberry seems to have had more contact between the races when its program was in the formative stage. Some people suggested that the evolving lack of interracial association at Newberry was caused by a preponderance of black members and an uncontrolled membership policy.[27]

Only in rare cases did blacks flood, or threaten to flood, the membership of previously white settlements in the 1930s. Much more typical was the situation facing Hull-House. While the second largest black colony in Chicago was in the Hull-House area, it never threatened to "take over" this unusually large settlement. In fact, blacks were hardly represented in the Hull-House program. Hull-House worker Dewey Jones told the Welfare Council he did not believe that the absence of blacks was the result of a specific Hull-House policy or decision to exclude them. Rather, the House had assumed that if they wanted to come they would. However, Jones thought blacks did not come because they were afraid of being rebuffed. As a result, the feeling developed that Hull-House was for whites only.[28]

Jones told the Council that the one exception to this development was a black mothers' club. Jane Addams had organized it in 1927. Every year since then, the *Hull-House Yearbook* included a picture of this club and a statement "that Negroes were taking part in the program." Yet, when Jones talked to one of the original founders of this club, he learned that they were not invited to participate in general activities for the community nor did their names appear on any of the Hull-House mailing lists. In actual fact, they were not getting anything out of the Hull-House program.[29]

Jones said that headworker Charlotte Carr, who arrived in 1937, noticed the absence of black participation and determined to do something about it. However, the years of ignoring the people had left their mark. Other nationality groups opposed the efforts to bring blacks into Hull-House activities. Nevertheless, Hull-House went ahead. In 1938, blacks attended the settlement's camp for the first time. Also, the staff made a deliberate effort to bring them into the game room. By talking to the neighborhood boys already there, the staff was able to overcome their resentment. Soon there were a number of black boys in the game room. However, as of March 1939 Hull-House had yet to achieve complete integration. Neither the music school nor the art department drew any racial lines, but they had few black participants. Also, few had joined clubs.[30] Clearly, Hull-House had a long way to go before achieving its goal of an integrated program.

Unfortunately, its progress was cut short by the death of Dewey Jones the month after he presented the above analysis of Hull-House to the Welfare Council. He had been the only black staff member at Hull-House.[31] Previously Jones had worked as a journalist[32] and was an advisor on race relations with the WPA at the time he received the Hull-House appointment.[33] Charlotte Carr also invited Jones and his wife to become residents.[34] When Jones died in 1939, Hull-House was facing the necessity of cutting back on paid staff. Therefore, Carr did not immediately recommend a replacement.[35] Had Hull-House made a point of inviting the blacks into the settlement when the blacks first began to move into the neighborhood, perhaps some of the racial problems of later years might have been averted. Unfortunately, the tendency to ignore blacks was all too common among settlements.

The major exceptions to this tendency were the settlements established for the definite purpose of working with the black community. Very often a city possessed only one settlement of this type. Because they specialized in working with blacks, these settlements had a definite sense of mission and were often called upon to perform certain functions which set them apart from other settlements. New York settlement worker Albert J. Kennedy attributed the establishment of these settlements to "the desire of Negroes to strengthen their own life, give effect to their own talent, establish their own standards, and create organizations that could be used to fight and trade with other population groups." [36]

One of the strongest of these settlements was Phyllis Wheatley House in Minneapolis. The black population in Minneapolis around 1938 numbered between 4,000 and 5,000. They were scattered in several ghettoes, Phyllis Wheatley being located among the largest concentration of blacks. Nevertheless, as the only black settlement in Minneapolis, Phyllis Wheatley attempted to serve all the blacks in the city.[37] The settlement was founded in 1924 [38] and opened a new building in 1929. At that time, Phyllis Wheatley claimed to be "the best Settlement House for Negroes in the country." [39] Several years later an unidentified person from Milwaukee paid Phyllis Wheatley the compliment of a visit in order to observe the program prior to the beginning of a black settlement in the Wisconsin city.[40]

During the inter-war years, settlement leader Albert J. Kennedy noted, "The white boards of settlements in Negro localities increasingly employed Negro leaders and staff members . . . and were increasingly ready to be advised on racial matters by such leaders." [41] In fact, Kennedy claimed that Negro settlements by 1935 were "almost wholly led and staffed by members of their own race." He attributed this development to changing attitudes on the settlement boards, which whites still dominated, and the rise in the number of Negroes with professional training and ability.[42] Minneapolis's Phyllis Wheatley House was no exception; it made a point of employing black headworkers and staff members from the start.

W. Gertrude Brown led Phyllis Wheatley House from its inception until her resignation in 1937. Prior to coming to Phyllis Wheatley, Brown earned a B.S. from Columbia University and attended the New York School of Social Work for two summer terms. She also took a summer course at Oxford University in England. She had taught public school for six years in Charlotte, North Carolina, and had done group work with Community Service Incorporated and the Linden Community Center in Dayton, Ohio.[43] At the time of her appointment as headworker of Phyllis Wheatley House, she was the executive secretary of a black social service organization in Dayton which had a staff of twenty-one workers.[44] Her salary at Phyllis Wheatley during the Depression was slightly less than the Twin City average for headworkers of $2,567.50.[45]

Brown took her professional obligations seriously and was deeply committed to the advancement of the black race. An avid convention-goer, in 1930 she attended the National Urban League convention, the National Federation of Settlements conference, the National Conference of Social Welfare, and the Interracial Conference.[46] She also became involved in organizations on the local level, including serving on the board of directors of the Urban League.[47] In addition, Brown was a speaker much in demand. During the first half of 1936, for example, she fulfilled eighteen speaking engagements.[48] Such occasions gave her an opportunity both to interpret blacks to the rest of the community and to expand the influence of blacks in general.

Unfortunately, Brown's extensive involvement in outside activities brought criticism from the Council of Social Agencies. A 1936 study by the Council suggested that as a result of her outside commitments, Brown was shirking her duties at Phyllis Wheatley. The Council recommended that the Phyllis Wheatley board limit Brown's speaking engagements so she would have more time to give to administer the settlement.[49] The Council also said she should hold regularly scheduled staff meetings.[50] At the same time, the settlement board decided to appoint a personnel committee, thus relieving Brown of primary responsibility for engaging and discharging staff and for other personnel matters.[51] In its report, the Council was guilty of putting efficiency above Brown's value as an interpreter and defender of the black to the rest of the community. Much of the criticism then leveled at W. Gertrude Brown appears to have been unjustified.

Added to the problems created by the Council report was a poor relationship between the board president and Brown. Brown, who was a sensitive person, found it increasingly difficult to communicate with the board president on vital issues; on the other hand, the board president was unwilling to take up vital issues with the headworker.[52] A clash of personalities contributed to the impasse. The petty criticisms of the board also bothered Brown, and eventually prompted her resignation.[53] The treatment of Brown was quite unfair in view of her accomplishments. She had built Phyllis Wheatley from the beginning and was an outstanding and well-loved member of the community. Although the board soon replaced Brown with another black woman,[54] and later with a third black woman,[55] the black community was up in arms against the board.

The major criticism of the black community was directed against white domination of the settlement's board of trustees. The resentment broke into the open when the Negro Business and Professional Association asked the Phyllis Wheatley board for a conference about the choice of a new head resident. Instead of granting this request, the board decided to stage a hearing on the question, " 'What is the matter with Phyllis Wheatley House?' " Although the Business and Professional Association was invited, along with more than a dozen other organizations, it boycotted the hearing. The association felt the hearing was a tactic to switch the issue from the coming choice of a head resident to generalities. Also, the invitations were extended on such short notice that delegates lacked sufficient time to ascertain their organizations' viewpoints.[56] Nevertheless, the hearing was well attended. Only one delegate expressed satisfaction with the settlement's board, explaining "that while the colored people might be capable of handling their own affairs the white people were in a position to do more for them." The rest of the delegates argued in favor of larger black representation on the board. The black representative from the American Legion proposed that the board's black membership be increased from its current four (out of eighteen) to at least fifty percent.[57] This position was supported by other delegates, including representatives from the Minneapolis Association of Colored Women's Clubs,[58] the Minneapolis Ministerial Alliance,[59] and the "chairman of a group of twenty-five families living in the immediate vicinity of Phyllis Wheatley House." [60] Blacks told the board that if granted increased representation, the board would have a better idea what the black community needed [61] plus interest in the house would revive.[62]

No sweeping changes were made in the board immediately following the hearing; and the other recommendation of the delegates, that Phyllis Wheatley hire a head resident from Minneapolis, was ignored. Yet, as time passed, black representation on the board increased. One of the blacks subsequently elected was the president of the Business and Professional Association who had brought the above controversy into the open.[63] The hearing also caused the settlement to draw up a list of qualifications for board membership. While race was ignored, the settlement did try to find board members free of prejudice and with some knowledge of problems facing blacks.[64] On the other hand, the board accepted the resignations of those members who could not comfortably associate with blacks at board meetings and social functions and whose sense of resentment was heightened by blacks eager for recognition or critical of social barriers. Officially, the board avoided prospective members with patronizing attitudes while it looked for "a sustained moral energy, a patience and a toughness of fibre." The actual result was a gradual increase in black membership during the 1940s,[65] probably due to the 1939 hearings.

Because of the special problems facing its clientele, Phyllis Wheatley was more involved in social action than any other settlement in Minneapolis. It cooperated with the Urban League in forming a black Workers Alliance and in the Workers Education program.[66] The settlement was also active in having the revival of a film which contributed to racial prejudice, *Birth of a Nation*, discontinued in Minneapolis.[67] Another successful project was to secure the appointment of the first black policewoman in Minneapolis.[68] Although Phyllis Wheatley was constantly involved in social action, it was nearly always social action with reference to racial prejudice and the advancement of blacks in Minneapolis.

Because it was the only black settlement in Minneapolis, Phyllis Wheatley was called upon in many instances where a settlement would have normally been by-passed. For example, Minnepolis hotels discriminated against blacks in the 1930s, and Phyllis Wheatley had residence facilities. Therefore, from the beginning of 1930 to the middle of 1936, Phyllis Wheatley functioned as a hotel for 362 transients from Canada and thirty-four states. Guests included such famous persons as Langston Hughes, W. E. B. DuBois, and Roland Hayes. When the settlement lacked room, it found lodging for black travelers in private homes.[69] In this regard, the University of Minnesota created a special problem for Phyllis Wheatley by excluding black students from its dormitories.[70] Phyllis Wheatley's head resident met with the president of the university to protest the situation. All the university president did was to promise another meeting with university officials.[71] Meanwhile, Phyllis Wheatley housed some of the students and found rooms for others.[72] Besides securing lodgings, Phyllis Wheatley was asked to perform a number of other tasks not usually performed by settlements in the 1930s. They included locating relatives, providing care for delinquent juveniles, finding boarding homes for youngsters, counseling families, securing hospital treatment, and acting on cases of discrimination.[73] New York headworker Albert J. Kennedy observed that the program of Negro settlements resembled that of the pioneer settlements more than the programs of the older settlements,[74] perhaps because the general scarcity of social service organizations during the Progressive Era still applied to the black in the 1930s. Unfortunately, social agencies did not discover the black as clientele on a large scale until the following decades.

Other types of black settlements included the black branch of a white settlement and the settlement activities of the Urban League, a black organization. The league maintained community centers in seventeen cities, but did not bother with National Federation of Settlements membership.[75] Nevertheless, the thirty-nine member national executive board of the Urban League included New York settlement worker Mary Simkhovitch.[76] In Philadelphia Whittier Center established Susan Parrish Wharton Settlement to work with blacks, with a black headworker in 1931.[77] Boston's Robert Gould Shaw House, with an all-black staff and clientele,[78] was organized under the auspices of South End House.[79] In New Orleans, Kinglsey House also established a black branch.[80] However, the typical southern settlement for blacks was church-sponsored. The Methodist Episcopal Church designated its black settlements "Bethlehem Houses" and its white settlements "Wesley Houses." [81] None of these settlements bothered with National Federation membership in the 1930s.[82] Many of the black settlements, particularly the branch houses, were poorly financed operations. Furthermore, they were not always established to give expression to the black race, but to enforce existing patterns of racial segregation.

Godman Guild in Columbus was a unique example of a settlement serving both races, but with a segregated program. Godman Guild designated three days of the week when blacks were welcome and three other days for whites.[83] It required pressure from the NAACP and the National Federation of Settlements, with the NAACP finally asking the Columbus Community Chest to withhold funds for the settlement before segregation was gradually dropped in 1956–57.[84]

Clearly, the settlement response to race relations during the depression reflected wide-ranging attitudes. It was quite common for a single city to house settlements reflecting diverse practices. During the depression Chicago was the home of an integrated Abraham Lincoln Centre, a de facto segregated Hull-House, and Eli Bates House which decided to close rather than serve the blacks moving into its neighborhood. Chicago also had its black settlement, Ada McKinley Center. To meet the need for services among the blacks, the black settlement developed. While some of these were created in response to existing patterns of segregation, others, like Phyllis Wheatley and Ada McKinley, were efforts to give expression to their black communities. With such varying practices, it was not surprising that the National Federation of Settlements, except for holding its conventions at integrated facilities, skirted the race relations issue.

Yet in 1936 two social workers, Sidney J. Lindenberg and Ruth Ellen Zittel, predicted that the black would soon relegate the "settlement problem of the immigrant . . . to the background." [85] Urban blacks suffered from poor housing and inadequate recreational, educational, social welfare, sanitary, and health programs. Lindenberg and Zittel asked, " 'What is the Settlement, the sponsor of the underprivileged and the champion of the immigrant, doing for the Negro who has settled on its doorstep?' " Their answer was "very little." [86]

Why did the settlements not do more? The United States of the 1930s was a more openly racist society in that the civil rights cause lacked the wide support it achieved later. Furthermore, some settlement workers themselves were blind to racial problems. They still thought of their movement primarily in terms of white middle-class workers living in poor white neighborhoods. Their greatest successes had been in helping immigrants to assimilate, and by the 1930s they had not totally adjusted to the decline in immigration. When certain leaders did speak out, they met with little support. Opportunities did appear in the 1930s for the settlements to do more for better race relations, but as in the case of Eli Bates, which decided to close rather than serve blacks, these opportunities fell by the wayside.

Insufficient work with blacks coupled with segregated policies on the part of some settlements did nothing to lay a groundwork of trust and friendly relations when the black migration northward swelled in the 1940s and 1950s, completely changing many settlement neighborhoods. Some settlements were then faced with a task made more difficult by year of traditions and inactivity which had to be overcome. The most serious lack of foresight displayed by settlements in the 1930s was their failure to do more for blacks.

10. Funding Reform

*T*HE settlement function is not fulfilled by a program of clubs and classes, however admirable," wrote Grace Abbott, professor of social work at the University of Chicago during the Depression. "The improvement of neighborhood conditions is a first objective." [1] Yet, many settlements were never really involved in social action. While most were eager to cooperate with private relief-giving efforts, some never went beyond this stage. New York and Chicago settlement leaders, however, actively worked to shape and secure passage of the Social Security Act, while the National Federation of Settlements tried to secure national health insurance. New York and Chicago settlements became involved with radical groups of the unemployed in sharp contrast to settlements in other cities which virtually shunned them. The socially conscious settlements of New York and Chicago also ran pro-labor programs. Yet outside these cities settlements were too intimidated by the Chests and their large contributors to do much for labor. Only when the issues became less directly related to economic questions, as was the case with race relations and the psuedo-reform of housing, did the distinction between Chest and non-Chest cities begin to fade. Generally speaking, reform activity in the settlement movement centered in the National Federation and in the local settlements of New York and Chicago.

Social workers and historians have advanced various reasons for the decline in reform activity on the part of settlements following the Progressive Era. It may not be fair to expect a social institution such as the settlement to maintain its original impetus for reform. Certain factors work in the opposite direction. Some people have a tendency to distrust rapid change and to long for tradition and stability. Also, many social institutions, settlements included, try to avoid being criticized for radicalism, which could result in the canceling of certain programs; even more likely, such criticism would contribute to an oppressive and stifling atmosphere, ruling out social action programs from the beginning. Certainly, social workers and settlement leaders became less inclined after the advent of the Community Chest to adopt controversial programs and risk criticism.

Another explanation for the decline in settlement social action during the New Deal, as compared to the Progressive Era, lies in the nature of the two reform movements. The economic side of Progressive reform seldom went beyond regulation—in factory conditions, housing, or industrial monopoly. By contrast, the New Deal brought aggressive intervention on the part of the federal government. Social welfare policy and social experimentation ceased to be the prerogatives of private agencies. Settlements, of course, were still free to experiment; but they had never been able to experiment on a large scale, and then their funds were cut. The depression of the 1930s was simply too vast for the resources of private agencies. The times demanded programs quickly and on a large scale—programs that only the resources of the federal government could supply. The settlements could still provide "models," but the Depression was impatient of small-scale experimentation. The temptation for many private social workers was to abandon the formulation of social policy to the government entirely.

Not only was the nature of reform different in the 1930s than before World War I, but so was the nature of social services. The Progressive Era lacked the network of specialized agencies which had sprung up by the 1930s. One by one these agencies took over the former functions of the settlements. For example, by 1929 local governments commonly provided playgrounds, kindergartens, adult education, and Americanization programs. Often settlements merely supplemented their former programs in order to maintain their initial investment in buildings and equipment. Originally, these services had been advanced as reforms. Having proven their worth, however, services replaced the reform impulse as the paramount concern of the settlements. In effect, buildings plus fixed costs dictated adherence to a recreation program, which further tied the settlements to their financial supporters.

Also, by the time of the Depression special interest associations dedicated to a number of reforms had arisen. These associations, without the overhead in staff and buildings which burdened the settlements, were free to agitate on behalf of their causes. An excellent example is the American Association for Social Security. Under its executive director, Abraham Epstein, this association sought support among settlements; but the impetus came from Epstein, not the settlements. Formerly, during the Progressive Era, the settlements had served to bring reformers together as residents. Settlements were then a novelty. They offered the reformer a home base, stimulating companionship from like-minded people, and a flexible program which perhaps the reformer could bend to his needs. By the time of the New Deal, reformers tended to regard the settlements as one possible source of support among many. Reformers no longer felt the old need or desire to identify themselves with settlements. As for settlement participation in these special interest reform organizations, it was usually a matter of individual, not institutional, involvement. As Nathan E. Cohen, author of *Social Work in the American Tradition*, put it, "Some things could be done within the agency setting, more could be done in the professional organization, and most could be done as individual citizens." [2] In other words, the farther the social worker was from the control of board and Chest, the more the worker could do to further social reorganization.

Perhaps professionalism in the field of social work could have served more effectively as a counterweight to the board and Chest. However, the social work schools were enamored with psychological concepts and focused on the individual. In doing so, their primary concern was to adjust the individual to the environment, not change the environment. Occasionally a social work educator such as Grace Coyle or Grace Abbott did speak out in favor of social action, but nothing much happened in settlements as a result. In any case, very few settlement workers had completed the full social work course leading to the master's degree in the 1930s. The advent of professionalism is inadequate as an explanation for the decline in settlement social reform.

The key to the demise lies within the structure of the settlement itself. Settlement workers did not make policy; they were hired by a board of trustees which was usually dominated by the employer group. That settlement work had become an occupation to these social workers did not necessarily make them less reform-minded, but it did place them more directly under the control of the boards.

During the Progressive Era, unpaid residents and volunteers supplied much of the reform impulse; and even during the New Deal, the two people connected with settlements who worked most actively with radical groups of the unemployed were Karl Borders and Frank W. McCulloch, a resident and a volunteer respectively. Not being on the settlement payroll enhanced their freedom of action.

Yet if some individuals could be financially independent, the settlement as an institution could not. It had considerable overhead in staff and buildings, which meant it had to raise money. During the Progressive Era each settlement raised its own funds, and usually large contributors sat on the board of trustees. With the arrival of the Chest, the same large contributors were still sitting on the boards. In addition, the major givers enlarged their control, not just over individual agencies, but over the whole network of Chest-supported institutions. Formerly a large contributor could put pressure only on the agencies to which he had contributed. Later he could influence all of them by applying pressure on the Chest. In addition, the Chest added one more layer of administration—one more hurdle—to overcome before a program could be launched. At least in non-Chest cities, there was the possibility that one or two agencies might have liberal boards and could lead the way in social action. In other cities, the Chest effectively stifled such initiative while imposing a rigid conformity.

However, the less centralized fund system did not automatically mean social action. All the deficit fund did was to give more opportunity to workers who might want to engage in reform activities. New York and Chicago were centers of social change within the settlement movement because they had a remarkable group of reform-minded leaders who could take advantage of their relative freedom of action. Perhaps some were attracted to non-Chest cities because the environment was more conducive to reform, but these cities also remained centers of reform because these leaders opposed efforts to establish Community Chests. For social action to occur, skilled and committed workers needed a fair degree of freedom.

How to supply this freedom for action within the agency context is a dilemma facing social reformers. From the standpoint of social action, are agencies better off without the Chest? Independence would increase the power of the individual boards, but it would end the concentration of agencies which magnifies the power of the big contributors. There is much to be said for the Chest in terms of eliminating waste and duplication and contributing efficiency in fund raising. Although Chests come under attack from time to time by groups who feel they have not gotten their fair share of funds or have been intimidated, no very attractive alternatives have been proposed. As long as America is a divided society of rich and poor, the rich and well-off will be able to contribute more to private agencies or Chests, and their contributions will give them a disproportionate amount of control. Even in a loose fund system, the wealthy still dominate individual agency boards. Without an alternative source of funds, it is doubtful whether private social agencies, such as settlements, can ever effectively challenge the economic status quo.

But if centrally funded private agencies cannot engage freely in certain types of social change activity, what is the alternative? The Great Society program of the mid-1960s tackled this problem. In some ways, the Great Society picked up where the New Deal left off. Indeed its emphasis on the community unit and community action were reminiscent of the best of old settlement theory. Since the Great Society made a point of by-passing the planning bodies of the United Funds (formerly known as Community Chests), the government's poverty program of the sixties provides some lessons for contemporary settlements, as well as for social change in general.

Since the Depression, the organization of public and private welfare has remained basically unchanged. To this welfare establishment, the Great Society added major additional federal funds, much of which went directly to private agencies. The private foundations, especially the Ford Foundation, also added to the revenue. Together, the federal government and the foundations began financing a new breed of social worker, the one to whom "community organization" meant "professional reform." These professionals brought with them techniques of agitation and a commitment to local participation which fit into the federal government's plans for the war on poverty.

The immediate precursors to the Great Society programs were two community action programs, Mobilization for Youth and the Ford Foundation's "grey area" projects. Both had some settlement connections. It was at a Henry Street Settlement board meeting in May 1957 that a philanthropist and businessman, J. M. Kaplan, proposed to underwrite preparation of a wide-ranging program to deal with juvenile delinquency.[3] Henry Street submitted a proposal to the National Institute of Mental Health for a settlement house-based program of community organization. The National Institute of Mental Health imposed a two year planning period, during which the planning committee decided that the settlement house concept of community organization, as represented by the Lower East Side Neighborhood Association, was too formal, "would intimidate the unsophisticated," and was "largely controlled by middle-class white leaders, who might resent the intrusion of newcomers upon their power." [4] The settlements retreated to the background as representatives from Lower East Side institutions and the New York School of Social Work organized Mobilization for Youth. The new agency was first financed by the Kaplan Foundation, the Taconic Foundation, the National Institute for Mental Health, and the New York School of Social Work[5] and later by the Ford Foundation, the City of New York, and other federal agencies.[6] Mobilization for Youth included subsidized job training for disadvantaged youth, the first such federally financed program since the Depression's National Youth Administration and the forerunner of the Great Society's job training programs.[7] Mobilization's program of voter registration, legal aid, rent strikes, and protest demonstrations eventually culminated in rather far-fetched charges of Communist infiltration,[8] but not until Mobilization for Youth had pointed the way for the poverty program.[9]

The Ford Foundation's "grey area" projects played a similar path-breaking role. During the Depression, Boston settlement houses had laid the basis for a network of community councils to work on neighborhood redevelopment. The Boston "grey area" project, dubbed "ABCD," was organized to work largely through existing agencies to encourage each neighborhood to participate in planning its own redevelopment. ABCD assigned its own community organization staff to settlement houses. The use of settlements occurred in spite of the Ford Foundation's doubts about "the settlement house approach to community organization." Apparently, the Boston settlements were more concerned with democratic procedures than specific issues.[10]

That private philanthropy at all should be involved may seem unusual in view of the conservatism of the Community Chests. However, the foundation's structure was quite different. In the case of the Ford Foundation, the Fords turned over a tremendous amount of money to the foundation in 1950. The trustees then employed what

Dwight MacDonald called "professional philanthropoids" to disburse
the money. In Daniel Moynihan's analysis, the professionals "were far
more politically liberal than the trustees. Rather as television took
editorializing away from Republican publishers and turned it over to
Democratic reporters, the huge contemporary foundation has done
something of the same to what was once termed charity." [11] Also,
agencies have no choice about which Chest finances them, but they
can always approach another foundation. Furthermore, the Community Chest (United Fund) finances permanent institutions indefinitely
whereas the foundation typically undertakes temporary programs or
limits the time of its commitment. Once the grant has been made, the
foundation has little control. The Ford Foundation dates from 1936,
and its pioneering in social change came after the Depression and
before recent legislation curbing the activities of tax-exempt foundations.

The pre-Great Society programs sponsored by the Ford
Foundation, the National Institute of Mental Health, and others
emphasized community organization along with vocational and
educational experiments, pre-school classes, and legal services. Except
for the legal services and in spite of a certain bias against the
settlement, these functions were remarkably similar to those of the
traditional settlement house. The Great Society gave national scope to
these activities.

The objective of Mobilization for Youth was the reduction of
juvenile delinquency by focusing on social and environmental causes;
the stated goal of the Great Society was the elimination of hard-core
poverty. In practice, the Great Society goal was less clear. The Civil
Rights movement had entered its militant phase and much of the
Great Society was geared to the urban black and to the young. Social
workers Francis Fox Piven and Richard A. Cloward observed, "The
political circumstances of the 1960's made it crucial . . . that blacks
get something in order to solidify their allegiance to the national
Democratic Party, and in order to quiet them." [12] However, less
cynical reasons also existed for the emphasis on blacks and the young.
Great Society planners were concerned about the emergence of a
cycle of inherited poverty, caused in part by racial discrimination. To
break the cycle, they focused on youth; and to counteract discrimination, they focused on blacks.[13] The urban emphasis also suggests a
commitment to revitalize the inner city. However, if the Great

Society's goal of elimination of hard-core poverty is taken at face value, one might ask why more jobs were not created to absorb the manpower trainees? Why was the welfare system not reformed to eliminate inadequate incomes? Yet there was no doubt about the New Deal commitment to economic and welfare reform.

Perhaps political reasons existed for not making the goals of the Great Society clearer. A sense of crisis was present during the New Deal that made coalition politics possible. People at all levels personally experienced the effects of the Depression. If a man had not lost his job, chances were that his wages had been cut, perhaps his hours had been reduced, and he was worried about being laid off. Finding another job could well be impossible. It is reasonable to assume that such a worker would have sympathy, if not empathy, for the unemployed. In spite of considerable griping over such things as "boondoggling," during the thirties the middle and working classes were disposed towards basic institutional changes in the welfare system, especially when these were accompanied by new programs for federally guaranteed home loan mortgages and savings deposits and a tough, pro-union stance. The welfare demonstrations and relief confrontations of the Depression hardly alienated those lucky enough to have jobs. A political center existed that the radicals could pull leftward.

By contrast, no such sense of economic crisis held the Roosevelt coalition together for Lyndon Johnson in the sixties. Instead, the middle and working classes came to feel threatened by the Great Society. A white suburbanite's support for civil rights and the poor might well evaporate if he saw slum schools competing with his own for good teachers, blacks reducing the number of college places for his youngsters, or the disadvantaged getting priority for the remaining skilled jobs.[14] Apparently, government economists also feared greater inflation if the artificial creation of additional jobs brought the unemployment rate below four percent.[15] Furthermore, Great Society reformers thought that institutions serving the poor would do better if they were not dependent on middle class approval or control.[16] Daniel Moynihan described what usually followed:

> Once and again, the attempt by official and quasi-official agencies (such as the Ford Foundation) to organize poor communities led first to the radicalization of the middle-class

persons who began the effort; next to a certain amount of stirring among the poor, but accompanied by heightened racial antagonism *on the part of the poor* if they happened to be black; next to retaliation from the larger white community; whereupon it would emerge that the community action agency, which had talked so much, been so much in the headlines, promised so much in the way of change in the fundamentals of things, was powerless.[17]

Whatever middle or working class support might have existed at the beginning was gone by the end.

Moynihan suggests it was "a fairly small number of men in banks and law firms whose names are not generally known, who do not run for Congress, who do not run for mayor," but who support those who do, that killed the community action programs.[18] The New Deal had caught the upper class weak and temporarily disoriented; but during the Great Society, the establishment was in full health and fairly quick to retaliate. Beginning with Mobilization for Youth, the community action workers followed a deliberate strategy of conflict in order to increase community participation, which would lend weight to the forces for change. These workers were aware of the possibility that their funds might be terminated. However, they felt that the risk was justified.[19]

The poor show the most continuity between the Depression and the Great Society. For example, during the New Deal, some settlements began experimenting with neighborhood participation on boards and in community planning. "Maximum feasible participation" of the poor became the hallmark of the Great Society. In practice, this meant the creation of what Moynihan called "a new level of American government, the inner-city community action agency," [20] to which the poor elected representatives. This agency enabled the federal government to by-pass established state and local agencies in the distribution of poverty funds. This was essential if the money was to go to where the federal government wanted. The participation of the poor also served "as a means of legitimizing the reformist aims" [21] of the Great Society. Psychologically, it helped to restore dignity to the poor. Economically, it saw that the poor were hired to staff the poverty projects wherever possible.[22] However, not surprisingly, the procedure tended to alienate local politicians and the established welfare councils, and led to the downfall of the Great Society.

Without a clear concept of the exact goal of the Great Society, it is difficult to evaluate its success. During the sixties, the poor were not much better off than before. They did not find it much easier to get jobs. Instead, more of them learned about existing welfare programs, and the relief rolls expanded. A few of the more successful Great Society programs, like Head Start, managed to survive into the seventies. However, the organization and type of welfare services remain basically the same as at the end of the Depression. To what extent the Great Society may have significantly expanded opportunities for the disadvantaged is unclear. Certainly, it heightened the political consciousness and sophistication of the blacks. Indeed, that was probably its area of greatest success.

In the aftermath of its demise, the Great Society left behind a legacy for settlements. The VISTA (Volunteers in Service to America) program was a domestic version of the Peace Corps, which revived the original settlement idea of actually living among those one seeks to help.

Consumer participation in social agencies in a policy-making capacity is another legacy of the Great Society. Recently, Chicago Commons supervised the organization of six state-financed day care centers in Chicago public housing projects. The Commons began by asking the tenant-elected Advisory Councils of the projects to nominate tenants to an interim committee. This committee recruited parents, children, and nonprofessional staff for the day care centers from fellow project dwellers. A "Parent Congress" consisting of parents with children in the centers then succeeded the interim committee. The Congress elects the centers' governing committees, including its policy committee, and half the members of the centers' board of directors.[23]

In addition, the Great Society also broke new ground in establishing a direct relationship between the federal government and local social agencies. The Housing and Urban Development (HUD) Act of 1965 inaugurated the Neighborhood Facilities Program, which continues in the seventies to mean money for new construction and rehabilitation of settlements and community centers. Also, some settlement programs may be funded through other federal departments. The HUD objective is to foster "multipurpose facilities which provide a variety of services, such as health, welfare, education, recreation, cultural, social, employment, training, or similar activities." [24] Gone is federal funding for controversial community action programs.

Kingsley House in New Orleans was founded in 1896. Recently, it carried out a $1 million renovation program, of which HUD contributed $700,000. Kingsley still depends primarily on the United Fund for support, but it also gets money for programs from the Departments of Justice, Labor, Agriculture, and Health, Education, and Welfare, plus the state government. This settlement carries on recreational, educational and day care activities. Its social services include family counseling, a project for the prevention of juvenile delinquency, a drug program, a mental health clinic, and "a social activity program for Spanish-speaking families." [25] Much of this is reminiscent of settlements back in the New Deal or Progressive Era; but gone is the excitement of residence, of social change, and of community action.

Perhaps settlements and social action in general have drawn several lessons from the Great Society of the sixties. The first is probably a sense of the limitations of professional reform. Expertise in social action cannot totally substitute for a sense of crisis in the larger community; and confrontation tactics that leave the poor increasingly more isolated may make them wiser, but these tactics may not result in fundamental social changes. Secondly, while most settlements are still basically dependent on United Funds for support, additional money may be obtained for specific programs from the federal government. If that government is indifferent to social change, this source is not likely to be much better for reform than the United Fund. However, the possibility remains that once again a government may favor social action, and private agencies will have an alternative funding source. Perhaps then substantial changes in the structure of our welfare system and of society will occur.

Appendix
LIST OF SETTLEMENTS IN THE 1930s

*T*HE following is a list of settlements affiliated with the National
Federation of Settlements, the United Neighborhood Houses of
New York, and the Chicago Federation of Settlements. In 1936,
202 settlements were members of one or more of these organizations.
No major settlement neglected its professional affiliations. In addition, minor settlements eagerly sought membership in the National
Federation and local federations as a badge of legitimacy. Hence, the
more than two hundred settlements listed below represent most of
those in the United States.

Settlements in the United Neighborhood Houses or the
Chicago Federation but not in the National are listed separately.
Because of the absence of a Chest in New York and Chicago, it was
quite common for these settlements to maintain religious ties for
financial as well as other reasons. However, these religious affiliations
barred them from membership in the National Federation, even
though their programs might be quite secular in nature. Consequently,
it may be assumed that religious denominations sponsored most of the
settlements listed separately under the local federations.

Unless otherwise marked, the following cities are all Chest
cities. The dates after some of the National Federation settlements
refer to the inclusion or exclusion of the agency in the National's
directory and do not necessarily refer to the beginning or end of the
settlement.

National Federation of Settlements

    * Non-Chest.
  ** Some settlements were almost entirely dependent on central
financing; others were largely independent.
*** Boston instituted a fund in the early 1930s which it tried hard
to develop into a Chest.
**** Insufficient data.

***** The one settlement here was financed by tours conducted through the original House of the Seven Gables.

Alabama, Ensley****
    Ensley Community House
California, Los Angeles****
    Los Angeles Settlement Association
    Neighborhood House
    Pasadena Settlement Association (from 1939)
    Santa Rita House (to 1939)
California, Riverside****
    Community Settlement Association
California, San Francisco
    Community Music School
    Telegraph Hill Neighborhood Association
    Visitacion Valley Community Center (to 1936)
Connecticut, Bridgeport
    Hall Home Settlement
Connecticut, Hartford
    Hartford Social Settlement
Connecticut, New Haven
    Lowell House (to 1936)
    Neighborhood House
Connecticut, Stamford
    Italian Center of Stamford (from 1936)
Delaware, Wilmington****
    People's Settlement Association (to 1936)
    Wilmington Music School (to 1936)
District of Columbia, Washington
    Friendship House
    Georgetown Children's House (from 1939)
    Juanita K. Nye Council House (from 1939)
    Neighborhood House
    North West Settlement House (from 1939)
    South East House (from 1939)
    South West Community House (from 1939)
Illinois, Chicago*
    Chicago Commons
    Christopher House (to 1939)
    Eli Bates House (to 1939)
    Emerson House
    Fellowship House
    Gads Hill Center
    Henry Booth House
    House of Happiness (to 1939)
    Hull-House
    Hyde Park Neighborhood Club (from 1939)

Jewish People's Institute (to 1936)
Northwestern University Settlement
South Chicago Neighborhood House (from 1936 to 1939)
University of Chicago Settlement
Illinois, Peoria
        Neighborhood House
Indiana, Indianapolis
        Christamore House
        Flanner House
Iowa, Des Moines
        Roadside Settlement
Kentucky, Louisville
        Neighborhood House
Louisiana, New Orleans
        Kingsley House
Massachusetts, Beverly Farms****
        Beverly Farms Music School (to 1936)
Massachusetts, Boston***
        Boston Music School Settlement (to 1936)
        Denison House
        East Boston Social Centers Council (from 1939)
        Elizabeth Peabody House
        Ellis Memorial
        Hale House
        Hecht Neighborhood House (from 1936)
        Jamaica Plain Neighborhood House
        Lincoln House
        Norfolk House Centre
        North Bennet Street Industrial School
        North Brighton Community House
        North End Union (from 1939)
        Robert Gould Shaw House
        Roxbury Neighborhood House
        South End House
        South End Music School (to 1936)
        Trinity Neighborhood House and Day Nursery (from 1936)
Massachusetts, Cambridge***
        Cambridge Neighborhood House
Massachusetts, Fall River****
        King Philip Settlement House
Massachusetts, Newton***
        All Newton Music School (to 1939)
        Stearns School Centre
Massachusetts, Salem*****
        House of Seven Gables Settlement (from 1936)
Michigan, Detroit
        Brightmoor Community Center

Dodge Community House
Franklin Street Settlement
Neighborhood House
St. Elizabeth Community House
Sophie Wright Settlement
Michigan, Grosse Pointe
Neighborhood Club
Michigan, Hamtramck
Tau Beta Community House
Michigan, Highland Park
Community Center
Minnesota, Minneapolis
B. F. Nelson Memorial (from 1936)
Elliot Park Neighborhood House
Goodwill Center (to 1936)
Margaret Barry House
North East Neighborhood House
Phyllis Wheatley House
Pillsbury House
Unity House
Wells Memorial Settlement House
Minnesota, St. Paul
Central Community House (to 1936)
Neighborhood House
Missouri, Kansas City
Mattie Rhodes Neighborhood Center
Minute Circle Friendly House
Thomas H. Swope Settlement
Missouri, St. Louis****
Neighborhood House
Community Music Schools Foundation
Nebraska, Omaha
Omaha Social Settlement
Woodson Center (from 1936)
New Jersey, New Brunswick
Neighborhood House (from 1936)
New Jersey, Newark
Catholic Neighborhood House (to 1936)
Ironbound Community House
Jewish Day Nursery and Neighborhood House
New Jersey, Orange
Orange Valley Social Settlement
New Jersey, Silver Lake****
Community House
New Jersey, South Orange
South Orange Community House

New Jersey, West Orange
      West Orange Community League
New York, Buffalo****
      Memorial Chapel Social Center (to 1936)
      Neighborhood House
      Welcome Hall (to 1936)
      Westminster House
New York, New York City*
      Beth-El Sisterhood (to 1939)
      Christodora House
      Crotona Community Club
      East Side House (from 1936)
      Federation Settlement (to 1939)
      Goddard Neighborhood Center (from 1936)
      Greenwich House
      Haarlem House
      Hamilton House
      Hartley House
      Hebrew Educational Society (to 1936)
      Henry Street Settlement
      Hudson Guild
      Jacob A. Riis Neighborhood Settlement
      Lenox Hill Neighborhood Association
      Madison House
      Music School Settlement
      Neighborhood House of the Central Presbyterian Church (to 1936)
      Neighborhood Music School (to 1939)
      Recreation Rooms and Settlement
      School Settlement Association
      Stuyvesant Neighborhood House
      Union Settlement
      University Settlement
      Willoughby House Settlement
      Yorkville Music School (to 1939)
New York, Rochester
      Baden Street Settlement
      Charles House Settlement (to 1936)
      David Hochstein Memorial Music School (to 1939)
      The Lewis Street Center
Ohio, Cleveland
      Alta Social Settlement
      The Cleveland Music School Settlement
      Council Educational Alliance
      East End Neighborhood House
      Friendly Inn
      Goodrich Social Settlement
      Hiram House

Merrick House
The Playhouse Settlement
University Neighborhood Centers
West Side Community House (from 1939)
Ohio, Columbus
Gladden Community House
Godman Guild House
Ohio, Lorain
Neighborhood House
Ohio, Mansfield****
Friendly House Social Settlement
Ohio, Springfield
Union Settlement House (to 1936)
Ohio, Toledo****
North Toledo Community House
Pennsylvania, Philadelphia**
Beth Eden House (from 1939)
College Settlement
Friends' Neighborhood Guild
House of Industry
The Lighthouse
Lutheran Settlement
Neighborhood Centre
Philadelphia Deaconess Home and Settlement
Reed Street Neighborhood House (to 1939)
St. Agnes House
St. Martha's House
Settlement Music School
Southwark Neighborhood House
Susan Parrish Wharton Settlement (from 1936)
University House
Webster House
Workman Place Neighborhood House
Pennsylvania, Pittsburgh
The Brashear Settlement
Irene Kaufmann Settlement
Kingsley House
Munhall Neighborhood Settlement (from 1939)
Soho Community House
Woods Run Settlement
Pennsylvania, Wilkes-Barre
Georgetown Community House
Rhode Island, Providence
Federal Hill House
Nickerson House
Tennessee, Nashville
Bertha Fensterwald Social Center (to 1936)
Bethlehem Center (from 1936)

Texas, Houston
> Rusk Settlement

Utah, Salt Lake City
> Neighborhood House

Virginia, Richmond
> William Byrd Community House

Wisconsin, Madison
> Neighborhood House

Wisconsin, Milwaukee
> Jewish Center (to 1936)

United Neighborhood Houses of New York

Note: These houses did not belong to the National Federation of Settlements.

> Bronx House
> Christ Church House
> Church of All Nations and Neighborhood House
> Clark Neighborhood House
> Council House
> Educational Alliance
> God's Providence House
> Grace Chapel
> Grand Street Settlement
> Home Thrift Association
> Judson Neighborhood House
> Labor Temple
> Lavanburg Homes
> New York Urban League, Incorporated
> 110th Street Neighborhood Club
> Prescott House
> Riis Neighborhood House
> 79th Street Neighborhood House
> Utopia Children's House
> White Door Settlement

Brooklyn
> Brooklyn Philanthropic League
> Colony House
> Italian Settlement
> Lincoln Settlement Association
> Little Italy Neighborhood Association
> School Settlement

Englewood, New Jersey
> Memorial House

Chicago Federation of Settlements

Note: These houses did not belong to the National Federation of Settlements.

Abraham Lincoln Centre
Association House
Bethlehem Creche
Chase House
Erie Chapel Institute
Garibaldi Institute
Halsted Street Institutional Church
Howell Neighborhood House
Laird Community House
Madonna Center
Marcy Center
New Marcy Center
Off-the-Street Club
Olivet Institute
Onward Neighborhood House
Red, White and Blue Club
South Chicago Community Center
South Side Settlement House
Union League Boys' Club

Notes

INTRODUCTION

1. This comparison of the Progressive Era and the New Deal draws heavily on Richard Hofstadter, *The Age of Reform: from Bryan to F.D.R.* (New York: Vintage, 1955) and Harvey Wish, *Contemporary America: the National Scene since 1900*, 4th ed. (New York: Harper & Row, 1966).

2. Historians have noted that, in general, social workers had turned away from reform by the 1930s, and have attributed the cause to the rise of professionalism within the discipline. They see the profession of social work as closely allied to the discipline of psychology, yet view psychology and social action as antagonistic to each other. Historians feel that, rather than reform society to suit the individual, the psychologist tries to adjust the individual to society. For example, historian Roy Lubove develops this thesis in *The Professional Altruist* (Cambridge: Harvard University Press, 1965).

CHAPTER 1

1. Headworker's report, 28 Jan. [1913] as quoted in "A. J. Kennedy Notes—Strikes in Settlement papers—2," University Settlement Papers, State Historical Society of Wisconsin (microfilm edition, 1972), reel 8.

2. Robbins Gilman to Lee Sharp of South Side Neighborhood House, North East Neighborhood House Papers, box 29, 30 Oct. 1937, Minnesota Historical Society.

3. Daniel Levine, *Jane Addams and the Liberal Tradition* (Madison: State Historical Society of Wisconsin, 1971), pp. 43–44.

4. "Report of the Headworker, 17 Feb. 1914, University Settlement Society Papers, reel 14.

5. Robbins Gilman to Robert A. Woods, headworker of South End House in Boston, 23 Mar. 1914, University Settlement Society Papers, reel 14.

6. Robert Bremner, *From the Depths: the Discovery of Poverty in the United States* (New York: New York University Press, 1956), p. 61.

7. Bremner, p. 15.

8. Allen F. Davis, *Spearheads for Reform: the Social Settlements and the Progressive Movement, 1890–1914* (New York: Oxford University Press, 1967), pp. 103–4.

9. Levine, p. 160.

10. Davis, pp. 105–8.

11. Davis, pp. 105–8.

12. Bremner, p. 241.

13. Davis, pp. 124–32.

14. Alice Gannett to Lillie Peck, secretary of the National Federation of Settlements, 15 Dec. 1934, University Settlement Papers, reel 8.

15. William M. Leiserson of the Pacific Coast Regional Office of the Social Security Board to "Friends of the University Settlement," 21 April 1937, University Settlement Society Papers, reel 14.

16. Judith Ann Trolander, "Twenty Years at Hiram House," *Ohio History* 78 (1969), p. 28.

17. Davis, p. 66.

18. Roy Lubove, *Community Planning in the 1920s: the Contribution of the Regional Planning Association of America* (Pittsburgh: University of Pittsburgh Press, 1963), pp. 5–15.

19. Davis, pp. 69–70.

20. Levine, pp. 58–59.

21. Davis, p. 62.

22. Trolander, pp. 29–33.

23. Trolander, pp. 30–32.

24. Davis, pp. 172–73.

25. Davis, pp. 94–102.

26. Jane Addams as quoted in Mary Lynn McCree, "The First Year of Hull-House, 1889–1890, in Letters by Jane Addams and Ellen Gates Starr," *Chicago History*, Fall 1970, p. 110.

27. Levine, p. 68.

28. Trolander, p. 70.

29. Trolander, p. 36.

30. "Extent of Settlement Work in the United States," 3 Dec. 1936, Lea Taylor Papers, box 4, Chicago Historical Society.

31. Albert J. Kennedy, "Social Settlements," *Social Work Year Book* (New York: Russell Sage Foundation, 1933), p. 480.

32. "Assistant Secretary" of the NFS to Carolyn E. Tufts of House of the Seven Gables Settlement, 16 March 1931, NFS Papers, fol. 349, Social Welfare History Archives, University of Minnesota.

33. "Memo for Mr. Kennedy," 4 Dec. 1935, NFS Papers, fol. 12.

34. Pamphlet, "Chicago Commons: 1937," p. 5, Ephemera Collection, SWHA, U. of Minn.

35. White House Conference for Jefferson County, Kentucky, "Youth Outside the Home and School Committee," typescript, University of Louisville, 31 Dec. 1933, p. 14, NFS Papers.

36. Directory issue, *Neighborhood*, 3 (Dec. 1930) and NFS membership lists, 1936 and 1939, Albert J. Kennedy Papers, Paige box 8, SWHA, U. of Minn.

37. Sina K. Evans, "Just One Day," typescript, 6 Aug. 1935, NFS Papers, fol. 477.

38. Pamphlet, "Chicago Commons: 1937," p. 5, Ephemera Collection.

39. Lillie Peck to Ellen W. Coolidge, then a board member of South End House, 24 March 1937, NFS Papers, fol. 343.

40. Lea D. Taylor, interview with the author, 20 July 1970.

41. Helen Hall, "Forward" to *The Helen Hall Settlement Papers: A Descriptive Bibliography of Community Studies and Other Reports, 1928–1938*, compiled by Susan Jenkins Brown (New York: Henry Street Settlement, 1959), p. 3.

42. Edith Abbott, "Boston Settlement Study," p. 5, Abbott Papers, Box 32, fol. 14, University of Chicago.

CHAPTER 2

1. See Roy Lubove, *The Professional Altruist* (Cambridge: Harvard University Press, 1965), and Clarke Chambers, *Paul U. Kellogg and the Survey* (Minneapolis: University of Minnesota Press, 1971).

2. Irwin Epstein, "Organizational Careers, Professionalization, and Social-Worker Radicalism," *Social Service Review*, 44 (June 1970), p. 130.

3. "Club Study Report—Leadership—Betas, St. Martha's House; Philadelphia," NFS Papers, fol. 75, SWHA, U. of Minn.

4. Clara A. Kaiser to Grace Gosselin of United Neighborhood Houses of New York, 9 May 1933, United Neighborhood Houses Papers, fol. 477, SWHA, U. of Minn.

5. Grace Coyle, "Group Work and Social Change," National Conference of Social Work *Proceedings* (Chicago: University of Chicago Pr., 1935), pp. 393–405.

6. Minutes of the Group Work Committee, School of Applied Social Science, Western Reserve University, 28 Oct. 1929, Case Western Reserve University.

7. Minutes, Group Work Committee, 1 June 1932.

8. Minutes of the Advisory Committee on Group Work, School of Applied Social Science, 18 May 1937, Case Western Reserve University.

9. The anonymous graduate is cited by Thomas F. Campbell in *SASS: Fifty Years of Social Work Education* (Cleveland: Press of Case Western Reserve University, 1967), p. 69.

10. Kathryn Farra, "The Organization and Administration of New York Settlements," mimeographed, 1931, p. 19, NFS Papers, fol. 537.

11. Mary M. Phinny, Resident Headworker, Neighborhood House, New Haven, Connecticut to Lillie Peck, executive secretary, NFS, 5 March 1934, NFS Papers, fol. 72.

12. "Chicago Settlements in 1932," Lea Taylor Papers, Chicago Historical Society.

13. Philip Klein, *From Philanthropy to Social Welfare* (San Francisco: Jossey-Bass, 1968), pp. 204–7.

14. According to Roy Lubove, *The Professional Altruist* (Cambridge: Harvard University Press, 1965), p. 136, to become a member of the AASW after July 1, 1933, the applicant needed to have completed from two to four or more years of college, including twenty semester credits in biological and social science and twenty-four credits in social work courses. This required a total of 300 hours in supervised field work plus four or five years of employment in an agency.

15. Helen Hall as paraphrased in the NFS board minutes, 3–4 Dec. 1938, NFS microfilm, reel 3, SWHA, U. of Minn.

16. "Study of Personnel Practices in Settlements—1936," NFS Papers, fol. 72.

17. Lillie Peck to Ellen W. Coolidge, then a board member of South End House, 24 March 1937, NFS Papers, fol. 343.

18. "Personal Facts about Lillie Peck," 12 Nov. 1937, NFS Papers, fol. 190.

19. Clipping, "Lillie Peck Dead; Social Worker, 68," *New York Times*, 22 Feb. 1957, NFS Papers, fol. 190.

20. Report to "Mr. Lewis" of the Buhl Foundation describing the NFS in

hopes of securing financial support [early 1930s], University Settlement Papers, Urban Archives, Temple University.

21. Helen Hall, "Introducing Our Neighbors," *Case Studies of Unemployment* (Philadelphia: University of Pennsylvania, 1931), pp. xxxiii–xxxiv.

22. Clinch Calkins, *Some Folks Won't Work* (New York: Harcourt, Brace, 1930).

23. Helen Hall, *Case Studies.*

24. "Heads of Divisions," 1934, NFS Papers, fol. 11.

25. United Neighborhood Houses, budgets for 1931, 1937, and 1939, United Neighborhood Houses Papers, fol. 79.

26. "Some Questions for Consideration in Selecting United Neighborhood Houses Board Members," 1939, United Neighborhood Houses Papers, fol. 52.

27. "Notes on Some of the New York Settlement 'Folks' 1937–38," United Neighborhood Houses Papers, fol. 22.

28. Chicago Federation of Settlements minutes, 7 Feb. 1933, Chicago Federation of Settlements.

29. George Bellamy to John A. Penton of the Penton Publishing Company, 2 June 1939, Hiram House Records, Western Reserve Historical Society.

30. Bellamy refers approvingly to Horatio Alger in "The businessman picks up his newspaper . . . ," 23 May 1938, Hiram House Records.

31. George Bellamy, "Group Work," 22 Aug. 1934, Hiram House Records.

32. George Bellamy, "High Points of Fifty Years Financial Service to Hiram House," 4 Oct. 1948, Hiram House Records.

33. "Salaries in Settlements in 1937," March 1937, Gads Hill Center Papers, box 10, fol. 59, Chicago Historical Society.

34. Personal tax and insurance records, 1936–37, Hiram House Records.

35. William F. Michalske, secretary of the Union Club to Bellamy, 29 June 1938, Hiram House Records.

36. William F. Michalske to "Dr. George Bellamy" (an HH.D, conferred by Western Reserve University), 3 Aug. 1939, Hiram House Records.

37. "Progress has been reached . . . ," 24 July 1934, Hiram House Records.

38. George Bellamy to William G. Mather, Cleveland industrialist, 23 Feb. 1931, Hiram House Records.

39. "Honors Clevelanders," *Plain Dealer*, 6 June 1938, p. 18.

40. Otis L. Graham, Jr., *An Encore for Reform* (New York: Oxford University Press, 1967), p. 192.

41. Eva Whiting White to Grace Abbott, 24 July 1936, Abbott Papers, box 68, fol. 10, University of Chicago.

42. Graham, p. 192.

43. John C. Farrell, *Beloved Lady: A History of Jane Addams' Ideas on Reform and Peace* (Baltimore: Johns Hopkins University Press, 1967), p. 213.

44. They were *The Second Twenty Years at Hull-House* (New York: Macmillan, 1932); *The Excellent Becomes the Permanent* (New York: Macmillan, 1932); and *My Friend, Julia Lathrop* (New York: Macmillan, 1935).

45. Chicago Commons annual report, 1932, pp. 3–4, Chicago Commons Papers, box 5, Chicago Historical Society.

46. Lea Taylor, transcript of an interview, University of Illinois, Chicago Circle, Special Collections.

47. "Directory," *Neighborhood*, 3 (Dec. 1930), pp. 190–239.

48. Lea Taylor to Albert J. Kennedy, 12 Sept. 1932, NFS Papers, fol. 551.

49. Albert J. Kennedy to Lea Taylor, 15 Sept. 1932, NFS Papers, fol. 551.

50. Sina K. Evans to Lillie M. Peck, "Labor Day," 1936, NFS Papers, fol. 477.

51. Lillian Wald to Jane Addams, 20 Feb. 1935, Abbott Papers, box 28, fol. 1.

52. Chambers, *Paul Kellogg*, p. 138.

53. "Facts about Helen Hall," NFS Papers, box 1, unnumbered fol.

54. "Helen Hall," *Tide*, 15 April 1937, p. 26.

55. Helen Hall, *Unfinished Business* (New York: Macmillan, 1971), p. 77.

56. Letter from "The House Committee" to "Miss Donaldson," 20 July 1932, Lillian Wald Papers, Mss. Div., New York Public Library.

57. Karl D. Hesley, director of social work, Henry Street Settlement to Leland Olds of the Community Councils of New York, 29 Jan. 1930, Lillian Wald Papers, Columbia University.

58. House of Industry, "Headworker's Report," 9 Dec. 1935, United Neighbors Association Papers, Urban Archives, Temple University.

59. Harriet E. Vittum, "A Time and Money Budget for a Department of Civics and Politics in a Settlement," *Neighborhood*, 3 (March 1930), p. 20.

60. Ruth Gage Thompson, President of the board of Phyllis Wheatley House in Minneapolis to "Board Member," 25 June 1939, Phyllis Wheatley Settlement House Papers, box 3, Minnesota Historical Society.

61. "Alta Social Settlement—40th Anniversary" pamphlet, Alta House Papers, box 3, Western Reserve Historical Society.

62. Ruth Austin to John K. Butler, applicant for a job at Gads Hill, 18 March 1932, Gads Hill Center Papers, box 9, fol. 52.

63. "Report of the Fall Program, University of Chicago Settlement," 12 Oct. 1936, McDowell Papers, fol. 25, Chicago Historical Society.

64. Mollie R. Carroll to Dr. Dudley B. Reed, 27 Dec. 1934 in McDowell Papers, fol. 36.

65. Memo by Russel Drake, Research Secretary, Council of Social Agencies, Minneapolis regarding such a situation at Unity House, 23 May 1939, North East Neighborhood House Papers, box 22, Minnesota Historical Society.

66. Adena Miller Rich, headworker, "Report to the Hull-House Trustees," 27 Nov. 1935, p. 4, Rich Papers, "Board" fol., University of Illinois, Chicago Circle.

67. Adena Miller Rich, "Some Responsibilities for an Administrative Assistant at Present at Hull-House," 20 Jan. 1937, Rich Papers, "Hull-House" fol.

68. Adena Miller Rich, "Report to the Hull-House Trustees," 27 Nov. 1935, p. 3, Rich Papers, "Board" fol.

69. "To the Residents of Hull-House," 13 April 1937, Esther Loeb Kohn Papers, fol. 142, University of Illinois, Chicago Circle.

70. Adena Miller Rich, "Report to the Hull-House Trustees," 27 Nov. 1935, p. 3, Rich Papers, "Board" fol.

71. Hull-House *Year-Book*, 1939, p. 48, Special Collections, University of Illinois, Chicago Circle.

72. Kathryn Farra, "The Organization and Administration of New York Settlements," mimeographed, 1931, p. 24, NFS Papers, fol. 537.

73. Clarke A. Chambers, *Seedtime of Reform* (Minneapolis: University of Minnesota Press, 1963), p. 123.

74. Only four settlements with residents were found in 1970. They were Henry Street and Lenox Hill in New York, and Gads Hill and Association House in Chicago.

75. "Salaries in Settlements in 1937," March 1937, Gads Hill Center Papers, box 10, fol. 59.

76. Report, 1 April 1933, Baden Street Settlement Papers, fol. 37, SWHA, U. of Minn.

77. "Report of the Head Worker—Sept. 1934," North East Neighborhood House Papers, box 6.

78. "Annual Report of Friendly Inn—1934," Friendly Inn Papers, Western Reserve Historical Society.

79. Lubove, p. 18.

80. Jon Alvah Peterson, "The Origins and Development of a Social Settlement: A History of the Godman Guild Association, 1898–1958," M.A. thesis, Ohio State University, 1959, p. 78.

81. Gaynell Hawkins, *Educational Experiments in Social Settlements* (New York: American Association for Adult Education, 1937), p. 61.

82. Alice Gannett, "Bringing Goodrich House Up to Date," 7 Nov. 1937, Goodrich House Papers, box 7, Western Reserve Historical Society.

83. Annual report of H. D. Bodley, headworker, Jan. 1939, Alta House Papers, box 1.

84. Board minutes, 14 May 1942, Alta House Papers, box 1.

85. *Hiram House Life*, 34 (17 Dec. 1930), p. 5, Hiram House Records, box 43.

86. Hall, *Unfinished Business*, p. 11.

87. Helen Hall to Lillian Wald, 19 June 1935, Henry Street Papers, SWHA, U. of Minn.

88. Grace Abbott, vice president of the Hull-House board to Alice Hamilton, former resident of Hull-House, 2 June 1938, Abbott Papers, box 55, fol. 3.

89. Board minutes, Hull-House, 1 April 1938, Abbott Papers, box 55, fol. 5.

CHAPTER 3

1. Kathryn Farra, "The Organization and Administration of New York Settlements," 1931, p. 5 in NFS Papers, fol. 537, SWHA, U. of Minn.; and Mary Simkhovitch, *The Settlement Primer*, 2nd ed. (New York: NFS, 1936), pp. 34–35.

2. "A Settlement Board—Its Functions, Selection, Composition, and Various Relationships," 14 June 1939, North East Neighborhood House Papers, box 29, Minnesota Historical Society.

3. Twin City Federation of Settlements, "Self-Analysis Survey of Minneapolis Settlement Houses," Sept. 1934, p. 2, Waite Neighborhood House Papers, box 19, Minnesota Historical Society.

4. Mary Simkhovitch, *The Settlement Primer*, 2nd ed. (New York: NFS, 1936), p. 35.

5. Allen Davis and Mary Lynn McCree, *Eighty Years at Hull-House* (Chicago: Quadrangle, 1969), p. 182.

6. Louise Wade, *Graham Taylor* (Chicago: University of Chicago Press, 1964), p. 221.

7. George W. Alger, Columbia Oral History Project No. 111, vol. 2, p. 252, Columbia University.

8. "The 40th Anniversary of the Founding of Hiram House," 1936, Hiram House Records, Western Reserve Historical Society.

9. George Bellamy to Eugene Lies of the Cleveland Welfare Federation, 17 May 1935, Hiram House Records.

10. Board minutes, 26 Jan. 1938, Alta House Papers, Western Reserve Historical Society.

11. Workman Place Neighborhood House, "Annual Report, 1936–7," NFS Papers, fol. 502.

12. Letterhead, 2 June 1936, Adena Miller Rich Papers, "Jane Addams Memorial Fund" fol., University of Illinois, Chicago Circle.

13. Grace Abbott, vice president of the board, to Alice Hamilton, former resident, Abbott Papers, box 55, fol. 3, University of Chicago.

14. Helen Cody Baker, "Chicago's Mrs. Bowen," *Survey* 75 (April 1939), p. 106.

15. Board minutes, Hull-House, 24 Feb. 1938, Abbott Papers, box 55, fol. 5.

16. Clipping, Sydney J. Harris, "Resigns as Head after Disputes on Cost, Policy," 23 Dec. 1942, NFS Papers, fol. 294.

17. Board minutes, 18 Nov. 1935, Chicago Commons Papers, box 19, Chicago Historical Society.

18. Lea Taylor, interview with the author, 20 July 1970.

19. Her activities on behalf of peace and the American Civil Liberties Union earned her a listing in Elizabeth Dilling, *The Red Network* (Chicago: Elizabeth Dilling, 1934), p. 305.

20. Lea Taylor interview.

21. Nathan E. Cohen, *Social Work in the American Tradition* (New York: Dryden Press, 1958), p. 200.

22. Gaynell Hawkins, *Educational Experiments in Social Settlements* (New York: American Association for Adult Education, 1937), p. 24.

23. Farra, p. 4, NFS Papers, fol. 537.

24. Mrs. Carl Narten, chairman, "Settlement Boards and Headworkers" conference, 1939, NFS microfilm, reel 2, SWHA, U. of Minn.

25. Board minutes, 14 Feb. 1939, Alta House Papers, box 1.

26. "Minutes of division meeting held Saturday . . . ," NFS Papers, fol. 86.

27. Farra, p. 4, NFS Papers, fol. 537.

28. Grace Abbott to Paul Kellogg, ed. of the *Survey*, 22 Sept. 1936, *Survey* Papers, fol. 327, SWHA, U. of Minn.

29. A. E. Bryson to Ruth Austin, headworker, 16 May 1939, Gads Hill Center Papers, fol. 62, Chicago Historical Society.

30. Harriet E. Vittum, "A Time and Money Budget for a Department of Civics and Politics in a Settlement," *Neighborhood* 3 (March 1930), p. 20.

31. Francis F. Prentiss to George Bellamy, 23 Dec. 1929, Hiram House Records.

32. Prentiss.

33. Audit report, 31 Dec. 1939, Gads Hill Center Papers, fol. 67.

34. Budget, 1 March 1939, Hartley House Papers, fol. 12, U. of Minn.

35. Davis and McCree, p. 143.

36. Open letter by Louise Bowen, president and treasurer of the Hull-House board, 24 June 1935, Esther Loeb Kohn Papers, fol. 142, University of Illinois, Chicago Circle.

37. Edward L. Ryerson, Jr., "Joint Financing of Private Social Work, I: Chicago's Experience," National Conference of Social Work *Proceedings* (New York: Columbia University Press, 1939), p. 527.

38. Letterhead of the Community Fund of Chicago, 27 May 1935, Chicago Commons Papers, box 26.

39. Frank D. Loomis, Executive Secretary, Community Fund, to Fred A. Preston, complaine :, 3 July 1935, Adena Miller Rich Papers, "Social Settlements" fol., University of Illinois, Chicago Circle.

40. Minutes of the executive committee of the United Neighborhood Houses, 8 Feb. 1938, United Neighborhood Houses Papers, fol. 46, SWHA, U. of Minn.

41. Floyd Hunter, "Community Organization: Lever for Institutional Change?" in Rupert B. Vance and N. D. Demerath, eds., *The Urban South* (Chapel Hill, University of North Carolina Press, 1954), pp. 254–55.

42. "Summary of Discussions on Agency Financing Held Under the Three Council Divisions," 8–9 March 1934, p. 4, Chicago Commons Papers, box 25.

43. Morrell Heald, *The Social Responsibilities of Business* (Cleveland: Press of Case Western Reserve University, 1970), p. 151. The figures were $73,000,000 in 1929; $101,000,000 in 1932; and $78,000,000 in 1933.

44. Scott M. Cutlip, *Fund Raising in the United States: Its Role in America's Philanthropy* (New Brunswick, N.J.: Rutgers University Press, 1965), p. 317.

45. Heald, p. 155.

46. Isabel Taylor, "Problems of the Small Settlement," *Neighborhood* 3 (March 1930), p. 27.

47. Kingsley Association, Pittsburgh, *Year Book*, 1930.

48. NFS board minutes, 19–23 May 1937, NFS microfilm, reel 3.

49. "Report of the Head Worker—Nov. 1929," North East Neighborhood House Papers, box 6, Minnesota Historical Society.

50. A listing of the budget committee members dated 25 May 1939, University Settlement Papers, Urban Archives, Temple University.

51. "Report of the Head Worker . . . February 1938," North East Neighborhood House Papers, box 7.

52. Board minutes, 20 Sept. 1937, Alta House, Alta House Papers, box 1.

53. NFS board minutes, 16–18 June 1939, NFS microfilm, reel 3.

54. NFS board minutes, 4–7 June 1936, NFS microfilm, reel 3.

55. Nellie Margaret Gilroy, "Social Education and Action in Settlements," M.S. thesis, School of Applied Social Science, Western Reserve University.

56. Mrs. Carl Narten, chairman, "Settlement Boards and Headworkers" conference, 1939, NFS microfilm, reel 2.

57. Narten.

58. Helen Hall, "The Consequences of Social Action for the Group Work Agency," address presented at the National Conference of Social Work, Atlantic City, 28 May 1936, p. 6, NFS Papers, fol. 75.

59. Glenford Lawrence, chairman, "Adult Workers and Club Representatives" conference, 1939, NFS microfilm, reel 2.

60. Charles C. Cooper to Lea Taylor, soon to replace Cooper as president of the NFS, 4 Oct. 1930, Lea Taylor Papers, box 2, Chicago Historical Society.

61. Albert J. Kennedy to Lea Taylor, 15 Sept. 1932 in NFS Papers, fol. 551.

62. Mary Simkhovitch, *The Settlement Primer*, 2nd ed. (New York: NFS, 1936), p. 40.

63. NFS board minutes, 4–5 Dec. 1937, NFS microfilm, reel 3.

64. NFS board minutes, 4–5 Dec. 1937.

CHAPTER 4

1. Lucia Johnson Bing, *Social Work in Greater Cleveland* (Cleveland: Welfare Federation, 1938), p. 16.

2. Bing, p. 17.

3. Bing, p. 19.

4. Louise Bowen to Jane Addams, 18 Feb. 1932, Abbott Papers, box 28, fol. 1, University of Chicago.

5. Helen Hall, "On Family Life in America, Hard Times Lay Heavy Load," *New York Times*, 3 Dec. 1933, p. 12, col. 2.

6. Helen Hall, *Unfinished Business* (New York: Macmillan, 1971), p. 11.

7. Helen Hall, "Rents," *Survey*, 15 April 1932, pp. 43–44.

8. Hall, "Rents," p. 43.

9. Hall, "On Family Life," p. 12, cols. 1–2.

10. Lea Taylor, interview with the author, 20 July 1970.

11. Annual report, Chicago Commons, 1931, p. 1, Chicago Commons Papers, box 5, Chicago Historical Society.

12. Cynthia Knowles, Acting Executive Secretary, United Neighborhood Houses to Dr. Chaffee of Labor Temple, 15 Aug. 1934; and unsigned letter to Stanley Isaacs, president of United Neighborhood Houses, 13 Aug. 1934, United Neighborhood Houses Papers, fol. 458, SWHA, U. of Minn.

13. Lillian Wald, radio talk over station WOR on 9 Nov. 1931, Wald Papers, Manuscript Division, New York Public Library.

14. Lea Taylor, radio talk, 3 June 1932, Lea Taylor Papers, box 24, Chicago Historical Society.

15. Annual report, Gads Hill Center, 1930, Gads Hill Center Papers, box 9, fol. 49, Chicago Historical Society.

16. Ruth Austin, head, Gads Hill Center to Mary Henson, United Charities, 23 Jan. 1932, Gads Hill Center Papers, box 9, fol. 52.

17. Minutes of the Executive Committee, Chicago Federation of Settlements, 9 Feb. 1932, possession Chicago Federation of Settlements.

18. Minutes of the New York City Welfare Council, 20 July 1932, Wald Papers, box 34, "Welfare Council" fol., Columbia University.

19. Minutes of the Executive Board of the Chicago Federation of Settlements, 11 Dec. 1931, Chicago Federation of Settlements.

20. Minutes of the general meeting of the Chicago Federation of Settlements, 4 Oct. 1932, Chicago Federation of Settlements.

21. Minutes of the Committee on Unemployment Relief of United Neighborhood Houses, 3 Jan. 1934, United Neighborhood Houses Papers, fol. 173.

22. Karl Borders, "Charity—the Betrayal of the Workers," *Unemployed*, no. 4, 1931, pp. 22–23. The *Unemployed* was a socialist (League for Industrial Democracy) publication which some of the unemployed tried to sell to make money.

23. Lea D. Taylor, "Decent Standards of Relief," *Survey*, 68 (15 May 1932), pp. 181–82.

24. Hall, "Rents," pp. 42–44.

25. Hall, *Unfinished Business*, p. 42.

26. Union Settlement, "Behind the Lines," 1932, uncatalogued pamphlet, New York Public Library.

27. Gaylord S. White, head of Union Settlement to Ellen S. Marvin, board member, 11 Nov. 1931, quoted in Ellen S. Marvin, "As I Remember Union Settlement," p. 53, NFS Papers, fol. 688, SWHA, U. of M.

28. Ellen S. Marvin, "As I Remember Union Settlement," p. 55, NFS Papers, fol. 688.

29. "Report of the Head Worker—November 1929," North East Neighborhood House Papers, box 6, Minnesota Historical Society.

30. "Report of the Head Worker for the Month of January, 1930," North East Neighborhood House Papers, box 6.

31. "Report of the Head Worker . . . February 1932," North East Neighborhood House Papers, box 6.

32. "Report of the Head Worker—May and June, 1932," North East Neighborhood House Papers, box 6.

33. Elizabeth Ann Hoff, part-time staff worker, "A Neighborhood's Horizon," 1934?, p. 12, North East Neighborhood House Papers, box 1.

34. "Report of the Head Worker—June and July 1933," North East Neighborhood House Papers, box 6.

35. "Boys' Work Bulletin," June 1933, p. 4, NFS Papers, fol. 39.

36. "Boys' Work Bulletin."

37. Annual report, North East Neighborhood House, 1931, North East Neighborhood House Papers, box 6.

38. Jon Alvah Peterson, "The Origins and Development of a Social Settlement: A History of Godman Guild Association, 1898–1958," M.A. thesis, Ohio State University, 1959, p. 92.

39. Peterson, p. 82.

40. Annual report, Soho Community House, Sept. 1938 to Aug. 1939, Neighborhood Center Association Papers, box 1, "Miscellaneous Correspondence and Reports," University of Pittsburgh, Special Collections.

41. "Annual Report, The Farms Committee of the Cleveland Employment Commission, 'A Rehabilitation Project,'" 1933, Paul Walter Papers, box 1, Western Reserve Historical Society.

42. Chicago Federation of Settlements minutes, July 1934?, Chicago Federation of Settlements.

43. "Report of the Head Worker—November 1929," North East Neighborhood House Papers, box 6.

44. George Bellamy to Messrs. M. J. and O. P. Van Sweringen, 25 Sept. 1931, Hiram House Records, Western Reserve Historical Society.

45. George Bellamy to M. J. Van Sweringen, 5 Nov. 1931, Hiram House Records.

46. J. Laughlin, "The 'L' family—2531 E. 26th Street—Feb. 19, 1932," Hiram House Records.

47. "Workman Place House Report, 1933–4," NFS Papers, fol. 502.

48. Report, Wald Papers, box 25, "McCann Relief Fund" fol., Columbia University.

49. "Ryerson Out as Relief Tangle Becomes Worse," *The New Frontier*, 4 March 1933, Chicago Historical Society.

50. Edward L. Ryerson, Jr., "Out of the Depression," *Survey*, 70 (Jan. 1934), p. 7.

51. "Neighborhood Service as Financed by Governor's Commission, Oct. 1, 1930 to Oct. 1, 1931," Chicago Commons Papers, box 4, Chicago Historical Society.

52. Annual report, Chicago Commons, 1931, pp. 1–2, Chicago Commons Papers, box 5.

53. Ryerson, "Out of the Depression," p. 6.

54. "Boys' Work Bulletin," June 1933, pp. 4–5.

55. "Boys' Work Bulletin," June 1933, p. 5.

CHAPTER 5

1. Draft of a radio speech by Jane Addams sent to Esther Loeb Kohn, Hull-House resident, Kohn Papers, fol. 180, University of Illinois, Chicago Circle.

2. Annual report, Chicago Commons, 1933, p. 6, Chicago Commons Papers, box 5, Chicago Historical Society.

3. "The law is an attempt . . . ," 28 Nov. 1934, Hiram House Records, Western Reserve Historical Society.

4. "Progress Through Play," 21 April 1936, Hiram House Records.

5. Lucia Johnson Bing, *Social Work in Greater Cleveland* (Cleveland: Welfare Federation, 1938), p. 19.

6. Edith Abbott, Boston Settlement Study, Abbott Papers, box 22, fol. 14, University of Chicago, pp. 16–16A.

7. Bing, p. 20.

8. Annual report, Shaw House, 1932–33, NFS Papers, fol. 341, SWHA, U. of Minn.

9. Board minutes, 3 Jan. 1934, Goodrich House Papers, box 1, Western Reserve Historical Society.

10. Annual report, 1933, Phyllis Wheatley Settlement House Papers, box 1, Minnesota Historical Society.

11. Walter Johnson, *1600 Pennsylvania Avenue* (Boston: Little, Brown, 1960), pp. 60–61.

12. "Drawing on the experience . . . ," 1934, Lea Taylor Papers, box 3, Chicago Historical Society.

13. "Memorandum for the Administrator of the Federal Emergency Relief Administration," 5 Feb. 1935, NFS Papers, fol. 545.

14. "The NFS, at its 23rd Conference at Montreal, passed the following resolution," 9 June 1935, NFS Papers, fol. 81.

15. Mark A. McCloskey to "Boys' Workers of the National Federation of Settlements," n.d., NFS Papers, fol. 36.

16. "Educational Director at South End House," NEWS, 2 (March 1934), p. 3, NFS Papers, fol. 208.

17. Joel D. Hunter, Chairman, Advisory Committee, Cook County Bureau of Public Welfare, Lea Taylor, et al. to Harry Hopkins, 16 Aug. 1935, Kohn Papers, fol. 56.

18. Miss McKenzie, "Reports of Meetings of Current Discussion Group, Chicago Commons, 1935–6," Chicago Commons Papers, box 12.

19. Lea Taylor, president of the Chicago Federation of Settlements to Howard O. Hunter, Field Representative, WPA (1935?), Lea Taylor Papers, box 10, Chicago Historical Society.

20. Paul Walter, "Report of the Mayor's Board of Suggestions for WPA Projects," 9 March 1936, Walter Papers, box 4, Western Reserve Historical Society.

21. Day letter, Lea Taylor, president of the Chicago Federation of Settlements, to Harry Hopkins, WPA Administrator, 16 Dec. 1937; and H. K. Seltzer, Director, Chicago WPA to Lea Taylor, 22 Jan. 1938, Chicago Commons Papers, box 26.

22. Lea Taylor, "Social Settlements," Social Work Year Book (New York: Russell Sage Foundation, 1935), p. 477.

23. Lea Taylor, transcript of an interview, p. 60, University of Illinois, Chicago Circle, Special Collections.

24. Anna Bramble, "Headworker's Report to the Board" [late 1937 or early 1938], House of Industry, United Neighbors Association Papers, box 24, Urban Archives, Temple University.

25. Helen Hall to Hallie Flanagan, director, Federal Theater Project, 29 July 1937, Henry Street Settlement Papers, SWHA, U. of Minn.

26. Hilda W. Smith, Specialist in Workers Education, Washington, D.C. to Lillie Peck, executive secretary, NFS, 24 June 1937, NFS Papers, fol. 76.

27. Press release, 1936, NFS Papers, fol. 81.

28. Resolution passed by the board, 5–6 Dec. 1936, NFS microfilm, reel 3, SWHA, U. of Minn.

29. Mary Simkhovitch, Neighborhood: My Story of Greenwich House (New York: Norton, 1938), p. 226.

30. "Report on the Follow-up Study on Workers Dismissed from the C.L.T.S. Project on or about July 1, 1937," Chicago Commons Papers, box 26.

31. "Report of the Head Worker—December 1937," North East Neighborhood House Papers, box 7, Minnesota Historical Society.

32. Press release, 5 Dec. 1937, NFS microfilm, reel 3.

33. Clipping, "Tells Delegates that Fascism can be Eliminated," 1939, NFS Papers, fol. 86.

34. "Dinner Conference Held at Merchandise Mart Club," 25 April 1939, p. 9, Lea Taylor Papers, box 13, Chicago Historical Society.

35. "Social Workers Protest Proposal to Cut WPA Fund," *Buffalo Times*, 19 June 1939 in Lea Taylor Papers, box 22, Chicago Historical Society.

36. Annual report, University of Chicago Settlement, 1939, p. 11, Russell Sage Collection, City College of New York.

37. "A Brief History of Marcy Center," 1940, Marcy Center Papers, box 35, University of Illinois, Chicago Circle.

38. George Bauer, Hiram House staff worker, "Work Relief Notes," 1 Dec. 1936, Hiram House Records, box 4.

39. George Bellamy to the Cleveland Foundation, 20 Nov. 1936, Hiram House Records, box 23.

40. Walter Johnson, *1600 Pennsylvania Avenue* (Boston: Little, Brown, 1960), p. 63.

41. "Timely Townsend Tunes" by "Seesil the Mill Levy," Dec. 1935, Hiram House Records, box 16.

42. Letterhead of the American Association for Social Security, 18 April 1934, NFS Papers, fol. 557.

43. Board minutes, 22–23 Nov. 1930, pp. 161–62, NFS microfilm, reel 3.

44. Directory," *Neighborhood*, 3 (Dec. 1930), p. 184.

45. Minutes of the Finance Committee of the Cleveland Committee for Unemployment Insurance," 29 Jan. 1931, Consumers League of Ohio Papers, Western Reserve Historical Society.

46. Form letter signed by Alice Gannett, 17 Oct. 1930; and "Calendar of the Campaign" (1931?), Consumers League of Ohio Papers.

47. Board minutes, 29–30 Jan. 1932, NFS microfilm, reel 3.

48. Form letter, W. H. McPherson, Chairman, Committee on Arrangements for Unemployment Insurance Rally sent to senators and representatives from Cuyahoga County except M. C. Harrison (May 1933), Consumers' League of Ohio Papers.

49. Bellamy to Gov. George White, 14 May 1933, Hiram House Records.

50. Chicago Federation of Settlements, minutes, 21 April 1931, Chicago Federation of Settlements.

51. Chicago Federation of Settlements, minutes, 7 March 1933, Chicago Federation of Settlements.

52. Board minutes, 18 May 1933, Chicago Commons Papers, box 19.

53. Gaynell Hawkins, *Educational Experiments in Social Settlements* (New York: American Association for Adult Education, 1937), p. 30.

54. Lillie Peck, open letter, 21 May 1932, NFS Papers, fol. 78.

55. Press release, 10 June 1934, NFS Papers, fol. 80.

56. Jane Addams, "Social Consequences of Business Depressions," pamphlet (Chicago: University of Chicago, 1931), p. 7, NFS Papers, fol. 2.

57. See Mollie Ray Carroll, "Unemployment Insurance by Industry: Some Suggestions from Germany," National Conference of Social Work *Proceedings* (Chicago: University of Chicago, 1930), pp. 258–64; Mollie Ray Carroll, "Social Insurance," National Conference of Social Work *Proceedings* (Chicago: University of

Chicago, 1930), pp. 251–62; Helen Hall, "English Dole and American Charity," *Atlantic Monthly*, 151 (May 1933), pp. 538–49; Helen Hall, "Charity in the Market Place," *New Outlook*, 161 (May 1933), pp. 48–50; Helen Hall, "Miners Must Eat: The Workings of English Dole and American Charity," *Atlantic Monthly*, 152 (Aug. 1933), pp. 153–62; Helen Hall, "Insure the Worker!" *Forum and Century*, 91 (June 1934), pp. 344–47.

58. Frances Perkins, et al. to President Franklin D. Roosevelt, 15 Jan. 1935 (carbon), Helen Hall Papers, Columbia University.

59. Paul Kellogg, et al. to Frances Perkins, Chairman of the President's Committee on Economic Security, 21 Dec. 1934, Albert J. Kennedy Papers, Paige box 7, "Unemployment" fol., SWHA, U. of Minn.

60. Board minutes, 26–27 Jan. 1935, NFS microfilm, reel 3.

61. Edwin E. Witte to Edith Abbott, sister of Grace Abbott, 18 Oct. 1939 quoted in Edith Abbott typescript, "The Social Security Act," pp. 1–2, Abbott Papers, box 4, fol. 1.

62. "The National Federation of Settlements at its 23rd Conference at Montreal, passed the following resolution," 9 June 1935, NFS Papers, fol. 81.

63. Press release (1936?), NFS Papers, fol. 81.

64. Board minutes, 13 Jan. 1937, North East Neighborhood House Papers, box 1.

65. "Report of the Head Resident . . . October 1930," North East Neighborhood House Papers, box 6.

66. Twin City Federation of Settlements, *Self-Analysis Survey of Minneapolis Settlement Houses*, Sept. 1934, p. 36, Waite Neighborhood House Papers, box 19, Minnesota Historical Society.

67. "University of Chicago Settlement—Report for February, 1933," McDowell Papers, fol. 22, Chicago Historical Society.

68. Lillie Peck, executive secretary, NFS to James J. Mallon, headworker, Toynbee Hall, London, 9 Dec. 1935, NFS Papers, fol. 25. *See also* Douglas W. Orr and Jean Orr, *Health Insurance with Medical Care: The British Experience* (New York: Macmillan, 1938).

69. "Statement Adopted at 26th Annual Conference, June 1–5, 1938: Pittsburgh, Pennsylvania," in NFS Papers, fol. 85.

70. Roy Lubove, "The New Deal and National Health," *Current History* 45 (Aug. 1963), p. 85.

71. Chronological Index (The "Bible") to NFS Activities, p. 104, NFS Papers, fol. 611.

72. Helen Hall, "When Sickness Strikes," address presented to the National Conference of Social Work, Buffalo, New York, 30 June 1939, Lea Taylor Papers, University of Illinois, Chicago Circle.

73. Lubove, pp. 85–86.

74. Press release, 10 June 1934, NFS Papers, fol. 80.

75. Press release (1936?), NFS Papers, fol. 81.

76. George Bellamy to John A. Penton, a prospective contributor, 2 June 1939, Hiram House Records.

77. George Bellamy to Nathan L. Dauby, May Co., 4 Feb. 1939, Hiram House Records.

CHAPTER 6

1. Robert Morrison, "North East Neighborhood House—Evaluation Schedule —Group Work Department—Men and Boys—July 1939," North East Neighborhood House Papers, box 8, Minnesota Historical Society.

2. Board minutes, Lincoln House, 21 Nov. 1938, South End House, Boston.

3. Annual report, Gladden Community House, 1935, NFS Papers, fol. 472, SWHA, U. of Minn.

4. Report, Oct. 1931, Baden Street Settlement Papers, fol. 37, SWHA, U. of Minn.

5. Franklin I. Harbach, chairman, Boys and Girls Workers, NFS Conference, 1939, NFS microfilm, reel 2, SWHA, U. of Minn.

6. Robert Eller Asher, "The Influence of the Chicago Workers Committee on Unemployment upon the Administration of Relief, 1931–1934," M.A. Thesis, University of Chicago, 1934, p. 10.

7. Lea Taylor, transcript of an interview, p. 57, University of Illinois, Chicago Circle, Special Collections.

8. Annual report, Chicago Commons, 1930, p. 4, Chicago Commons Papers, box 5, Chicago Historical Society.

9. "Karl Borders, 61, U.N. Welfare Aide, Chief Officer of International Children's Emergency Fund Dies—Former Supply Head," New York Times, 31 Jan. 1953.

10. Robert Eller Asher, "The Influence of the Chicago Workers Committee . . ." M. A. Thesis, University of Chicago, 1934, p. 34.

11. "Borders." This somewhat official biographical sketch jumps from the Chicago Commons post to the WPA, ignoring the LID and CWCOU positions. The omission may have been due to McCarthyism, still rampant in 1953.

12. Asher, "Influence," p. 34.

13. Aileen S. Kraditor, ed., Up from the Pedestal (Chicago: Quadrangle, 1968), p. 119.

14. Frank W. McCulloch to author, 19 Aug. 1970.

15. Asher, "Influence," p. 10.

16. Asher, "Influence," p. 12.

17. Asher, "Influence," p. 13.

18. Asher, "Influence," p. 13.

19. Elizabeth Dilling, The Red Network (Chicago: Elizabeth Dilling, 1934), p. 133. Dilling's list of settlements with locals included Lincoln Center, Chicago Commons, Olivet Institute, Chase House, Hyde Park Neighborhood Club, Hull-House, Christopher House, Marcy Center, Howell Neighborhood House, Garibaldi Institute, Association House, Eli Bates House, University of Chicago Settlement, and Emerson House. For some reason, she omitted Northwestern University Settlement.

20. Asher, "Influence," pp. 13–14.

21. Dilling, p. 133.

22. Asher, "Influence," p. 33.

23. Nathaniel Weyl, "Organizing Hunger," New Republic 77 (14 Dec. 1932), p. 119.

24. Asher, "Influence," p. 33.

25. Chicago Federation of Settlements minutes, 22 Nov. 1932, Chicago Federation of Settlements.

26. Asher, "Influence," p. 17.

27. "An Urban Famine," mimeograph of the CWCOU hearings, 5–12 Jan. 1932, p. 2, Chicago Commons Papers, box 24, Chicago Historical Society.

28. Annual report, Chicago Commons, 1932, p. 3, Chicago Commons Papers, box 5.

29. "Urban Famine," p. 12.

30. "Urban Famine," p. 5.

31. Asher, "Influence," pp. 15–17.

32. "Urban Famine," p. 5.

33. Asher, "Influence," p. 24.

34. Edmund B. Chaffee, et al. to "Friend," 2 June 1933, Albert J. Kennedy Papers, Paige box 7, "Unemployment" fol., SWHA, U. of Minn.

35. Robert Eller Asher, "The Jobless Help Themselves," New Republic 72 (28 Sept. 1932), p. 168.

36. Lea Taylor, transcript of interview, p. 58, University of Illinois, Chicago Circle, Special Collections.

37. Asher, "Jobless," pp. 168–69.

38. Lea Taylor, transcript of interview, p. 58, University of Illinois, Chicago Circle, Special Collections.

39. Asher, "Jobless," p. 169.

40. Edmund Wilson, "Hull-House in 1932: II," New Republic 73 (25 Jan. 1933), p. 287.

41. Lea Taylor, interview with the author, 20 July 1970.

42. Wilson, p. 287.

43. Lea Taylor, interview with the author, 20 July 1970.

44. Wilson, p. 287.

45. Wilson, p. 288.

46. Lea Taylor, interview with the author, 20 July 1970.

47. Handbill on the Hunger March, 31 Oct. 1932, Chicago Commons Papers, box 25.

48. Nathaniel Weyl, "Organizing Hunger," New Republic 77 (14 Dec. 1932), p. 118.

49. Asher, "Influence," p. 22.

50. The constitution is reprinted as "Appendix A" in Robert Eller Asher, "Influence," p. 77.

51. Laura A. Friedman, "100 Unemployed Families in Chicago," M.A. Thesis, University of Chicago, 1933, p. 175.

52. Asher, "Jobless," p. 168.

53. Gertrude Springer, "Shock Troops to the Rescue," Survey 69 (Jan. 1933), p. 11.

54. Wicker Park Conference minutes, 21 July 1932, Graham Taylor Papers, incoming papers box, Newberry Library.

55. Asher, "Influence," p. 22.

56. Springer, p. 10.

57. Springer, p. 11.

58. Asher, "Influence," p. 27.

59. Asher, "Influence," p. 28.

60. Asher, "Influence," p. 29.

61. Asher, "Influence," p. 6 quoting "The Right to Alms," *Chicago Tribune*, 9 Nov. 1932.

62. Dilling, p. 133.

63. "Nobody is Starving," *New Frontier* 2 (22 March 1933), Graham Taylor Papers, "Chicago Workers Committee on Unemployment" fol., Newberry Library.

64. "Nobody is Starving," *New Frontier* 2 (4 March 1933), Chicago Historical Society.

65. "Garbage Dumps Still Furnishing Food for Many," *New Frontier* 2 (8 Feb. 1933), Graham Taylor Papers.

66. "Your Paper," *New Frontier* 1 (12 Dec. 1932), Graham Taylor Papers.

67. Springer, p. 11.

68. "The University of Chicago Settlement—Report for October, 1933," McDowell Papers, fol. 22, Chicago Historical Society.

69. Springer, p. 11.

70. Asher, "Influence," pp. 35–36.

71. "Thousands in March 4 Mass Meeting," *New Frontier* 2 (4 March 1933), Chicago Historical Society.

72. *Howeller*, 27 Oct. 1933, Howell House Papers, box 1, University of Illinois, Chicago Circle.

73. *Howeller*, 2 March 1934, Howell House Papers, box 1.

74. "1,000 May Day Paraders March through Loop," *Chicago Daily News*, 1 May 1933, p. 1 and "March on May 1st [1935]," Chicago Commons Papers, box 26.

75. Chicago Federation of Settlements minutes, 27 Nov. 1934, Chicago Federation of Settlements.

76. Annual report, Chicago Commons, 1933, p. 10, Chicago Commons Papers, box 5.

77. "Workers Back These Eight for Alderman," *New Frontier* 2 (25 Jan. 1933), Graham Taylor Papers, CWCOU fol.

78. Frank W. McCulloch to Lea Taylor, 3 May 1935, Lea Taylor Papers, box 3, Chicago Historical Society.

79. "Annual Report—1934" of the CWCOU, Graham Taylor Papers, CWCOU fol.

80. Mary Fox, executive secretary, New York Workers Committee on Unemployment to Albert J. Kennedy, head of University Settlement, 25 April 1933, in Kennedy Papers, Paige box 7, "Unemployment" fol. Lists Church of All Nations, Henry Street Settlement, Hudson Guild, Union Settlement, Greenwich House, Federation Settlement, and Christ Church House. Also Harry Laidler, "Cementing the Relationship between the Settlement and the Workers Unemployed Union," 23 May 1935, Kennedy Papers, Paige box 7, "United Neighborhood Houses" fol. Additional houses in 1935 included University Settlement, Recreation Rooms, Hamilton House, Riis House, and Lenox Hill Settlement.

81. Karl Hesley, assistant headworker, Henry Street Settlement, " 'Projects of Self-Help and Self-Expression by and for the Unemployed in Settlements,' " 15 May 1933, United Neighborhood Houses Papers, fol. 176, SWHA, U. of Minn.

82. Harry Laidler, LID, "Cementing the Relationship between the Settlement and the Workers Unemployed Union," Albert J. Kennedy Papers, Paige box 7, "United Neighborhood Houses, 1933–37" fol.

83. Copy of telegram (?), Graham Taylor to Barnett Hodes, corporation counsel, City Hall, Chicago, 8 July 1936, Graham Taylor Papers.

84. "Relief Workers March in Loop; Issue Demands; Horner and Roosevelt are Assailed," *Chicago Tribune*, 19 July 1936. In 1936 the Workers Alliance claimed a national dues-paying membership of 300,000. *See* Francis Fox Piven and Richard A. Cloward, *Regulating the Poor: the Functions of Public Welfare* (New York: Random House, 1971), p. 108.

85. "Mighty Convention Lays Basis for Greater Workers Alliance," *Workers Alliance* 1, April [1936], Graham Taylor Papers, "Workers Alliance" fol.

86. One such instance occurred in August 1935 when the Workers Unemployed Union, a New York affiliate of the Workers Alliance, endorsed a strike action. See "President Bars U.S. Relief to All who Quit WPA Jobs; More Strike on City Works," *New York Times*, 10 Aug. 1935, p. 1, col. 8.

87. "Agreement on Unity of W.A.A. and National Unemployment Councils," *Workers Alliance* 1 (1 March 1936), Graham Taylor Papers, "Workers Alliance" fol.

88. "Annual Report of the Adult Education Department, Chicago Commons . . . 1935–36," p. 9, Chicago Commons Papers, box 12.

89. "Annual Report—1938–1939—Adult Workers Education Department," p. 3, Chicago Commons Papers, box 12.

90. "Thomas Condemns Reds' Relief Aims," *New York Times*, 19 Feb. 1939, p. 21, cols. 1–2.

91. Minutes of staff meeting, Chicago Commons, 25 Feb. 1939, Graham Taylor Papers.

92. "Back-to-Job Move in WPA Strike Row Begun by One Group," *New York Times*, 9 July 1939, p. 2, col. 8.

93. Frank W. McCulloch to author, 19 Aug. 1970.

94. Clipping, "Legion Charges 30 City Leaders Help the Reds," 24 Jan. 1933, Adena Miller Rich Papers, "Addams" fol., University of Illinois, Chicago Circle.

95. Dilling, passim.

96. Frank D. Loomis, "To Social Settlements Participating in the Community Fund," 8 July 1935, Benton House Papers, box 3, Chicago Historical Society.

97. "Mr. X" to Fred A. Preston, who forwarded the correspondence to Frank Loomis, 29 May 1935, in Adena Miller Rich Papers, "Social Settlements" fol.

98. Curtis Reese to Frank Loomis, 18 June 1935, Adena Miller Rich Papers, "Social Settlements" fol.

99. Adena Miller Rich, headworker, Hull-House, "Hull-House, November 20, 1936 to February 19, 1937," Adena Miller Rich Papers.

100. Minutes, United Neighborhood Houses Unemployment Committee, 6 Aug. 1935, United Neighborhood Houses Papers, fol. 173.

101. Mary Simkhovitch, *The Settlement Primer*, 2nd ed. (New York: NFS, 1935), p. 33.

102. Helen Hall, "The Consequences of Social Action for the Group Work Agency," address presented at the NFS Conference, 6 June 1936, Lea Taylor Papers, fol. 36, University of Illinois, Chicago Circle.

103. Chicago Federation of Settlements minutes, 23 Feb. 1937, Lea Taylor Papers, box 10, Chicago Historical Society.

104. "Disturbing the Inertia of Young People," *Round Table*, April 1938, NFS Papers, fol. 202.

105. "Memo for Mr. Kennedy," 4 Dec. 1936, NFS Papers, fol. 12.

106. Florence T. Waite, *A Warm Friend for the Spirit: A History of the Family Service Association of Cleveland and Its Forbears, 1830–1952* (Cleveland: Family Service Association, 1960), pp. 263–84.

107. Frank W. McCulloch to author, 19 Aug. 1970.

CHAPTER 7

1. Philip Klein, *A Social Study of Pittsburgh* (New York: Columbia University Press, 1938), pp. 308–09.

2. Robbins Gilman to Lee Sharp, South Side Neighborhood House, Minneapolis, 30 Sept. 1937, North East Neighborhood House Papers, box 29, Minnesota Historical Society.

3. Elizabeth Ann Hoff, part-time staff worker, North East Neighborhood House, "A Neighborhood's Horizon," (1934?), p. 12, North East Neighborhood House Papers, box 1.

4. "Report of the Head Worker for the Month of October 1929" in North East Neighborhood House Papers, box 6.

5. Alice Gannett quoted in "Sees Child Labor on Increase Here," *Plain Dealer*, 17 Jan. 1933, p. 8, col. 3.

6. Lillian Wald, *Windows on Henry Street* (Boston: Little, Brown, 1934), p. 197.

7. Board minutes, Denison House, 16 Feb. 1937, Denison House Papers, Schlesinger Library, Radcliffe College.

8. George Bellamy, "Child Labor Law," 3 April 1936, Hiram House Records, Western Reserve Historical Society.

9. Courtenay Dinwiddie, General Secretary, National Child Labor Committee to Jane Addams, 14 Dec. 1933, Kohn Papers, fol. 247, University of Illinois, Chicago Circle.

10. Lillian Wald, "The Child and the Law," p. 20, Wald Papers, "Speeches and Writings," Manuscript Division, New York Public Library.

11. Lillian Wald, "The Race Marches Forward on the Feet of Little Children," 1932, Wald Papers, "Speeches and Writings."

12. Lillian Wald to Gov. Herbert Lehman, 28 July 1933. Wald Papers.

13. Lillian Wald to Katherine Lenroot, 28 Dec. 1934, Wald Papers.

14. Lillian Wald to Gen. Hugh S. Johnson, 17 July 1933, Wald Papers.

15. Minutes, staff meeting, 10 Jan. 1931, Graham Taylor Papers, Newberry Library.

16. Board minutes, 4–7 June 1936, NFS microfilm, reel 3, SWHA, U. of Minn.

17. Resolution of the board, 5–6 Dec. 1936, NFS microfilm, reel 3.

18. Walter Johnson, *1600 Pennsylvania Avenue* (Boston: Little, Brown, 1960), p. 94.

19. Edith Abbott, "The Lost Children's Amendment," typescript, p. 91, Abbott Papers, box III, fol. 1, University of Chicago.

20. "Resolutions Adopted by the NFS," 8–11 June 1933, NFS Papers, fol. 79, SWHA, U. of Minn.

21. Press release (1936?), NFS Papers, fol. 81.

22. Judith Laughlin, "Lena Scaglione, 19, 3510 Orange," 15 April 1933, Hiram House Records.

23. George Bellamy to Grace Abbott, 21 April 1933; and Grace Abbott to George Bellamy, 25 April 1933, Hiram House Records.

24. "Release from Labor Standards Committee," 15 June 1933, Consumers League of Ohio Papers, Western Reserve Historical Society.

25. "Organizations which have endorsed Minimum Wage," 3 June 1933, Consumers League of Ohio Papers.

26. "Boys' Work Bulletin," Jan. 1936, p. 4, NFS Papers, fol. 39.

27. Lea Taylor to Mrs. Baker, 5 Nov. 1937, Lea Taylor Papers, box 19, Chicago Historical Society.

28. Report, Lea Taylor to Martin P. Durkin, Director, Illinois Department of Labor, 13 Aug. 1937, p. 7, Chicago Commons Papers, box 26, Chicago Historical Society.

29. Clipping, "Dress Industry Wage Approved," Lea Taylor Papers, box 19, Chicago Historical Society.

30. *Newsletter to Auxiliaries of Chicago Commons* 1 (8 March 1937), Chicago Commons Papers, box 26.

31. Bulletin, "State Labor Legislation," NFS Papers, fol. 144.

32. Press release, 10 June 1934, NFS Papers, fol. 80.

33. Notes on a symposium, "The Place of the Settlement in Industrial Relations," held as part of the NFS Conference, 1938, NFS Papers, fol. 82.

34. Norma Moe, executive secretary, Twin Cities Chapter, AASW to Lee Sharp, Chairman, Twin Cities Federation of Settlements, 26 Nov. 1937, North East Neighborhood House Papers, box 29.

35. "Frank Crosswaith," *New Frontier* 2 (4 March 1933), Chicago Historical Society.

36. "To Strike or Not to Strike . . ." (22 April 1937), Chicago Commons Papers, box 6.

37. Gaynell Hawkins, *Educational Experiments in Social Settlements* (New York: American Association for Adult Education, 1937), p. 72. Hawkins attributes the story to Mark Starr of the International Ladies Garment Workers Union.

38. "Boys' and Girls' Work Divisions, Joint Delegate Conference, Eastern Section, Nov. 7th and 8th, 1936, N.Y.C.," NFS Papers, fol. 110.

39. Emeric Kurtagh, "Workers Education in the Settlement—Report given at the 10th Annual Meeting of the American Association for Adult Education," 19 May 1936, p. 3, NFS Papers, fol. 425.

40. "The NFS, at its 23rd Conference at Montreal, passed the following resolution," 9 June 1935, NFS Papers, fol. 81.

41. Press release (1936?), NFS Papers, fol. 81.

42. Resolution passed by the NFS board, 19–23 May 1937, NFS microfilm, reel 3.

43. Hilda W. Smith, Specialist in Workers Education, Washington, D.C. to Lillie Peck, 24 June 1937, NFS Papers, fol. 76.

44. Hilda Smith to Lillie Peck, executive secretary of the NFS, 27 June 1939, NFS Papers, fol. 599.

45. Emeric Kurtagh, "Workers Education in the Settlement—Report of the American Association for Adult Education," 19 May 1936, p. 3, NFS Papers, fol. 425.

46. "Conference Bulletin No. 2—Workers' Education," May–June 1934, NFS Papers, fol. 76.

47. "The following houses have Workers' Education programs," 2 April 1936, NFS Papers, fol. 76.

48. Leon Werch, ed., "Workers' Education in the Settlements," pamphlet of Committee on Workers Education, NFS, June 1938, p. 9, NFS Papers, fol. 76.

49. "Workers' Education in the Settlement—Report given at the 10th Annual Meeting of the American Association for Adult Education," 19 May 1936, pp. 3–5, NFS Papers.

50. Alice Hamilton, ex-resident, to Grace Abbott, vice-president of the Hull-House board, 30 May 1938, Abbott Papers, box 55, fol. 3, University of Chicago.

51. Allen Davis and Mary Lynn McCree, *Eighty Years at Hull-House* (Chicago: Quadrangle, 1969), p. 190.

52. Clipping, "Settlements urge Free Speech Right as Real Essential," 1935?, NFS Papers, fol. 81.

53. Gaynell Hawkins, pp. 45–46.

54. "Report of the Mid-Western Section, Boys' and Girls' Work Division," 30–31 Jan. 1937, p. 3, NFS Papers, fol. 111.

55. Hilda Smith quoted in minutes of the 6th New England Regional Conference of the Boys' Work Division of the United Settlements of Greater Boston," 15–16 May 1937, p. 3, NFS Papers, fol. 110.

56. Robbins Gilman to Glenford Lawrence, 1 Dec. 1938, North East Neighborhood House Papers, box 26.

57. "Preliminary Workers' Education Report, 1937–38," pp. 10–11, Chicago Commons Papers, box 12.

58. Letterhead, Citizens' Emergency Committee on Industrial Relations stationery, 1937, Chicago Commons Papers, box 26.

59. "Citizens' Emergency Committee on Industrial Relations," 5 Feb.–21 May 1937 in Chicago Commons Papers, box 26.

60. Walter Johnson, p. 102.

61. Glenford Lawrence, "The Place of the Settlement in Industrial Relations," notes on a symposium, NFS Conference, 1928, NFS Papers, fol. 82.

62. Louise Bowen to Lillian Wald, former head of Henry Street Settlement, 14 Feb. 1938, NFS Papers, fol. 294.

63. Lea Taylor, interview with the author, 20 July 1970.

64. Helen Hall, "The Consequences of Social Action for the Group Work Agency," presented at the NFS Conference, June 1936, Lea Taylor Papers, fol. 36, University of Illinois, Chicago Circle.

CHAPTER 8

1. Edith Elmer Wood to Albert J. Kennedy, quoted in Kennedy, "The Part of the Settlements in Cultivating Civic and Social Order," mimeograph, 1933, p. 33, Wald Papers, box 22, "Housing (mimeos)" fol., Columbia University.

2. Lillian Robbins, headworker, Hamilton House, "Radio-Continuity: Housing Information Bureau," 27 Aug. 1936, Hamilton-Madison Papers, fol. 14, SWHA, U. of Minn. Dialogue among Mrs. Frazier, Mrs. Samuel L. Rosenman, and Stanley Isaacs, March 1937, United Neighborhood Houses Papers, fol. 98, SWHA, U. of Minn.

3. Henry Street Settlement, *A Dutchman's Farm* (New York: Henry Street, 1939), p. 8, Helen Hall Papers, Columbia University.

4. George Gove to Lillian Wald, 17 Dec. 1929, Wald Papers, box 21, "Housing (N.Y. State and Municipal)" fol., Columbia University.

5. "Address of Stanley M. Isaacs, candidate for Borough [President] of Manhattan," 13 Oct. 1937, p. 3, Kennedy Papers, Paige box 7, "Stanley Isaacs" fol., SWHA, U. of Minn.

6. "General Session—Evening—June 3, 1938," NFS Papers, fol. 85, SWHA, U. of Minn.

7. Noted in resolution passed by the Woman's City Club, 16 Sept. 1935, Lea Taylor Papers, box 17, Chicago Historical Society.

8. Lea Taylor to Elizabeth Hughes, Secretary of the Housing Committee, Council of Social Agencies, 27 June 1935, Lea Taylor Papers, box 21, Chicago Historical Society.

9. D. E. Mackelmann, Secretary, Committee on Housing, Council of Social Agencies "to the Head Residents of the Settlements," 14 Jan. 1937, Lea Taylor Papers, "Council of Social Agencies" fol., University of Illinois, Chicago Circle.

10. Board minutes, University of Chicago Settlement, 11 May 1936, McDowell Papers, fol. 25, Chicago Historical Society.

11. Board minutes, Chicago Commons, 22 May 1936, Chicago Commons Papers, box 19, Chicago Historical Society.

12. Minutes, Committee on Housing, Council of Social Agencies, 9 Feb. 1936, Lea Taylor Papers, box 21, Chicago Historical Society.

13. Charles M. Glaab and A. Theodore Brown in *A History of Urban America* (New York: Macmillan, 1967), p. 291, say zoning was largely a post-World War I movement. Nine hundred eighty-one cities had passed zoning regulations by 1930.

14. "Report of the Head Worker . . . April 1939," North East Neighborhood House Papers, box 7, Minnesota Historical Society.

15. "Report of the Head Worker . . . March 1939," North East Neighborhood House Papers, box 7.

16. "Report of the Head Worker . . . April 1939," North East Neighborhood House Papers, Box 7.

17. Catheryne Cooke Gilman, "Neighbors United Through Social Settlement Services . . . 1914–1948," typescript, p. 874, Minnesota Historical Society.

18. Alexander Bing, president of City Housing Corporation to Lillian Wald, 21 Oct. 1930, Wald Papers, box 21, "Housing (City Housing Corporation)" fol., Columbia University.

19. Glaab and Brown, p. 298.

20. Albert J. Kennedy, "The Part of the Settlements in Cultivating Civic and Social Order," 1933, p. 25, Wald Papers, box 22, "Housing (mimeographs)" fol., Columbia University.

21. James Ford, "Housing," *Social Work Year Book* (New York: Russell Sage Foundation, 1935), p. 188.

22. J. A. Wolf to Albert J. Kennedy, 14 Jan. 1933, NFS Papers, fol. 137.

23. Wolf to Kennedy, 14 Jan. 1933, NFS Papers, fol. 137.

24. Clipping, "$500,000 Federal Loan for Local Housing Project," NFS Papers, fol. 137.

25. Committee on Workers Education, NFS, "Workers Education in the Settlements," June 1938, p. 20, NFS Papers, fol. 76.

26. Fred L. Lavanburg Foundation and Hamilton House, *What Happened to 386 Families Who Were Compelled to Vacate their Slum Dwellings to Make Way for a Large Housing Project* (New York: Fred L. Lavanburg Foundation, 1933), p. 2.

27. Lillian Wald, "Jane Addams: the Last Years," Wald Papers, Speeches and Writings, Manuscript Division, New York Public Library.

28. Kennedy, "Part of the Settlements," pp. 24–25. The settlements were Union, Christodora, and Lenox Hill.

29. Lea Taylor to Albert J. Kennedy, 29 Nov. 1933, NFS Papers, fol. 551.

30. Annual report, 1933, Phyllis Wheatley Settlement House Papers, box 1, Minnesota Historical Society.

31. Annual report, 1935, Phyllis Wheatley Settlement House Papers, box 1.

32. Annual report, 1935, Phyllis Wheatley Papers.

33. Board minutes, 18 March 1936, Phyllis Wheatley Settlement House Papers, box 1.

34. Board minutes, 15 April 1936, Phyllis Wheatley Settlement House Papers, box 1.

35. Board minutes, 15 April 1936, Phyllis Wheatley.

36. Board minutes, 17 Feb. 1937, Phyllis Wheatley Settlement House Papers, box 2.

37. Ruth Gage Thompson, president of the Board to Dr. Stuart Chapin, professor of sociology, University of Minnesota, 23 Feb. 1937, Phyllis Wheatley Settlement House Papers, box 11.

38. Board minutes, 17 March 1937, Phyllis Wheatley Settlement House Papers, box 2.

39. "Sumner Field Housing Project Mass Meeting," March 1938, Phyllis Wheatley Settlement House Papers, box 11.

40. Monthly report, Nov. 1938, Phyllis Wheatley Settlement House Papers, box 2.

41. Board minutes, 2 Feb. 1938, Goodrich House Papers, box 1, Western Reserve Historical Society.

42. "Meeting on Housing, Feb. 1, 1938," Goodrich House Papers, box 4.

43. Report of Housing Committee meeting held 4 Oct. 1938, Goodrich House Papers, box 1.

44. "Meeting of Board Members with Mr. Ernest Bohn," 18 Oct. 1938, Goodrich House Papers, box 1.

45. Board minutes, 31 Oct. 1938, Goodrich House Papers, box 1.

46. Clarke A. Chambers, *Seedtime of Reform* (Minneapolis: University of Minnesota, 1963), p. 137.

47. Helen Alfred to the secretary of the League of Mothers' Clubs, 4 Oct. 1937, United Neighborhood House Papers, fol. 513.

48. Chambers, p. 137.

49. Lea Taylor to Lillie Peck, secretary, NFS, 28 Nov. 1931, NFS Papers, fol. 551.

50. Open letter, 21 May 1932, NFS Papers, fol. 78.

51. Press release, 10 June 1934, NFS Papers, fol. 80.

52. "League of Mothers' Clubs" fol., United Neighborhood Houses Papers, fol. 547.

53. Helen Hall, "The Consequences of Social Action for the Group Work Agency," June 1936, Lea Taylor Papers, fol. 36, University of Illinois, Chicago Circle.

54. Mrs. Julius C. Bernheim, Honorary Chairman to Mr. Charney Vladek, N.Y.C. Housing Authority, 20 Nov. 1935, United Neighborhood Houses Papers, fol. 512.

55. Letterhead of Lower East Side Community Council, 29 May 1930, Wald Papers, box 18, "Lower East Side Community Council" fol., Columbia University.

56. *Henry Bulletin* 7 (7 Jan. 1935), p. 3, Wald Papers, box 60, "Henry News" fol., Columbia University.

57. Lillie M. Peck, "Adult Education in Settlements," 1 Feb. 1936, p. 1. NFS Papers, fol. 4.

58. *Kips Bay Neighbor* 9 (Jan. 1930).

59. Annual report, Goddard Neighborhood Center (N.Y.C.), 1935, NFS Papers, fol. 418.

60. "Helping a Complex Neighborhood to become Community Conscious," NFS Papers, fol. 539.

61. "An Enlarging South End Joint Planning Committee," *NEWS* 2 (March 1934), p. 5, NFS Papers, fol. 208.

62. Annual report, Robert Gould Shaw House, 1932–33, NFS Papers, fol. 341.

63. "West End Planning Board," *NEWS* 2 (June 1934), p. 2, NFS Papers, fol. 208.

64. "North End Planning Board Achieves Practical Results," *NEWS* 3 (Jan. 1934), p. 8, NFS Papers, fol. 208.

65. "Successful Hearing," *NEWS* 3 (April 1935), p. 3, NFS Papers, fol. 208.

66. "An Enlarging South End Joint Planning Committee," *NEWS* 2 (March 1934), p. 5, NFS Papers, fol. 208.

67. Minutes, Robert A. Woods Associates, 30 Nov. 1932, South End House, Boston.

68. "Opposes Liquor License," *South End House*, 6 (Nov. 1936), p. 1, South End House.

69. Richard S. Winslow, "South End House Association," 1938, NFS Papers, fol. 343.

70. Albert Boer, *The Development of USES: A Chronology of the United South End Settlements, 1891–1966* (Boston: USES, 1966), p. 69.

71. "Further Progress for Tenement Clearance," *NEWS* 2 (June 1934), p. 5, NFS Papers, fol. 208.

72. Albert H. Stoneman, "South End House Association," 1933, p. 5, NFS Papers, fol. 343.

73. Stoneman, p. 6.

74. Allen Davis and Mary Lynn McCree, *Eighty Years at Hull-House* (Chicago: Quadrangle, 1969), p. 189.

75. Davis and McCree, p. 190.

76. Ralph S. Hudson, Resident Director, to "Honorable President and Members of City Council," 24 Nov. 1941, Neighborhood Association Papers, box 5, "Bath Study" fol., University of Pittsburgh, Special Collections.

77. Minutes of budget committee [1936?], Community Chest of Allegheny County Records, 1937–1959, box 4, University of Pittsburgh, Special Collections.

78. Ralph S. Hudson, director, Woods Run Settlement to Mayor Cornelius D. Scully, 9 Dec. 1938, Neighborhood Center Association, box 4, "Reports, Minutes and Correspondence—1938" fol.

79. "In the Boys and Girls work . . ." [1932?], Neighborhood Center Association Papers, box 4, "Reports 1931, 1932, 1936, 1938" fol.

80. Michael Kazel, "Woods Run Settlement's Neighborhood Beautification Projects," June–July 1939, Neighborhood Center Association Papers, box 6, "Neighborhood Beautification" fol.

CHAPTER 9

1. "Statement of Facts Regarding the Negro Delegates . . . Kansas City, May 1934," Lea Taylor Papers, box 3, Chicago Historical Society.

2. Clipping, "Settlement Workers are Segregated: Negro Delegates Withdraw from Meeting When Jim Crowed," *Call*, 25 May 1934, Lea Taylor Papers, box 3.

3. Clipping, Taylor.

4. Violet Robbin, Acting Secretary (National Conference of Social Work?) to Emma Adams, head resident, Mattie Rhodes Neighborhood Center, Kansas City, Missouri, 25 May 1934, Lea Taylor Papers, box 3.

5. Twin Cities headworkers to Lea Taylor, 1 June 1934, Lea Taylor Papers, box 3.

6. Lea Taylor to Robbins Gilman, 8 June 1934, Lea Taylor Papers, box 3.

7. "Announcement to Members of the NFS," 1936, NFS Papers, fol. 82, SWHA, U. of Minn.

8. Lillie Peck to Robbins Gilman, headworker, North East Neighborhood House, 23 March 1936, North East Neighborhood House Papers, box 26, Minnesota Historical Society.

9. Lea Taylor to Lillie Peck, 17 June 1934, Lea Taylor Papers, box 3.

10. Grace Gosselin to Lea Taylor, 6 Nov. 1931, Lea Taylor Papers, box 2.

11. "Senior club representatives," NFS Papers, fol. 70.

12. Kathryn Farra, "The Organization and Administration of New York Settlements," mimeograph, 1931, p. 42, NFS Papers, fol. 537.

13. Philip Klein, *A Social Study of Pittsburgh* (New York: Columbia University Press, 1938), p. 282.

14. Mary Simkhovitch, *The Settlement Primer*, 2nd ed. (New York: NFS, 1936), p. 48.

15. Gaynell Hawkins, *Educational Experiments in Social Settlements* (New York: American Association for Adult Education, 1937), pp. 54–55.

16. Annual report, 1938, p. 9, Abraham Lincoln Centre Papers, Chicago Historical Society.

17. Annual report, 1930, pp. 23–24, Abraham Lincoln Centre Papers.

18. Minutes, Joint meeting with committee from Council of Social Agencies, 18 April 1938, Welfare Council Papers, Chicago Historical Society.

19. "Eli Bates House," 17 Sept. 1937, Welfare Council Papers.

20. Board minutes, 18 Feb. 1930, Marcy Center Papers, box 33, University of Illinois, Chicago Circle.

21. "Building the New Marcy Center in a Jewish Neighborhood," Marcy Center Papers, box 20.

22. "Facts about Marcy Center," Marcy Center Papers, box 31.

23. Elizabeth E. Marcy Center," 28 April 1935, Welfare Council Papers.

24. "Elizabeth E. Marcy Center," 27 April 1935, Welfare Council Papers.

25. Annual report, 1938, Newberry Center Papers, box 100, University of Illinois, Chicago Circle.

26. Annual report, 1938, Newberry Center Papers.

27. Arlington Smith, Newberry Center, report to the Executive Committee, Division of Education and Recreation, 15 March 1939, Welfare Council Papers, "Minorities" fol.

28. Dewey Jones, Hull-House, report to Executive Committee, Division of Education and Recreation, 15 March 1939, Welfare Council Papers, "Minorities" fol.

29. Jones.

30. Jones.

31. "Monthly Report—September 1938," Phyllis Wheatley Settlement House Papers, box 2, Minnesota Historical Society.

32. "Monthly Report—Sept. 1938," Phyllis Wheatley.

33. Board minutes, Hull-House, 21 Jan. 1938, Abbott Papers, box 55, fol. 5, University of Chicago.

34. Board minutes, Hull-House, 21 Jan. 1938, Abbott Papers.

35. Board minutes, Hull-House, 21 April 1939, Abbott Papers, box 55, fol. 5.

36. Albert J. Kennedy, unpublished typescript on settlements and race relations, pp. 9–10, Kennedy Papers, fol. 40, SWHA, U. of Minn.

37. J. A. Davis, Chairman of Staff Committee, Phyllis Wheatley board to Lois Diehl, General Secretary, St. Louis YWCA, 12 Dec. 1938, Phyllis Wheatley Settlement House Papers, box 6.

38. "Twenty-five Years a Neighbor: the Story of Phyllis Wheatley Settlement House," Ephemera, SWHA, U. of Minn.

39. "Monthly Report—October 1929," Phyllis Wheatley Settlement House Papers, box 1.

40. Annual report, 1932, Phyllis Wheatley Settlement House Papers, box 1.

41. Kennedy, p. 9.

42. Kennedy, p. 12.

43. Study of Phyllis Wheatley House by Council of Social Agencies, 15 Nov. 1936, p. 59, Phyllis Wheatley Settlement House Papers, box 1.

44. "Phyllis Wheatley Settlement House," n.d., Phyllis Wheatley Settlement House Papers, box 1.

45. Study of Phyllis Wheatley House, p. 69.

46. Board minutes, 14 May 1930, Phyllis Wheatley Settlement House Papers, box 1.

47. "Board of Directors—Twin City Urban League," Phyllis Wheatley Settlement House Papers, box 10.

48. Study of Phyllis Wheatley House, p. 65.

49. Study of Phyllis Wheatley House, pp. 67–68.

50. Study of Phyllis Wheatley House, p. 70.

51. Study of Phyllis Wheatley House, p. 64.

52. Ruth Gage Thompson, board president to T. Arnold Hill, National Urban League, 21 June 1938, Phyllis Wheatley Settlement House Papers, box 6.

53. Margaret E. Chapmen, former member of the Phyllis Wheatley board to Lillie Peck, executive secretary of the NFS, 26 Oct. 1937, NFS Papers, fol. 376.

54. Louise Bromley Oswell, headworker to James A. Davis, Chairman, Personnel Committee, 14 Nov. 1938, Phyllis Wheatley Settlement House Papers, box 6.

55. Board minutes, 15 Feb. 1939, Phyllis Wheatley Settlement House Papers, box 2. The third head resident was Magnolia Latimer.

56. Clipping, "Brown, Business and Professional Head, Issues Statement," Minneapolis *Spokesman*, 3 Feb. 1939, Phyllis Wheatley Settlement House Papers, box 14.

57. Board minutes, 26 Jan. 1939, Phyllis Wheatley Settlement House Papers, box 2.

58. Fannie M. Shanks, President, Minneapolis Association of Colored Women's Clubs to "Phyllis Wheatley Board," 26 Jan. 1939, Phyllis Wheatley Settlement House Papers, box 3.

59. H. W. Boots, President, Minneapolis Ministerial Alliance to "Board of Directors," 15 Feb. 1939, Phyllis Wheatley Settlement House Papers, box 3.

60. Mildred B. Strader to Mrs. Ruth Gage Thompson, president of the board, 31 Jan. 1939, Phyllis Wheatley Settlement House Papers, box 3.

61. Board minutes, 26 Jan. 1939, Phyllis Wheatley Settlement House Papers, box 2.

62. Boots.

63. "Twenty-five Years a Neighbor."

64. "Suggested Qualifications of Board Members of Phyllis Wheatley House," 1939, Phyllis Wheatley Settlement House Papers, box 3.

65. "Twenty-five Years a Neighbor."

66. Leon Werch, ed., "Workers Education in the Settlements" pamphlet (Committee on Workers Education, NFS, June 1938), p. 9, NFS Papers, fol. 76.

67. Board minutes, 14 Jan. 1931, Phyllis Wheatley Settlement House Papers, box 1.

68. Ruth Gage Thompson, Corresponding Secretary to Mayor A. G. Bainbridge, 13 March 1935, Phyllis Wheatley Settlement House Papers, box 3. Minnesota

Historical Society; and "Twenty-five Years a Neighbor: the Story of Phyllis Wheatley Settlement House," Ephemera.

69. Study of Phyllis Wheatley House, pp. 20–21.

70. Study of Phyllis Wheatley House, p. 21.

71. Board minutes, 16 Dec. 1936, Phyllis Wheatley Settlement House Papers, box 1.

72. Study of Phyllis Wheatley House, p. 21.

73. Study of Phyllis Wheatley House, p. 7.

74. Kennedy, p. 13.

75. List of Urban Leagues maintaining community centers, NFS Papers, fol. 12.

76. Letterhead for National Urban League dated 4 Jan. 1937, Simkhovitch Papers, fol. 80, Schlesinger Library, Radcliffe College.

77. "Susan Parrish Wharton Settlement, Report of the Headworker," 1 Oct.– 1 Dec. 1931, Wharton Center Papers, Urban Archives, Temple University.

78. Grace Abbott, *A Survey of Boston Settlements* . . . , mimeograph, 1934, South End House, Boston.

79. Julian D. Steele, "Robert Gould Shaw House, Inc. Thirty Years, 1908–1938," NFS Papers, fol. 341.

80. Eleanor McMain, headworker, Kingsley House to Ellen Coolidge, Foreign Secretary, NFS, 10 July 1931, NFS Papers, fol. 148.

81. Frances Ingram, headworker, Neighborhood House, Louisville to Lillie Peck, NFS executive secretary, 28 Nov. 1936, NFS Papers, fol. 12.

82. "Directory," *Neighborhood*, 3 (Dec. 1930), pp. 178–239.

83. Lillie Peck, executive secretary, NFS, field report, 17 Nov. 1933, NFS Papers, fol. 473.

84. Jon A. Peterson, "The Origins and Development of a Social Settlement: a History of the Godman Guild Association, 1898–1955," M.A. thesis, Ohio State University, 1959, p. 112.

85. Sidney J. Lindenberg and Ruth Ellen Zittel, "The Settlement Scene Changes," *Social Forces*, 14 (May 1936), p. 509.

86. Lindenberg and Zittel, p. 503.

CHAPTER 10

1. "Summary of Conclusions and Recommendations" regarding the Boston Settlement study, Abbott Papers, box 32, fol. 13, University of Chicago.

2. Nathan E. Cohen, *Social Work in the American Tradition* (New York: Dryden Press, 1958), p. 201.

3. Helen Hall, *Unfinished Business* (New York: Macmillan, 1971), pp. 269–70.

4. Peter Marris and Martin Rein, *Dilemmas of Social Reform: Poverty and Community Action in the United States* (New York: Atherton, 1967), p. 177. The board of Mobilization for Youth in November 1958 was chaired by the president of the Henry Street Settlement board, Carlton Winslow. Out of twenty members, thirteen were directly connected with settlements. One was Helen Hall, still head of Henry Street Settlement. See "Henry Street Settlement Studies: Mobilization for Youth," mimeographed, Nov. 1958, Helen Hall Papers, box 10, SWHA, U. of Minn.

5. Daniel P. Moynihan, *Maximum Feasible Misunderstanding: Community Action in the War on Poverty* (New York: Free Press, 1969), pp. 44–45.

6. Moynihan, p. 58.

7. "Introduction," George A. Brager and Francis P. Purcell, eds., *Community Action against Poverty: Readings from the Mobilization Experience* (New Haven, Conn.: College and University Press, 1967), p. 19.

8. George A. Brager, then co-director of Mobilization for Youth, and Francis P. Purcell in the "Conclusion" to their *Community Action against Poverty*, p. 334, assert that Mobilization's community action program, especially the issue of whether the New York City government or nonpolitical neighborhood groups would control poverty funds, was the reason behind the Communist charges. Mobilization survived, but its community action efforts were considerably weakened.

9. Moynihan, pp. 56–58.

10. Peter Marris and Martin Rein, *Dilemmas of Social Reform: Poverty and Community Action in the United States* (New York: Atherton, 1967), pp. 181–83.

11. Moynihan, pp. 34–35.

12. Francis Fox Piven and Richard A. Cloward, *Regulating the Poor: the Functions of Public Welfare* (New York: Vintage, 1971), p. 286.

13. John C. Donovan, *The Politics of Poverty* (New York: Pegasus, 1967), pp. 97–99.

14. Peter Marris and Martin Rein, p. 42.

15. Richard M. Elman, *The Poorhouse State: The American Way of Life on Public Assistance* (New York: Dell, 1966), p. 14.

16. Marris and Rein, p. 46.

17. Moynihan, pp. 134–35.

18. Moynihan, p. 136.

19. George A. Brager, "Effecting Organization Change Through a Demonstration Project: the Case of the Schools," Brager and Purcell, eds., *Community Action against Poverty*, p. 118.

20. Moynihan, p. 42.

21. Marris and Rein, p. 143.

22. Marris and Rein, p. 210.

23. William H. Brueckner, "New Horizons Project," *Consumer Involvement in the Delivery of Social Service*, reprinted from *Human Needs*, 1 (Mar. 1973), pp. 15–18.

24. David Dresser, HUD Community Development, "Neighborhood Facilities," *HUD Challenge*, 4:2 (February 1973), p. 2. This article also explains how to apply for the HUD grants.

25. Lillian J. Fujimoto and David A. Johnston, both of Kingsley House, "Rehabilitated Kingsley House," *HUD Challenge*, 4:2 (February 1973), pp. 13–14.

Bibliography

Bibliographic Note

This study rests largely on settlement collections and the papers of people actively associated with settlements in the 1930s. Except for the Kingsley House Papers at Tulane University, all the existing settlement collections now in public archives were consulted. Manuscript collections were available for some forty settlements, roughly twenty percent of those houses in the National Federation of Settlements, United Neighborhood Houses of New York, and the Chicago Federation of Settlements, during any given year of the Depression. Supplementing these materials were theses, primary printed sources, and secondary sources. Interviews were relied on to a limited extent. Obviously because of the dependence upon manuscript collections available in public archives, this study is weighted in favor of those cities which have been most active in collecting these materials.

Manuscript Collections

Before describing the numerous local collections, a few collections of national scope should be noted. Perhaps the single most important collection is the National Federation of Settlements Papers located at the Social Welfare History Archives, University of Minnesota. In addition to extensive material on the national organization, these papers contain one of the two best collections of annual reports for individual settlements. The other major source for annual reports is the Russell Sage Collection at the City College of the City University of New York. While the number of annual reports in these two collections is extensive, some gaps remain.

Other collections of national scope, but of limited value for this study, are the *Survey* Papers, Social Welfare History Archives, University of Minnesota; the Abraham Epstein (American Association for Social Security) Papers, Cornell University; and the Hilda Smith (WPA Workers Education Program) Papers, Schlesinger Library, Radcliffe College. The National Federation of Settlements collection, valuable though it is, gives only a bird's eye view of the settlements. To get the real feeling of the movement, one must go to the grass-roots level and dig around in the local collections.

The Chicago collections are the most extensive and complete of any city. Several collections relate to Chicago settlements in general. For example, the minutes of the Chicago Federation of Settlements are in possession of the Chicago Federation. Also, the Welfare Council of Metropolitan Chicago Papers in the Chicago Historical Society is a superb source for candid evaluations of the various settlements. Collections of little value for this study were the Chicago Area Chapter of the National Association of Social Workers, Chicago Historical Society, and the Julius Rosenwald (philanthropist and Hull-House board member) Papers, University of Chicago.

The trustees of Hull-House, probably the most famous settlement of all, showed a distressing lack of concern for preserving its history. Fortunately, this was not true of a number of well-known individuals connected with the settlement. Thus material on Hull-House can be pieced together by consulting the papers of Edith and Grace Abbott, University of Chicago Library; Louise H. Bowen (scrapbooks only), Chicago Historical Society; Alice Hamilton, Schlesinger Library, Radcliffe; Florence Kelley, Columbia University; Esther Loeb Kohn, University of Illinois, Chicago Circle; and Adena Miller Rich, also at University of Illinois, Chicago Circle. The Abbott and Rich collections are of most value.

The papers of Chicago Commons are the most extensive of the individual settlement collections. Basically they consist of the Chicago Commons and the Lea D. Taylor Papers (the latter really an extension of the former) at the Chicago Historical Society. They are supplemented by the Tabernacle Church (Lea Taylor's assistant, Glenford Lawrence, doubled as pastor of this church, which was practically defunct by the time of the Depression) Papers, Chicago Historical Society; Lea Taylor Papers, University of Illinois, Chicago Circle; and Graham Taylor Papers, Newberry Library. Since Chicago Commons was one of the two or three most important settlements of the era, it is highly fortunate that so much has survived and is available.

The Chicago Historical Society also has the papers of Abraham Lincoln Centre, Benton House, Bethlehem House, Howell House, Christopher House, Emerson House, Erie Neighborhood House, Gads Hill Center, and Parkway Community House; but these papers are not extensive for the 1930s. Somewhat more extensive are the papers of the University of Chicago Settlement in the Mary E. McDowell Papers, also at the Chicago Historical Society. Other Chicago settlement collections are the Marcy Center Papers, University of Illinois, Chicago Circle; and Laird House in the Paul Fox Papers, Immigrant Archives, University of Minnesota.

Although New York had more settlements than any other city, the number and quality of the available collections falls far short of Chicago's. The only general New York settlement source is the United Neighborhood Houses of New York Papers in the Social Welfare History Archives, University of Minnesota. Other New York settlement papers located there include Five Towns Community House (Long Island), Hartley House, Hamilton House, Henry Street under Helen Hall, Madison House, and University Settlement in the Albert J. Kennedy Papers. The State Historical Society of Wisconsin has the rest of the University Settlement Papers and will lend them on microfilm. New York settlement papers in the Schlesinger Library, Radcliffe, are the 110th Street Neighborhood Club in the Maryal Knox Papers, and Greenwich House in the Mary Simkhovitch Papers. Both collections are small and superficial. The only New York settlement papers to remain in New York are those associated with Henry Street Settlement. Both Lillian Wald collections are sizable, the one at Columbia University being even larger than the New York Public Library's. The Helen Hall Papers at Columbia University is a small collection of speeches, articles, and studies. One will find more information on New York settlements at the University of Minnesota in Minneapolis than in New York. The papers of the Baden Street Settlement of Rochester, New York, are also in the Social Welfare Archives, University of Minnesota.

The available sources on Boston are quite meager. The Schlesinger Library at Radcliffe has the papers for Denison House and the scrapbooks of Eva Whiting White, director of Elizabeth Peabody House. Like the other Schlesinger Library collections cited, these are also shallow. One's time in Boston can be better spent, not at Harvard, but at South End House. Fairly extensive papers are still in the possession of this settlement.

Philadelphia owes its available settlement collections to the Urban Archives at Temple University. Although most of the collections are quite disorganized, they include papers for the Settlement Music School, United Neighbors Association (House of Industry in the 1930s), University Settlement, and Wharton Centre. Other relevant collections are the Housing Association Papers and the Health and Welfare Council Record, 1922–69 (Council of Social Agencies in the 1930s). Also, some of the Helen Hall Papers at the Social Welfare History Archives, University of Minnesota, contain material on Philadelphia's University Settlement.

Although a great deal of information on Pittsburgh settlements is lacking, the University of Pittsburgh has the prize Community Chest collection. Chest collections are rare, and when they do exist, they often consist of public relations material such as campaign posters and pamphlets. The Community Chest of Allegheny County Records, 1937–1959, contains the verbatim minutes of the various committees that decided exactly what programs in settlements would be financed with Chest funds at the end of the 1930s. Also at the University of Pittsburgh is the Neighborhood Center Association Papers (Woods Run Settlement in the 1930s) in addition to the American Service Institute Papers. The latter collection has very little material relating to the 1930s.

The University of Pittsburgh also possesses fairly extensive papers on a unique Cleveland settlement, University Neighborhood Centers, in the Wilbur I. Newstetter Collection. Information on Newstetter and University Neighborhood Centers is also in the possession of the School of Applied Social Sciences, Case Western Reserve University and at the Western Reserve Historical Society. The latter also has the papers for Alta House, East End Neighborhood House, Friendly Inn, Goodrich House, Hiram House, and Phyllis Wheatley Settlement House. The Hiram House Records are one of the largest collections available in the country and the best example of a settlement at the conservative end of the social reform spectrum, at least on economic issues. The papers of Paul Walter, Taft's campaign manager in the 1950s and a Hiram House resident in the 1930s, are also at the Western Reserve Historical Society. Another relevant collection at this institution is the Consumers' League of Ohio Papers. Altogether, papers for one-third of Cleveland's settlements are available.

Approximately the same percentage is also available for Twin Cities settlements in the Minnesota Historical Society. Minor collections include Wells Memorial House in Minneapolis, and Neighborhood House and Hallie Q. Brown House, both in St. Paul. The Edward F. Waite Neighborhood House (Elliot Park in the 1930s) collection is of good size. The Society's best collections, though, are the ones relating to North East Neighborhood House and Phyllis Wheatley Settlement House, both of Minneapolis. The latter settlement collection is the outstanding one in the country for a black settlement. Besides the sizable North East Neighborhood House Papers, the Society also has the very extensive Robbins and Catherine Cooke Gilman Papers, in addition to a three volume typescript by Mrs. Gilman, "Neighbors United Through Social Settlement Services at the North East Neighborhood House, Minneapolis, 1914–1948." The Society's Community Fund material is worthless, unless one is interested in campaign posters and badges.

Altogether, seventy-seven manuscript collections were utilized in the preparation of this study.

Theses and Dissertations

Asher, Robert Eller. "The Influence of the Chicago Workers Committee on Unemployment upon the Administration of Relief, 1931–1934." M.A. thesis, University
of Chicago, 1934.
Asher was active in the organization which formed the subject of his thesis and
served as the editor of that organization's newspaper.

Bond, Eleanor Margaret. "Factors in the Shift from the Evangelistic Approach to the
Education and Recreational Approach in the Program of the Bethlehem
Community Center." M.A. thesis, Chicago Theological Seminary, 1940.

Friedman, Laura A. "One Hundred Unemployed Families in Chicago." M.A. thesis,
Department of Economics, University of Chicago, 1933.
She drew her sample from members of the Chicago Workers Committee on
Unemployment.

Gilroy, Nellie Margaret. "Social Education and Action in Settlements." M.S. thesis,
School of Applied Social Sciences, Western Reserve University.

Hollander, Katharine Rawson. "The Family Service Department of Chicago Commons
Settlement House from Its Beginnings to March, 1938." Master's thesis, School
of Social Service Administration, University of Chicago, 1939.

Maloney, Sarah. "A History of Group Work Education in the United States." Ph.D.
diss., SASS, Western Reserve University, 1961.

Mixon, John L. "Work Relief in the Chicago Leisure Time Service Project in Chicago."
M.A. thesis, School of Social Service Administration, University of Chicago,
1937.

Moore, John F. "Origins and Development of the Council of Social Agencies in
Columbus and Franklin County, Ohio." M.A. thesis, Ohio State University,
1937.

Mould, Beryl F. "The People of Godman Guild Neighborhood of Columbus, Ohio,
1939." M.A. thesis, Ohio State University, 1939.

Peterson, Jon A. "The Origins and Development of a Social Settlement: A History of
the Godman Guild Association, 1898–1958." M.A. thesis, Ohio State University, 1959.

Oral History

The only interview the author conducted was with Lea Taylor on 20 July 1970.
A typescript by another interviewer of Taylor is available at the University of Illinois,
Chicago Circle. Though use was made of the Oral History Project of Columbia
University, particularly the Stanley Isaacs transcripts, in general the Columbia project
proved to be of little value for this study.

Primary Printed Sources

Books and Periodicals

Abbott, Edith. *The Tenements of Chicago, 1908–1935.* Chicago: University of Chicago Press, 1936.
Addams, Jane. *The Excellent Becomes the Permanent.* New York: Macmillan, 1932.
————. *My Friend, Julia Lathrop.* New York: Macmillan, 1935.
————. *The Second Twenty Years at Hull-House.* New York: Macmillan, 1930.
Anon. "Angel of Tenements." *Literary Digest* 121 (1 Feb. 1936): 34. The "angel" is Lillian Wald.
Anon. "In Jane Addams's Post; A. M. Rich Elected Head." *Literary Digest* 120 (24 Aug. 1935): 18.
Almond, Gabriel and Harold D. Lasswell. "Aggressive Behavior by Clients toward Public Relief Administrators: a Configurative Analysis." *American Political Science Review* 28 (Aug. 1934): 643–55.
Asher, Robert E. "Chicago Unemployed Show Their Fist." *Revolt,* Dec. 1932.
————. "The Jobless Help Themselves." *New Republic* 72 (28 Sept. 1932): 168–69.
Beatty, Jerome. "She Never Gave Up, Lifesaver Lillian Wald." *Forum* 96 (Aug. 1936): 70–73.
Bing, Lucia J. *Social Work in Greater Cleveland.* Cleveland: Welfare Federation, 1938.
Borders, Karl. "When the Unemployed Organize." *The Unemployed,* no. 5 (no date).
Bowen, Louise de Koven. *Speeches, Addresses and Letters of Louise de Koven Bowen.* Vol. 2. Ann Arbor: Edwards, 1937.
Brager, George A. and Francis P. Purcell. *Community Action Against Poverty: Readings from the Mobilization Experience.* New Haven, Conn.: College and University Press, 1967.
Brueckner, William H. "New Horizons Project," *Consumer Involvement in the Delivery of Social Service.* Reprinted from *Human Needs,* 1 (Mar. 1973): 15–18.
Buell, Bradley. "Eleanor McMain, One of the Pioneers." *Survey,* 65 (Jan. 1931): 375.
Calkins, Clinch. *Some Folks Won't Work.* New York: Harcourt, Brace, 1930.
Catlin, George B. "Neighborhood House, Detroit Industrial School." *Michigan History Magazine,* 18 (July 1934): 253–75.
Dilling, Elizabeth. *The Red Network.* Chicago: Elizabeth Dilling, 1934.
Donovan, John C. *The Politics of Poverty.* New York: Pegasus, 1967.
Dresser, David. "Neighborhood Facilities." *HUD Challenge,* 4 (Feb. 1973): 2–3.
DuBois, W.E.B. *The Philadelphia Negro: A Social Study.* Philadelphia: Published for the University, 1899.
Duffus, Robert L. *Lillian Wald: Neighbor and Crusader.* New York: Macmillan, 1938.
Dunlap, Flora. "Roadside Settlement of Des Moines." *Annals of Iowa,* Ser. 3, Vol. 21 (Jan. 1938): 161–89.
Elman, Richard M. *The Poorhouse State: The American Way of Life on Public Assistance.* New York: Dell, 1966.

Fujimoto, Lillian J. and David A. Johnston. "Rehabilitated Kingsley House." *HUD Challenge*, 4 (Feb. 1973): 13–14.

Green, Howard Whipple. "Cultural Areas in the City of Cleveland." *American Journal of Sociology*, Nov. 1932: 356.

———. "Slums—A City's Most Expensive Luxury." *A Sheet-a-Week*, 1 (22 Sept. 1934).

Hale, Mary T. *A History of Pillsbury House.* Minneapolis, 1935.

Hall, Helen. *Case Studies of Unemployment.* Philadelphia: University of Pennsylvania, 1931.

———. "Charity in the Market Place." *New Outlook*, 161 (May 1933): 48–50.

———. "Consumers: Consumers Emergency Council." *Tide Magazine*, 15 Apr. 1937.

———. "Digest of 'Report to the President of the Committee on Economic Security.'" Government Printing Office, 1935.

———. "English Dole and American Charity." *Atlantic Monthly*, 151 (May 1933): 538–49.

———. "Insure the Worker!" *Forum and Century*, 91 (June 1934): 344–47.

———. "The Little Green Card." *Survey Graphic*, May 1933.

———. "Miners Must Eat: the Workings of English Dole and American Charity." *Atlantic Monthly*, 152 (Aug. 1933): 153–62.

———. "On Family Life in America, Hard Times Lay Heavy Load." *New York Sunday Times*, 3 Dec. 1933: 12, col. 2.

———. "Shall We Stick to the American Dole?" *Survey Graphic.* Jan. 1931.

———. *Unfinished Business.* New York: Macmillan, 1971.

———. "When Detroit's Out of Gear." *Survey Graphic*, 1, Apr. 1930.

——— and Irene Hickok Nelson. "How Unemployment Strikes Home." *Survey Graphic*, 1 Apr. 1929.

Harman, Ruth and Charlotte Lekachman. "Jacobs House." *Wisconsin Magazine of History*, 16 (March 1933): 252–84.

Hart, Helen. "The Changing Function of the Settlement under Changing Conditions." National Conference of Social Work *Proceedings*, 1931: 289–95.

———. "Social Settlements and the Trend toward Specialization." *Social Forces*, 9 (June 1931): 526–32.

Hawkins, Gaynell. *Educational Experiments in Social Settlements.* New York: American Association for Adult Education, 1937.

Hendry, Charles E. and Margaret T. Svendsen. *Between Stacks and Spires.* Cleveland: Welfare Federation, 1936.

Herskovitz, Melville. *The Myth of the Negro Past.* Boston: Beacon, 1958.

Hoyt, Mabel F. "History of Community House, Sioux City, Iowa." *Annals of Iowa*, Scr. 3, Vol. 21 (Jan. 1938): 190.

Kellogg, Paul U. "Social Settlements." *Encyclopedia of the Social Sciences*, vol. 14, New York: Macmillan, 1934: 157–62.

Kennedy, Albert J. *Social Conditions in the 27th Ward.* A report made to the Buhl Foundation upon a study made between Nov. 1929 and Nov. 1930.

———. "Social Settlements." *Social Work Year Book*, 2 (1930–33): 480–87.

Klein, Philip. *A Social Study of Pittsburgh: Community Problems and Social Services of Allegheny County.* New York: Columbia University Press, 1938.

———. *From Philanthropy to Social Welfare* (San Francisco, Jossey-Bass, 1968).

Koch, Raymond L. "Politics and Relief in Minneapolis during the 1930s." *Minnesota History*, 41 (1968): 153–70.

Lindenberg, Sidney J. and Ruth Ellen Zittel. "The Settlement Scene Changes." *Social Forces*, 14 (May 1936): 599–66.

Linn, James Weber. *Jane Addams: a Biography.* New York: Appleton-Century, 1935.

Lovett, Robert Morss. *All Our Years.* New York: Viking, 1948.

———. "Hull House Chooses a New Head." *Christian Century*, 52 (2 Oct. 1935): 1239–40.

McDowell, Mary, et al. *Mary McDowell and Municipal Housekeeping.* Millar, 1936?.

Mayer, Milton. "Charlotte Carr—Settlement Lady." *Atlantic Monthly*, 162 (Dec. 1938): 741–48.

Mock, C. "Trends of Settlement Activities toward School Use." *Social Forces*, 9 (June 1931): 532–34.

Moynihan, Daniel P. *Maximum Feasible Misunderstanding: Community Action in the War on Poverty.* New York: The Free Press, 1969.

Orr, Douglas W. and Jean Walker Orr. *Health Insurance with Medical Care: the British Experience.* New York: Macmillan, 1938.

Ovington, Mary White. *Half a Man: The Status of the Negro in New York.* New York: Longman's Green, 1911.

Piven, Francis Fox and Richard A. Cloward. *Regulating the Poor: The Functions of Public Welfare.* New York: Random House, 1971.

Remuglia, Anthony. "The Unemployed Incorporate." *New Republic*, 77 (10 Jan. 1934): 244–46.

Simkhovitch, Mary. *Neighborhood: My Story of Greenwich House.* New York: Norton, 1938.

———. *The Settlement Primer: a Handbook for Neighborhood Workers.* New York: National Federation of Settlements, 1936.

Stoney, George. *Rooms of Their Own: a Survey of Twenty-Eight Lower East Side Social Clubs.* New York: Henry Street Settlement, 1939.

"Students in the Course in Group Work." *The Group Records of Four Clubs at the University Neighborhood Centers.* Cleveland: SASS, Western Reserve University, 1930.

Taylor, Graham. *Chicago Commons Through Forty Years.* Chicago: Chicago Commons, 1936.

———. *Pioneering on Social Frontiers.* Chicago: University of Chicago Press, 1930.

Taylor, Lea D. "The Future of the Settlement." Reprinted in Lorene M. Pacey, ed. *Readings in the Development of Settlement Work.* New York: Association Press, 1950: 245–60.

Terkel, Studs. *Hard Times: an Oral History of the Great Depression.* New York: Pantheon, 1970.

Towne, Florence H. *Neighbors.* Chicago: Donnelly, 1940.

Twin Cities Federation of Settlements. *Self-Analysis Survey of Minneapolis Settlement Houses.* Minneapolis: Royal, 1934.

Waite, Florence T. *A Warm Friend for the Spirit: A History of the Family Service Association of Cleveland and Its Forbears, 1830–1952.* Cleveland: Family Service Asso., 1960.

Wald, Lillian. "Change Comes to the East Side." *Atlantic Monthly*, 153 (Jan. 1934): 39–49.

———. "Lean Years." *Atlantic Monthly*, 152 (Dec. 1933): 650–59.

———. "People Who Have Crossed Our Threshold." *Atlantic Monthly*, 153 (Mar. 1934): 326–37.

———. *Windows on Henry Street*. Boston: Little, Brown, 1934.

Walker, Charles Rumford. "Relief and Revolution." *Forum*, 88 (Aug. & Sept. 1932): 73–78, 152–58.

Weyl, Nathaniel. "Organizing Hunger." *New Republic*, 77 (14 Dec. 1932): 117–20.

Williamson, Margaret. "Those Who Help Themselves." *Commonweal*, 17 (8 Mar. 1933): 516–17.

Wilson, Edmund. "Hull-House in 1932." *New Republic*, 73 (18 Jan.–1 Feb. 1933): 260–62, 287–90, 317–22.

Secondary Sources

Books and Periodicals

Boer, Albert. *The Development of USES; a Chronology of the United South End Settlements, 1891–1966*. Boston: United South End Settlements, 1966.

Bremner, Robert. *From the Depths. The Discovery of Poverty in the United States* (New York: New York University Press, 1956.

Brown, Susan Jenkins. *The Helen Hall Settlement Papers; a Descriptive Bibliography of Community Studies and Other Reports, 1928–1958*. Henry Street Settlement, 1959.

Bruno, Frank. *Trends in Social Work*. New York: Columbia University Press, 1948.

Campbell, Thomas F. *SASS: Fifty Years of Social Work Education*. Cleveland: Press of Case Western Reserve University, 1967.

Chambers, Clarke. *Paul A. Kellogg and the Survey of Minneapolis*. University of Minnesota Press, 1971.

———. *Seedtime of Reform: American Social Service and Social Action, 1918–33*. Minneapolis: University of Minnesota Press, 1963.

———. "Social Service and Social Reform: A Historical Essay." *Social Service Review*, 36 (March 1963): 76–90.

Cohen, Nathan E. *Social Work in the American Tradition*. New York: Dryden Press, 1958.

Cutlip, Scott M. *Fund Raising in the United States. Its Role in American Philanthropy*. New Brunswick: Rutgers University Press, 1965.

Davis, Allen. *Spearheads for Reform: the Social Settlements and the Progressive Movement, 1890–1914*. New York: Oxford University Press, 1967.

——— and Mary Lynn McCree. *Eighty Years at Hull-House*. Chicago: Quadrangle, 1969.

de Schweinitz, Karl. "The Past as a Guide to the Function and Pattern of Social Work." *Frontiers for Social Work*. Ed. W. Wallace Weaver. Philadelphia: University of Pennsylvania Press, 1960, pp. 59–94.

Epstein, Irwin. "Organizational Careers, Professionalization and Social Worker Radi-
    calism." *Social Service Review*, 44 (June 1970): 123–31.
———. "Professionalization, Professionalism, and Social Worker Radicalism." *Journal
    of Health and Social Behavior*, 11 (March 1970): 67–77.
Farrell, John C. *Beloved Lady: A History of Jane Addams' Ideas on Reform and Peace.*
    Baltimore: Johns Hopkins, 1967.
Glaab, Charles N. and A. Theodore Brown. *A History of Urban America.* New York:
    Macmillan, 1967.
Gosnell, Harold F. *Negro Politicians: the Rise of Negro Politics in Chicago.* Chicago:
    University of Chicago Press, 1966.
Graham, Jr., Otis L. *An Encore for Reform: the Old Progressives and the New Deal.* New
    York: Oxford University Press, 1967.
Handlin, Oscar. *The Uprooted.* Boston: Little, Brown, 1951.
Heald, Morrell. *The Social Responsibilities of Business.* Cleveland: Press of Case
    Western Reserve University, 1970.
Hofstadter, Richard. *The Age of Reform: from Bryan to F.D.R.* New York, Vintage,
    1955.
Howard, Donald S. "Social Work and Social Reform." *New Directions in Social Work.*
    Ed. Cora Kasiuss. New York: Harper, 1954, pp. 159–75.
Hunter, Floyd. "Community Organization: Lever for Institutional Change?" *The Urban
    South.* Eds. Rupert B. Vance and N. D. Demerath. Chapel Hill: University of
    North Carolina, 1954, pp. 252–67.
Konopka, Gisela. *Edward C. Lindeman and Social Work Philosophy.* Minneapolis:
    University of Minnesota Press, 1958.
Kraditor, Aileen S. ed. *Up from the Pedestal.* Chicago: Quadrangle, 1968.
Johnson, Walter. *1600 Pennsylvania Avenue.* Boston: Little, Brown, 1963 (1960).
Levine, Daniel. *Jane Addams and the Liberal Tradition.* Madison: State Historical
    Society of Wisconsin, 1971.
Lubove, Roy, *Community Planning in the 1920s: The Contribution of the Regional
    Planning Association of America* (Pittsburgh: University of Pittsburgh Press,
    1963).
———. "The New Deal and National Health." *Current History*, 45 (Aug. 1963): 77–86.
———. *The Professional Altruist: the Emergence of Social Work as a Career.* Cambridge:
    Harvard University Press, 1965.
———. *The Struggle for Social Security, 1900–1935.* Cambridge: Harvard University
    Press, 1968.
———. *Twentieth Century Pittsburgh.* New York: Wiley, 1969.
MacRae, Robert. "Social Work and Social Action." *Social Service Review*, 40 (March
    1966): 1–7.
Marris, Peter and Martin Rein, *Dilemmas of Social Reform.* New York: Atherton, 1967.
Miller, Doris K. "Social Reform and Organized Psychology." *Journal of Social Issues*,
    28 (1972): 217–31.
Peterson, Jon A. "From Social Settlement to Social Agency: Settlement Work in
    Columbus, Ohio, 1898–1958." *Social Service Review*, 39 (1965): 191–208.
Pumphrey, Ralph E. and Murial W. Pumphrey, eds. *The Heritage of American Social
    Work: Readings in Its Philosophical and Institutional Development.* New York:
    Columbia University Press, 1961.

Russell Sage Foundation. *Report of the Princeton Conference on the History of Philanthropy in the United States.* New York: Russell Sage Foundation, 1956.

Selby, John. *Beyond Civil Rights.* Cleveland: World, 1966. (Undocumented history of Playhouse Settlement.)

Shannon, David. *The Socialist Party of America.* Chicago: Quadrangle, 1967.

Speizman, M. D. "Movement of the Settlement House Idea into the South." *Southwestern Social Science Quarterly,* 44 (1963): 237–46.

Tims, Margaret. *Jane Addams of Hull-House, 1860–1935: a Centenary Study.* London: Allen and Unwin, 1961.

Trolander, Judith Ann. "The Response of Settlements to the Great Depression." *Social Work,* 18 (Sept. 1973): 92–102.

———. "Twenty Years at Hiram House." *Ohio History,* 78 (Winter 1969): 25–38; 69–71.

Wade, Louise C. "Chicago Settlement Papers." *Social Service Review,* 37 (1963): 461–63.

———. *Graham Taylor.* Chicago: University of Chicago, 1964.

———. "The Heritage from Chicago's Early Settlement Houses." *Journal of the Illinois State Historical Society,* 60 (1967): 411–41.

Warner, Sam Bass, Jr. *Private City: Philadelphia in Three Stages of Its Growth.* Philadelphia: University of Pennsylvania Press, 1968.

Wilensky, Harold L. and Charles N. Lebeaux. "The Emergence of a Social Work Profession." *Industrial Society and Social Welfare.* New York: Russell Sage Foundation, 1958, pp. 283–334.

Wish, Harvey. *Contemporary America: the National Scene since 1900.* 4th edition. New York: Harper and Row, 1966.

Index

Judith Ann Trolander, assistant professor of history at Western Illinois University, received a B.A. (1964) from the University of Minnesota, a M.S.L.S. (1966) from Western Reserve University, and an M.A. and Ph.D. (1972) from Case Western Reserve University. She is a frequent contributor of articles on history and social work to scholarly journals.

The manuscript was edited by Jean Spang. The book was designed by Joanne Kinney. The typeface for the text is Times Roman, the design of which was supervised by Stanley Morison about 1931. The display face is Garamond bold italic which is based on original designs by Aldus Manutius in the 16th century.

The text is printed on Nashoba antique text paper and the book is bound in Columbia Mills' Llamique cloth over binders boards. Manufactured in the United States of America.